Ide... ...rk St ...

The construction of narrative identity is a public – and hence potentially political – process. Telling and listening to stories about oneself involves narrative techniques. Using modern novels as a reference point, Maureen  Whitebrook asks what follows for political identity (be it of a person, group or nation) from taking the narrative element seriously: 'Who am I?' in conjunction with 'Who are we?', and 'Who tells the political story?'

Identity, Narrative and Politics argues that political theory is limited in its understanding of narrative identity, and explores the sophisticated ideas which emerge from novels as alternative expressions of political understanding. Using a broad international selection of twentieth-century English language works – by writers such as Virginia Woolf, Nadine Gordimer and Thomas Pynchon – this book considers each novel as a source of political ideas, in terms of content, structure, form and technique, and specifically in relation to narrative political identity.

The book assumes no prior knowledge of the literature discussed, and will be fascinating reading for students of politics, literature, cultural politics and political morality.

Maureen Whitebrook is Honorary Research Fellow in the Department of Politics, University of Sheffield. Her publications include *Reading Political Stories* and *Real Toads in Imaginary Gardens: Narrative Accounts of Liberalism.* She is the Chair/Convenor of the Politics and the Arts Group.

Identity, Narrative and Politics

Maureen Whitebrook

London and New York

First published 2001
by Routledge
11 New Fetter Lane, London EC4P 4EE

Simultaneously published in the USA and Canada
by Routledge
29 West 35th Street, New York, NY 10001

Routledge is an imprint of the Taylor & Francis Group

© 2001 Maureen Whitebrook

Typeset in Baskerville by BC Typesetting, Bristol
Printed and bound in Great Britain by
TJ International Ltd, Padstow, Cornwall

British Library Cataloguing in Publication Data
A catalogue record for this book is available from the British Library

Library of Congress Cataloging in Publication Data
Whitebrook, Maureen.
    Identity, narrative and politics/Maureen Whitebrook.
        p.   cm.
    Includes bibliographical references and index.
        1. English fiction – 20th century – History and criticism.   2. Politics and
    literature – English-speaking coountries – History – 20th century.   3. American
    fiction – 20th century – History and criticism.   4. Political fiction – History and
    criticism.   5. Identity (Psychology) in literature.   6. Group identity in literature.
    7. Narration (Rhetoric)   I. Title.

    PR888.P6 W47 2001
    823′.9109358–dc21   00-062790

ISBN 0–415–23894–3 (hbk)
ISBN 0–415–23895–1 (pbk)

Contents

Acknowledgements

The author and publisher are grateful for permission to reproduce copyrighted material: extracts from Philip Roth's *Operation Shylock* are reproduced by permission of The Random House Group; extracts from Virginia Woolf's *Mrs Dalloway* are reproduced by permission of the Society of Authors as the literary representative of the Estate of Virginia Woolf.

Between proposal and publication, this book has been subject to the unfortunately not uncommon vagaries of the publishing business. I am therefore grateful to both Caroline Wintersgill and Craig Fowlie; the former for taking the project on and encouraging me to develop it, the latter for showing real interest in a project that he did not initiate, and for seeing it through to completion with equal interest and encouragement.

I thank the various readers of the original proposal for this project and the first draft, all of whom made helpful comments and suggestions, most of which have found their way into the completed book. I thank John Horton for his continuing, and encouraging, interest in my work and, again, for his willingness to read draft versions of this book. I am greatly indebted to Susan Stephenson for her comments on and help with my work over the long period that this book has been in the making, and in particular for her careful reading of an early version.

Participation in a number of workshops and conference panels has enabled me to try out some of the ideas here and to receive many helpful comments, suggestions and references. While it has not been possible to acknowledge all this help in the text, I hope that those who recognize their contributions will accept the appearance of this book as a token of my thanks for their help.

I am, as always, most grateful to those friends who have patiently supported my work and helped it along in various entertaining ways – and especially thanks to Stuart Bennett.

1 Introduction

Identity, narrative, narratives and narrative identity

In 1991, in a lengthy article in the *New York Review of Books*, Joan Didion discusses the 'wilding' episode, an incident of rape which had taken place in Central Park, New York in 1989, when a white woman investment banker jogging in the park was attacked and raped by a gang of black and Hispanic youths (Didion 1991).[1] Didion's mode of analysis was to place the incident in relation to the city of New York and the 'story' or 'stories' of that city, taking off from the account of the rape and subsequent capture and trial of the alleged rapists to make certain points about the narrative of New York.

The victim of the crime was not generally identified by name, but 'abstracted' and her situation 'made to stand for that of the city itself'. Her employers thought her 'the personification of "what makes this city so vibrant and so great"' who had been 'struck down by a side of our city that is as awful and terrifying as the creative side is wonderful'. Didion comments:

> It was precisely in this conflation of victim and city, this confusion of personal woe with public distress, that the crime's 'story' would be found, its lesson, its encouraging promise of narrative resolution . . . For so long as this case held the city's febrile attention, then it offered a narrative for the city's distress, a frame in which the actual social and economic forces wrenching the city could be personalized and ultimately obscured.
>
> (Didion 1991: 46, 54)

As Didion comments on the case, she discusses this narrativization of both the particular incident and the life of the city as such. For instance, New York is 'rapidly vanishing into the chasm between its actual life and its preferred narratives'. As reportage switched from a pragmatic acceptance of the danger of open spaces at night to an ideal construct whereby New York – including Central Park – had been, or should be, safe, she notes that 'the insistent sentimentalization of experience' is habitual in New York, along with a 'preference for . . . the distortion and flattening of character', and 'the reduction of events to narrative' as the 'heart of the way the city presents itself'. And this narrative, 'with its dramatic line of "crisis" and resolution, or recovery', obscures race and class tensions, civic and commercial arrangements, 'the conspiracy of those in the know'. The history of Central Park is shown to be such a 'story' – an artificial construction, a 'story' that 'had to do with certain dramatic contrasts, or extremes, that were believed to characterize life in this as in no other city'.

From this reading of the crime, and its location, the park, Didion draws general conclusions. For example,

> Stories in which terrible crimes are inflicted on innocent victims, offering as they do a similarly sentimental reading of class differences and human suffering, a reading that promises both resolution and retribution, have long performed as the city's endorphins, a built-in source of natural morphine working to blur the edges of real and to a great extent insoluble problems.

And even more generally:

> The imposition of a sentimental, or false, narrative on the disparate and often random experience that constitutes the life of a city or a country means, necessarily, that much of what happens in that city or country will be rendered merely illustrative, a series of set pieces or performance opportunities.

So this case allowed, for example, 'a narrative based on the magical ability of "leaders" to improve the common weal'.

Didion's conclusion is that

> among the citizens of a New York come to grief on the sentimental stories told in defense of its own lazy criminality, the city's inevitability remained the given, the heart, the first and last word on which all the stories rested. We love New York, the narrative promises, because it matches our energy level.

Didion, herself a novelist, specifically voices an awareness of the dangers of narrative. Social scientists may well sympathize with her suspicions: narrative accounts are suspect, because they lack objectivity; stories promote a certain point of view; there is a tendency to romanticize or sentimentalize in the process of storytelling. However, not only is Didion's account itself a story, but, more importantly, her narrative analysis is flawed. Those factors taken together suggest that her attack on narrative deserves some attention, that her suspicions are unfounded and even, by extension, that narrative accounts can be positively helpful to analyses of the socio-political realm.

Her commentary on the city of New York takes the form of a narrative account: characters and events, together with commentary on them, have been put together to present – show – a certain interpretation of a set of facts. And her talk of conspiracy, or herself omitting to name the victim, are narrative or rhetorical devices employed in order to make her point the more strongly. Those features suggest how easily even the intentionally non-narrative writer slips into using narrative techniques. But Didion also makes explicit statements on narrative, which are misleading in their misunderstanding of 'narrative' and 'story'.

Didion thinks that narrative's effects can only obscure 'the real world' of facts and inferences to be drawn from those facts. 'Sentimentality' should not be a factor in political deliberation; nor should accounts that by their method distort or romanticize, that 'reduce events to narrative'. Such objections do not correspond, though, to the formulation whereby at its most basic 'narrative' denotes the patterning or ordering of events – the fundamental element of narrative. Didion speaks of 'a reading that promises both resolution and retribution' but the imposition of a narrative framework does not thereby entail 'resolution'. Narrative theory distinguishes between ending and closure; and indeed, Didion's own account ends (concludes), but there is little or no sense of closure – the 'story' of New York is not resolved, the characters are not neatly disposed of.

Two major points emerge from Didion's strictures on the (mis)use, or even danger, of narrative in real-life situations. One is that narrative method, explaining what is happening by way of narratives, is a commonplace human activity, and that the student of politics who seeks to understand that activity in more or less specific terms may need both to employ narrative techniques themself and to take other people's narratives into account. The second follows from that: the need to understand what narrative is, and what its use entails. I take up these points in the study that follows.

Argument

My specific interest is in the relationships between narrative, identity and politics. My discussion moves around the interconnections, drawing out where there is – actually or potentially – interplay between narrative identity and politics,[2] and finally suggesting how the connections can be developed for the benefit of political theory.[3]

As one of the more recent works that claim to apply narrative to political theory points out, 'At present there is a small cottage industry . . . awash in a sea of claims . . . about narrative' (Dienstag 1997: 209). Or again, 'References to narrative and storytelling have become an almost obligatory gesture for theorists who defy the academic norm of detached writing', and who 'use storytelling to shift knowledge from a center that purports to be impartial, uniform and omniscient, to a margin that acknowledges the heterogeneity and inevitable partiality of any standpoint' (Disch 1994: 1, 10, and cf. 5–9). However, the increasing frequency of assertions about narrative identity in theory is not matched by explanation or even acknowledgement of what is involved in adopting narrative as a term for social and political explanation.

References to narrative, the narrative self and even narrative identity are now frequent enough in political discourse to suggest that it is time to consider more carefully than heretofore just what narrative implies for political understanding. There is an awareness of the narrative mode in political theory, but narrative has to be further understood as more than just story-telling taken to be so natural an activity that it requires no attention to technique, or to underlying technical requirements. 'Narrative', like most theoretical concepts, carries with it an accompanying baggage of technicalities, allusions, connotations, references. Those wanting to use the idea of narrative as 'simply telling a story' may object that they have no need of intensive work on narrative as such. But 'telling a story' is far from simple, as narrative theory discloses – and so even that most basic usage leads back into the technicalities, if narrative is to be given proper attention in theorizing.

Although there are now several studies which have focused on specific aspects of narrative, identity and politics – for example, in Anglophone theory, Charles Taylor's *Sources of the Self* (Taylor 1989) on the self and identity, Alasdair MacIntyre's chapter in *After Virtue* (MacIntyre 1985) on identity and narrative, and Joshua Foe Dienstag's *Dancing in Chains* (Dienstag 1997) on narrative and political theory – this discussion though is based on a particular definition of identity: that identity is a matter of telling stories – hence *narrative* identity – and that this has political implications deriving from storytelling's public setting. The construction of narrative identity is a collective act, involving tellers and listeners. Certain aspects of narrative, its defining characteristics and elements, have a bearing on the political.

I suggest that identity is, primarily, a matter of the stories persons tell others about themselves, plus the stories others tell about those persons and/or other stories in which those persons are included. Defining identity in terms of narrative rests on claims about the naturalness of storytelling, and hence the construction of identity through stories (Nash 1994a: xi and *passim*). Then inasmuch as identity means something like 'what the self shows the world' or 'what of the self is shown to the world', together with 'what of the self is recognized by the world', the construction of identity – narrating identity – entails placing the self in the public sphere, and thus a capacity for taking on a political role. The political aspect of identity rests on an understanding of the self as social, 'situated', and narratives of identity as embedded in other stories, including the wider stories of social and cultural settings.

I examine the use of narrative for politics by way of narratives – novels – as a way of expanding on what narrative may be understood to mean for political theorizing, taking it that modern novels have something to say about modern lives. Such novels exhibit – show in practice – features of narrative that are politically relevant, and their characters depict the problems of constructing identity. I draw from narrative theory to suggest that certain elements of narrative relate to some of the current concerns of political theory, and thence assist political understanding.

Theorists may, of course, use 'narrative' merely adjectivally, or to refer to historical narratives – or, as in the case of Dienstag's *Dancing in Chains*, works of political theory may be classified as narratives. There would then be only tenuous reasons, if any, for links to literary narratives, and it would certainly seem over-scrupulous to apply narrative theory or the literary critical understanding of narrative to such usages. However, in the case of political uses of 'narrative identity', it might be expected that narrative identity would exhibit narrative features – and hence my attention to elements of narrative as understood in literary and philosophical studies.

The connection of identity to fictional narratives is not only a matter of the provision of appropriate models for, or occasions for reflection on, theoretical concerns but has a direct bearing on understanding narrative identity. I take it that there would be little or no point in yet another study of a political theme with literary examples – several theorists, notably Peter Johnson, have done that well enough already (e.g. Ingle 1979; Fishman 1989; Johnson, P. 1988). New work requires moving on from treating novels as exemplary or mimetic to look at narrative form as well as content, on the understanding that form is a metaphor for theme and/or that content is always mediated through form – both of which are commonplaces of literary criticism. If, then, a theme is politically significant – as I take identity to be – what can be learnt from the form of expression of that theme in literary narratives?

Storytelling that constructs identity is not a simple matter – there may be doubling, time shifts, gaps, any or all of the constituent and characteristic features of narrative. For that reason, I look at novels as accessible instances of narrative in practice. Turning to narratives – modern novels – allows for observation of how identity is constructed, through attention to content and form: plot and characterization; and narrative structure, style and techniques. The process of narrative construction is relevant inasmuch as it makes the point that identity is narratively made, and shows what that means for an understanding of political identity.

The outcome of this examination of narrative and reading of narratives is to show that identity is, or may be, uncertain: narrative does not necessarily ensure unity. Neither narrative theory nor modern narratives offer a direct link between narrative and unity, or order: narrative may exhibit lack of pattern, an absence of closure. Such instability may appear politically threatening, or even dangerous; but attention to narrative also shows how instability – disorder – can be a characteristic of coherent stories. The narrative process itself – narrative telling – is significant here. Narrative understood by way of process – form, narrative structure, style and techniques – suggests that coherence is in the telling. Uncertainty, fragmentation and disunity can be contained in the narrative by way of content and form, what is told and the telling of it.

Content

Identity

Identity is the subject of a vast literature in disciplines such as philosophy and psychoanalysis. I do not attempt to critique this work, or to enter into debates about the status of the self, the existence or not of an essential self, or a pre-existing, essential or core identity, as definitive of the self as, for instance, in the interest in memory, or continuity over time.[4] However, I do want to distinguish between the two terms, to establish a sense of *identity*, as distinct from *self*, beyond the understandings presently on offer, making the distinction in terms of the public – intersubjective, social, political – nature of identity.[5] My concern is with the process of identity formation, external identification and recognition. In this understanding of identity as the public manifestation of the self, identity expresses something of one's self, does so for public consumption, and in so doing allows that that expression may need to be modified by the reactions of others.

The two dominant conceptions of identity are that it is a product of ourselves or that it is a product of our social context, or our beings as social selves. These are not mutually exclusive. The concept of individual identity 'represents the convergence of the psychological development of the self with the social position of the individual' (Alford 1991: 6); and we 'become self-conscious in the process by which we are inducted into social life, and the forms of social life into which we are inducted provide the resources – primarily, but not only the linguistic resources – in terms of which we are conscious of ourselves' (Poole 1996: 55). It is such a combined understanding of identity that I want to work with.

Theories of identity relate closely to linguistic considerations, a matter of some relevance for a conception of narrative identity.

> The casting of thought in language makes the private and individual public and collective by accommodating individual experience and subjectivity within the concepts, categories, and order of a particular culture and political system. . . . Individuals make themselves out of the matter and according to the patterns that their language provides.
>
> (Norton 1988: 46–7)

It is significant that the language used to express identity is not a private possession but a given deriving from the culture: 'the private experience of a human being is shaped and ordered in learning to speak and write and in acquiring the know-how of other social and material practices', and 'that ordering is expressed in the use of language and other intentional, norm governed practices'. Then, 'our sense of our own identity' originates in 'appropriations of the structure of public discourse between particular and singular persons for the ordering of private experience and the expression of our personal identities as singularities in public space' (Harré 1998: 42, 43).

The embodiment of identity is also significant: '[t]he narratives of our lives are structured around the facts of birth, immaturity and dependence, growth and development, and finally decay and dissolution' (Poole 1996: 47). Benhabib insists that 'the subjects of reason are finite, embodied and fragile creatures, and not disembodied cogitos or abstract unities of transcendental aperception' (Benhabib 1992: 5; cf. Kerby 1991: 115 n. 4; Nicholson 1995: 40–4; Barron 1993: 95–6; Norton 1988; Bordo 1993).

Certain critical questions for politics are consequent upon these definitions and distinctions. Is identity self-constructed, self-defined, what the person takes themself to be, *or* a consequence of their social context – and in that latter case, is it self-assumed or ascribed? Is identity a matter of how the person sees themself or how others see them? And what of collective identity – 'we' as well as 'I'? Is identity a product of inherent or ascribed characteristics, given or chosen – 'given' by characteristics such as age or gender, which can be affirmed or denied, or 'chosen', either by affirming or denying given characteristics, or by adopting non-given characteristics, negotiating an identity? Then, what range can be chosen from, what connections are there to the 'given' situation – some must be necessary for a basic coherence?

Political identity

The available meanings of political identity range from citizenship, used almost as a neutral, merely descriptive term, a concomitant of the relationship of the individual and the state, to the characteristics of members of groups, or, in a wider meaning beyond the political identity of persons, to the identity of political entities – groups significant in the political realm or politically defined entities such as nations or states, intra-state or supranational groups ('Europeland', for example).

Noel O'Sullivan has identified three 'currently available' theories of the political, liberal, discourse and agonal, represented by Rawls, Habermas and Honig and Connolly, respectively and a fourth, 'the classical ideal of civil association' which he considers 'best suited to modern conditions of increasing diversity' (O'Sullivan 1997: 740). Each of these indicates a relevant form of political identity. The identity of the liberal/Rawlsian person is the individual, autonomous, rational chooser – as Sandel summarizes it, 'the human subject as a sovereign agent of choice, a creature whose ends are chosen rather than given, who comes by his aims and purposes by acts of will, as opposed, say, to acts of cognition' (Sandel 1982: 22; cf. Flathman 1992: 124; Parekh 1992: 161–2).[6] Discourse theory regards identity as product, in part at least, of the community – a 'negotiated' identity, and politically dependent on the existence of a political realm where 'conversation' as 'free and equal agents' is possible (cf. Taylor 1991: 47–50). Agonal theory is based on the 'decentring of the state', where political identity would be that of democratic citizens (O'Sullivan 1997: 745). For William Connolly, for example, the construction of identity demands awareness of the political as the arena within which a struggle with the problem of evil takes place (O'Sullivan 1997: 747). Civil association theory allows for diversity, 'radical and pluralist democracy' (O'Sullivan 1997: 749): political identity may be shifting, multiple in the sense that it follows from attachment to particular enterprises – 'causes'. It is political precisely because it rests on a collective identification with others.

By implication for all of the theories which O'Sullivan discusses, as with many usages of political identity, that identity might be expressed in terms of citizenship. Mouffe asserts that 'citizenship'

> is not one identity among others, as it is in liberalism, nor is it the domi-
> nant identity that overrides all others, as it is in civic republicanism . . .
> [but] an articulating principle that affects the different subject positions
> of the social agent while allowing for a plurality of specific allegiances
> and for the respect of individual liberty.
>
> (Mouffe 1995a: 38)

'Only citizenship enables us jointly to take charge of and take responsibility for the social forces that otherwise dominate our lives and limit our opinions, even though we produce them' (Pitkin 1981: 327–52; cf. Parekh 1995b). Political identity would then represent a movement from separate identity to collective identity, a movement from 'I' to 'we'. Indeed, Tracy Strong would make that move definitive of politics as such: 'The political is that form of human activity in which the answer to the question "who am I?" is also the answer to the question "who are we?"' (Strong 1990: 34; Connolly 1991: 158; cf. Booth and Rosamond 1996). There is always some collective element to political identity. The inter-relationality inherent in narrative identity implies this, in line with that understanding of political identity which assumes aggregation: 'in the political arena, those who encounter one another are collective actors contending about collective goals and the distribution of collective goods' (Habermas 1994: 108). Embedment and intertextuality, entailing that stories are always connected and often derive from other stories, also suggest that this might be the case. John Gray asserts 'the moral and political importance of *collective identification*' as

> the pervasive human phenomenon in virtue of which personal identities
> are constituted by membership in some nation, religion, tribe or other
> collectivity . . . the fact is that the man who conceives himself as a
> solitary individual, whose identity is unencumbered by any collective
> identification, though he is real, is vanishingly rare.
>
> (Gray, J. 1993: 7)

Indeed, Harré claims that identity is not to be treated as a singularity at all, but is now a group characteristic; his reason for this contention is the ubiquity of identity politics in recent discussions of identity (Harré 1998: 6; Appiah and Gates 1996: 1).

In general terms, political identity may be theorized in two rather different ways: either as a matter of (self-)awareness about the relationship of the person to the political order or as a function of inclusion in political units and as referring to certain characteristics whereby persons can be grouped for political purposes by a wide range of identificatory characteristics: nationality, geographical place or regional location, race, ethnicity, family or kinship, language, class, sex/gender, political affiliation, religion, or even football support. The first represents personal identity in a political context; the second is that of the political subject taken as a unit for political analysis, citizen, member of a group or nation. The person is identified, ascribed identity, by virtue of their belonging to, bearing the characteristics of, a political or politically relevant entity.

There are certain drawbacks to separating out political identity in terms of the political status of the individual or the person as member of a political collectivity. To concentrate on the separate person allows an over-emphasis on the separate self, whereas in the political context, these persons are also, and often, grouped – aggregated. Aggregation risks de-personifying and stereotyping; political identity understood in group terms also tends to depersonalize. In the world of International Relations, for instance, 'no children are ever born, and nobody ever dies, in this constructed world. There are states, and they are what is' (Elshtain 1987). The person whose identity is of interest to political theory can be strangely characterless: as Jacqueline Rose has noted, for example, Rawls's rational person does not feel envy (Rose 1996: 86). Such apparent deficiencies may be thought hardly surprising given the theoretical need to abstract, to define by reference to specifically political contexts and by characteristics held in common with others and taken as the relevant features for political analysis – disregarding, that is, the individual characteristics of political actors. (However, recent theory, in critiquing of such approaches, has worked towards alternative conceptualizations of the political self; some of these have connections to or a bearing on narrative identity as applied in the political sphere, and are referred to in the course of this study.)

Narrative identity

The conceptualization of narrative identity rests on the claim that narrating is a basic human activity. Persons understand their own lives as stories. Not only are 'stories being told endlessly by everyone, in public and private', but '[w]ithout the narrative structure they impose, our experience of the world and of ourselves would not be intelligible: it would only be a continuous given, in the way one supposes it must be for animals' (Cave 1995: 112;

cf. Bruner 1996; Hardy 1987; Hyvärinen 1992: 543). Taylor claims that in order to have 'a sense of who we are', to have an identity, 'we have to have a notion of how we have become, and of where we are going'; we grasp a sense of our lives *in* a narrative – 'I understand my present action in the form of an "and then"' (Taylor 1989: 47). Furthermore, 'social life itself is storied', and 'narrative is an ontological condition of social life' (Somers 1994: 614) – 'in offering an explanation of what we are doing, we relate it to our own intentions and thereby present it under the aspect of a further episode in the narrative of our lives' (and '[t]his is what explains the fact that both short- and long-term stretches of our lives can be and are characterized in terms appropriate to literary works') (Mulhall and Swift 1996: 76, 87). A specifi- cally political gloss is put on the understanding of the ubiquity of narrating as a human activity by the assertion that 'the formation of subjects is the primal political process', and 'the process by which energies are formed into subjects' is linked to 'the basic cultural act that is in the final analysis less that of knowing than of making coherent narrative explanations' (Siegle 1986: 13).

Narrative identity then consists of stories we tell to ourselves about our- selves and the stories we *or* others tell to others, or stories that are told to others about ourselves – all the stories in which we are included: 'my inside story that I convey to others' – the 'inside-out story', and 'impression' stories 'that are entertained about me *outside-in*, that are "read" into my life by all those who know me or encounter me in any way . . . "my" life in the sense of what is *made* of me by others' (Randall 1995: 54–6). There is a distinction to be made between self-identity as perceived and indeed constituted by, narrated by, the self and identity in a more general sense, including the per- ception by others of that which makes the self recognizable to self *and* to those others. Narrative identity is then at once subjective and intersubjective, and entails answerability and responsibility and the capacity for negotiation.

Narrative

'Narrative' refers to a variety of genres and a variety of forms of expression, usually verbal; including novels, epic poetry, history, biography and auto- biography, but also including non-verbal forms such as representational art and film (Chatman 1978). The term may convey some connotation of non-real, or imaginative; certainly it is a primary feature of narrative that all its forms are *constructed* (and so liable to 'creative ambiguity' (Lieblich and Josselon 1994)). The selection and arrangement of events, in a particular order, so as to suggest some relationship between them, distinguish narrative from mere descriptions of qualities, states or situations. Narratives are 'complex organizational schemata which involve agents, events, time, consciousness, memory, judgment, language'. They 'organize human experi- ence in such a way that it is rendered significant', providing 'a connective thread between one state of affairs and another such that they are given a continuity in the consciousness of the storyteller and the listener' (Stephenson 1996: 6). There is (often but not always) explanation that unfolds in time, with surprise during its progress and knowledge only by hindsight.

Somers defines narratives, in a social science context, as 'constellations of *relationships* (connected parts) embedded in *time and space*, constituted by *causal emplotment*'. The distinction from other forms of explanation is that meaning is not attributed by categorization: 'narrativity precludes sense-making of a singular isolated phenomenon'. It 'demands that we discern the meaning of any single event only in temporal or spatial relationship to other events': its chief characteristic is 'that it renders understanding only by *connecting* (however unstably) *parts* to a constructed *configuration* or a *social network* of relationships (however incoherent or unrealizable) composed of symbolic, institutional, and material practices' (Somers 1994: 616).

Narrative involves both the organization of events, *story*, and the process of organization, *narration* (Cohan and Shires 1988: 53): there are two over-lapping aspects, the 'question of content, the assemblage of material', and the 'rhetorical, how the material is presented to the audience' (Fowler, R. 1973; cf. Ross 1973: 122; Gray, M. 1992: 191). There is then a technical difference in meaning between 'narrative' used as synonymous with 'story' or 'storytelling', and 'narrative' as denoting a form or technique.[7] My argument is that more attention should be paid to the latter in order to better understand the former: I examine *how* in order to show *that*. (The point is made by the distinction between 'narrative' as the form and content, and 'story' as the untheorized practice, and thus a distinction familiar to theorists between a practice and its theorizing.) The narrative mode must be under-stood as more than storytelling, taken to be so natural an activity that it requires no attention to technique or underlying technical requirements (cf. Brodsky 1987; Lamarque and Olsen 1994: 227ff.).

I suggest that narration, voice and point of view, who is telling the story, from whose, or what, perspective, emplotment, especially in relation to contingency and chance), and closure are all relevant to an interest in the narrative construction of identity. Then, given that certain narrative terms are potentially explanatory for the construction of identity, attention is direc-ted to that form of narrative where those terms are most clearly deployed. Novels display the process of construction and the use and the effect of typical narrative elements and techniques, including those that are particularly rele-vant to narrative identity as understood in and/or relevant to contemporary political theory.

Narratives

The general injunction to turn to narrative, originating (in those words) in Anglophone theory with Richard Rorty and also expressed, rather differ-ently, by Alasdair MacIntyre, Charles Taylor and Martha Nussbaum, has been frequently cited in recent political theory; their terminology has been adopted to the extent that 'narrative', 'story' and 'storytelling' have become regular usages in political theory, beyond the work on or deriving directly from these particular theorists. A rather different, and longer-standing interest in storytelling derives from Hannah Arendt, who 'from her early writings to her unfinished lectures on judging . . . sustains the belief that political theory can be understood as a kind of storytelling'. Storytelling is 'an integral part of her political philosophy', 'a method she employed and a way she described what she was doing' (Disch 1994: 2; cf. Disch 1993: 689; Benhabib 1996: 112–13, 125–6; Lane 1997).

Beyond the utilization of storytelling as mode of political explanation or argument, in maintaining that the concept of narrative can be helpful for political understanding, I also argue that that understanding may be enhanced by attention to literary narratives – novels. Not surprisingly, literary studies have something to say about narrative identity. It is claimed that 'the history of identity is a good deal more visibly and colourfully exhibited in fiction than in philosophy as such', with that claim substantiated by reference to stories and lives, examples which bring out 'the power of narrative to determine our sense of what identity is and where it is located' (Cave 1995: 105). For example, Somer argues that it is novels that best account for aspects of Latin American national identities – hence 'foundational fictions' (Somer 1991; cf. Dolan 1994; Echevarria 1985).

Modern novels

While realist novels may seem the most accessible, with no apparent problems of narration, where identity is in question, the theorist needs to attend to more complex examples, post-realist modern novels, the narrative structuring of which calls into question simplistic conceptualizations of narrative. Modern fictional narratives disturb assumptions about sequentiality and causation; they put closure and conventional ideas of coherence into question; they allow for contingency and coincidence, and for the disordered or inaccurate recall of events that is a feature of lived life. Such novels have moved on from realism in so far as that is associated with the Enlightenment culture of classic liberalism and with a confidence about the establishment of modes of thinking based on reason. In realist novels the autonomous individual of the liberal tradition is reproduced in literary terms as the omniscient author/narrator figure. The depiction of characters with fixed motivation moves towards a fixed or conventional ending and emplotment is tied to clear pursuit of certain outcomes (marriage and money, for instance). Post-realist modern novels adopt a more questioning attitude in respect of form *and* content.

The techniques, structure, style and methods of characterization of the novels read in the following chapters are such as to distinguish them from the typical realist novel. All are 'experimental' to some extent; all draw on characteristic narrative features and techniques associated with modernism; several have been categorized as late-modernist; none is unarguably post-modernist. They have each been liable to a diversity of critical labelling. For example, the first novel examined, E. L. Doctorow's *The Book of Daniel* (1971), has been variously identified as modernist, experimental and post-modernist, the latter by several different definitions of that term. Thomas Pynchon, author of *The Crying of Lot 49* (1979), the last novel examined, is variously claimed as a modernist (McHale 1987; Tanner 1982: 31–56); as a postmodernist (Hite 1983: 4); either (Hilfer 1992: 99); or both (Madsen 1991: 114–15).

As Stevenson points out, writers write, critics label – modernism is a critical construct (Stevenson 1992: 8); and so are the other categorizations, including postmodernist. A comment on Auster makes the point: there are many definitions of postmodernism; critics read his novels 'through the screen of one or another of these', as illustration of the definition, but to do so 'is to severely limit it', given that 'which definition one begins with will make all the difference in how one reads his work' (Barone 1995: 16). There is a certain confusion outside of literary studies about the application of 'postmodern' as a label for fiction. Such labelling is highly contentious, as indicated by the variety of labelling attached to the novels I refer to. Novels commonly characterized as postmodernist inherit from and share with modernism features popularly applied solely to postmodernism such as authorial self-consciousness, narrative knowingness, or techniques such as structural disorder, non-linear sequentiality, or shifts of narrative voice. Indeed, the relevant features are common to many different novels across the history of the genre, from *Tristram Shandy* onwards (Hutcheon 1989).[8] Stipulating 'post-realist' or 'experimental' as the relevant label(s) for the novels I refer to avoids entering into digressionary and distracting debate on literary sub-genres.

There is also a strong case for avoiding entanglement with postmodernism as such which is more central to the main argument of this study than is the relatively minor matter of the categorization of the novels cited in exposition of that argument, and inherent in its focus on narrative identity. While acknowledging that the work of those Continental philosophers commonly cited in discussions of narrative – 'the usual suspects' on the subject, Ricoeur, Lyotard, Derrida in particular,[9] – underpins many of the sources that I do cite, there are reasons internal to this study for my apparent 'failure' to confront them directly, arising from why or how they pay attention to narrative. For example, just as I go on to show the limitations of Alasdair MacIntyre's discussion of narrative (in Chapter 6), despite its ubiquitous citation in the social sciences and philosophy, so similarly for these philosophers. Just as MacIntyre's attention to narrative is contained within his overall attention to the necessity of restoring the virtues, so for example Ricoeur's discussion of narrative is said to be concerned with questions of time and of the self and the other, and is judged to be directed towards ethical outcomes (Rainwater 1995: 105, 107; Kearney 1995: 182ff.), and as such not directly relevant to this study of narrative identity and political outcomes.

Narrative political identity links identity with agency: postmodernism, tending to decentre the subject, is therefore outside of the scope of this study (Schrag 1997: 27; cf. Brodsky 1987: 13; Cave 1995: 109; Johnson, B. 1994: 28, 29; Madsen 1991: 118–19; White 1991: 19; Warren 1988: 1). Inasmuch as the late-twentieth-century, 'postmodernist' novel is 'preoccupied with . . . the death of the central subject' (Bradbury 1982: 16; cf. Altieri 1994; Cadava *et al.* 1991), that too precludes attention to postmodernism in a discussion of narrative(s) in relation to politics. The link between agency and responsibility also entails that postmodern narrative theory is inappropriate for this study where it is associated with 'an aesthetic of "deliberate irresponsibility"' or '"indecisive indifference"' – as Foucault's and Derrida's respectively are said to be (Kearney 1995: 184 and *passim*; Critchley and Schroeder 1998: 398). Kearney also notes that 'politically radical critics of deconstruction' have long attacked postmodernism for 'its quietistic, apolitical neutrality, its inaptitude to lead to political intervention, its privileging of analysis over action . . . it paralyzes, or at least cannot authorize, action' (Kearney 1995: 173–90, 184 and *passim*).

Schrag notes that for Lyotard, '[T]he self is simply dispersed into a panorama of radically diversified and changing language games' (Schrag 1997: 27; cf. Brodsky 1987: 13). More particularly, for identity politics,

> deconstruction has been seen by critics as undermining, rather than enabling, political agency . . . while political activists are critiquing deconstruction for analyzing the world without intervening to change it, deconstruction is warning against the identity-based grounds on which such an intervention has been conceptualized.
>
> (Johnson, B. 1994: 29)

In this view, 'Derrida renders epistemologically groundless *all* identities, even those of women or racial minorities who would attempt to assert themselves oppositionally' (Johnson, B. 1994: 28). The link between agency and responsibility then again makes postmodern narrative theory inappropriate for this study. The inapplicability of these theorists to my discussion is exemplified in the remark that 'the postmodern counteractant of celebrating plurality, incompleteness, and difference may well be an over-reaction that leaves us with a subject too thin to bear the responsibilities of its narrative involvements' (Schrag 1997: 28). It would be more than somewhat ironic if the thinness of the self which is complained of as a feature of some political theory was replaced with an equally thin figure from postmodernism.

The use of novels for theory

In an Introduction to a collection of papers on identity, the editors say (referring to the arguments, examples and counter-arguments in that volume)
that '[I]n negotiating the myriad complex dimensions of our human identities we surely need all the tools we can borrow or invent' (Appiah and Gates
1996: 6). I 'borrow' novels.

My case for bringing narratives into the theoretical argument of this study
is that political understanding would benefit from a development of the idea
of narrative identity which goes beyond current theoretical usages, and such
a development is possible by reference to certain modern novels. There is a
need to see the person in context, both extra-politically and across time, and
to account for 'the dense construction of the normal individual', or the
'abnormalities' of the ordinary self (Connolly 1991; cf. Taylor 1989: 18).
Novels allow this, presenting 'the awkward couplings of experience non-
analytically, holistically, and . . . in all their cultural and historical particularity' (Cave 1995: 118–19).

Some forms of theorizing depersonalize the political, or tend towards the
presentation of 'thin' political actors: 'a substantive self, thick with particular
traits, is progressively shorn of characteristics once taken to be essential to
its identity' with 'features [that] are seen to be arbitrarily given . . . relegated
from presumed constituents to mere attributes of the self' (Sandel 1982: 93).
Theory frequently fails to make the political agent concrete: for example,
Harpham says of Charles Altieri's *Subjective Agency* that it is '[R]elentlessly
theoretical . . . and even somewhat phobic of examples (in his book there are
lots of first, second and third persons, but very few people)'; and that by
'choosing to talk about agency rather than agents . . . he seems even more
"inhuman" than his presumptive antagonists' (Harpham 1995: 12, 13). Or,
character is treated as a matter of 'the variables an observer must assess
when trying to understand or predict anyone's behaviour' (Rosenau and
Bredemeir 1993: 343, 347). A turn to narratives allows for the de-personalized
persons of theory, the bearers of a representative or typified identity, to be
understood as separate persons – characters – with singular sets of characteristics, including but not confined to their political context and/or group identity. Novels deal with persons not just as given agents, and not in isolation,
but in complex interrelationships, situated in a world.

Novels can be read as studies not only of political or other real-life situations, but of the narrative self, and the construction of narrative identity.
Novels provide more than merely illustration or example: literary narratives
raise distinctive technical questions for theoretical analysis. The process of
narrative construction is readily observable in modern novels; novels are
prime instances of the development of character, and many modern novels
'discuss', implicitly or, increasingly, explicitly the idea of authorship. Novels
also suggest, by way of content and structure, style and techniques, the

narrative form as such, that disorder is not necessarily dysfunctional, for the person *or* the socio-political order, or for the relationship between the two.

My case for bringing novels to the study of politics is strengthened by reference to Quentin Skinner's criticism of Charles Taylor for his assurance about certain aspects of modern identity – the centrality of marriage and the family. Skinner says that these are not questions for the moral philosopher: because the enquiry is 'about general structures of feeling', those who should be interrogated are 'the statisticians or, better still, the novelists'. Skinner continues by noting that though there is no difficulty about doing so, because many modern novels treat the subject of his questioning as a major theme,

> What is surely striking, as soon as we begin to reflect on this body of literature, is that hardly anyone who has pondered the question with any depth of imagination has felt able to answer it in a manner that even approaches Taylor's assurance and lack of ambivalence.

And he contrasts Taylor's 'crudely formulated dichotomies' with 'the ambiguities and complexities of feeling' that writers 'have so compassionately portrayed' (Skinner 1991: 141). I argue that it is just such ambiguities and complexities – achieved by way of content *and* form – that novels can bring to political theory.

Skinner's novels of choice in this respect are John Updike's *Couples* and Cyra McFadden's *The Serial* – not titles that are regularly cited even where politics and literature are connected. But such a move is encouraging: the use of literature need not be confined to Greek drama, the works of Shakespeare and nineteenth-century classic realist novels. I have chosen to read a number of novels that show not only the processes of construction but also the effects of that construction, the social and political interactions involved: E.L. Doctorow's *The Book of Daniel* (1971), Philip Roth's *Operation Shylock* (1993), Nadine Gordimer's *A Sport of Nature* (1987), Virginia Woolf's *Mrs Dalloway* (1925), Paul Auster's *Leviathan* (1992), and Thomas Pynchon's *The Crying of Lot 49* (1979).

I have selected novels for discussion on the basis of an equality of treatment between literary and political texts: that is, I do not look for novels to illustrate political themes, but move between the two, reading novels for their depiction of political ideas in conjunction with relevant works of theory. In this context these novels share common characteristics: somewhat tautologically, they are capable of a political reading; they offer politically relevant examples of narrative structuring; they display a certain self-consciousness about the narrative process. The process of the narrative construction of identity is foregrounded in each novel. What relates them is a common concern with the substantive and methodological features of this process: all of them reveal a preoccupation with both the characterization of and the narrative means of depicting how persons narratively construct their identity and the outcomes – including the political – of so doing.

Method

My method is to read a number of modern, post-realist, experimental novels in conjunction with given positions in political theory and relevant theory from other disciplines; and thence to suggest modification of, or addition to, political thinking on narrative identity. By way of this series of critical readings, I show what narrative texts – narrative accounts of lives – present of the construction of narrative identity. Each novel is discussed in terms of this overall theme, and specific aspects of narrative are distinguished, building up an understanding of narrative which has a bearing on political identity.

An immediate methodological issue is *how* to read the novels. The appropriate strategy is close reading, as necessary for attention to the narrative forms and techniques employed in literary works. This is similar to the method advocated and employed by Nussbaum in *Love's Knowledge* (1990), her collected essays on philosophy and literature. Nussbaum's project there 'involves supplementing abstract philosophical attempts at self-understanding with concrete narrative fictions': there are certain 'plausible views' about human life that can only be stated in 'a literary narrative of a certain sort'. At the core of that project is the claim that 'literary form and human life are inseparable: that forms themselves express a content'. She maintains that 'certain truths about human life can only be fittingly and accurately stated in the language and forms characteristic of the narrative artist'. Therefore, 'form and style are not incidental features'; and so 'the selection of genre, formal structures, sentences, vocabulary, of the whole manner of addressing the reader's sense of life' – all express 'a sense of life and of value, a sense of what matters and what does not, of what learning and communication are, of life's relations and connections' (Nussbaum 1990: 5, 7, 288, 289–90, 312). She is concerned, then, with 'the sense of the deep connections between content and form' (in her case, in relation to questions of ethics) through 'the detailed study of complex particular cases' (Nussbaum 1990: 23).

Nussbaum's project rests on the idea that certain features of human life, including 'the priorities of particulars over generalities', 'resist systematic theoretical treatment' and can only be conveyed by literature (Parker 1994: 35). I want to stress the importance of 'particulars' in a treatment of political identity, but as a political theorist I do not want to elevate them over generalities (or abstractions), but rather to treat both as mutually significant. While Nussbaum has asserted that novels function *as* moral theory, I make a lesser claim: that novels include political ideas which relate to political theory, but theory is needed to systematize those political ideas which are part of the literary whole.

The recognition that the literary work is a whole and is to be approached as such is a necessary condition of using such texts in theoretical work. In any 'use' of works of literature for theoretical purposes, as Adam Newton has it, 'the voice of the text may always have the last word' (Newton 1995: 293). The reader must try to avoid extracting meaning from, or imposing meaning on, texts that do not carry those meanings of themselves. Newton maintains that works of literature are complete in themselves, not merely exemplary instances.[10] The response to a work of literature should not be applying, imitating or learning from, but regarding or 'facing', 'as one might face a person, having to confront the claims raised by that very immediacy, an immediacy of contact, not of meaning' (Newton 1995: 11). The method is to *look at* the novel – what goes on inside it – and respond to that. Such a usage respects the autonomy of the literary text while allowing it to be read politically.

There is an interesting precedent for the transposition of the pictorial and the literary. In 1866 George Eliot, in response to a suggestion by Frederick Harrison that she incorporate ideas of Comtian positivism in a novel, replied that she foresaw a difficulty, 'the severe effort of trying to make certain ideas thoroughly incarnate', and that,

> I think aesthetic teaching is the highest of all teaching because it deals with life in its highest complexity. But if it ceases to be purely aesthetic – if it lapses anywhere from the picture to the diagram – it becomes the most offensive of all teaching . . .
>
> (Haight 1956: 300)

The use of literature for politics should not cause the literary text to 'lapse from the picture to the diagram'; and indeed, the use of literary texts that are pictures not diagrams should of itself entail that they are 'used' – viewed, reflected on – in a certain way.

Metaphors relating to pictorial rather than literary (verbal) aesthetics are very pertinent for Newton's and, derivatively, my argument at this point. It is more obvious perhaps for painting than for narrative prose that there is not a message, *a* meaning to be derived from the aesthetic object, but the depiction is there, primarily, at least, to be looked at and, possibly, thought about. So one needs to look at the novel, and respond to that and only that (cf. Lamarque and Olsen 1994: 451).

There is a further methodological rider. The novels I read here are instances of 'process literature', which display 'aperture', the possibility that things could be other (Morson 1998). There is a rather fine distinction (as Newton comes close to admitting) between the 'argument' within the literary text – what is in the text rather than what is attached to it by way of criticism – and what is read into it. The moment a reader says what is in the text, they interpret. The novel must be taken as an entity: it is a complex and detailed picture to be looked at. However, as picture, inside the frame –

which acts not as limitation but as suggestive of the appropriate critical stance – while the reader cannot live in the world of the novel, they may interpret. In post-realist novels, indeterminate narration, multiple voice, and similar narrative techniques positively encourage reader involvement, and thence the possibility of judgement as to 'what is going on' in the world of the novel. This is not, however, an encouragement to identification – such narrative techniques prevent coherent (continuous) identification with a character in the very process of requiring the reader to participate in the telling of the story.

Development of the argument

The chapters that follow examine the issues and implications for political theory which arise from understanding narrative identity as story(ing) – involving various narrative features – by way of the reading of novels, each of which is discussed in terms of various aspects of the narrative construction of identity. These literary readings suggest problems inherent in the idea of narrative identity which are likely to complicate and challenge the use of that term for politics.

Chapters 2, 3 and 4 continue the introductory background to this discussion: that identities are constructed as narratives by means of narrative form, narrative structure, style and techniques. These readings indicate that identity is not necessarily stable, but may be shifting, fluid or multiple. This raises difficulties if narrative identity is linked to political identity: Chapters 5 and 6 address that problem in terms of the potential of narrative for containing contingency, through emplotment, narrative telling. Chapter 7 draws on the findings of the preceding chapters to summarize the implications of attention to narrative for political conceptions of narrative identity, and to suggest how the findings of this study might be further developed. This study does not move towards a conclusion – or, in literary terms, closure – and the arrangement of chapters is not sequential. Characteristic features of narrative and themes relevant to narrative identity recur and interconnect in these readings: each novel includes features that are dealt with in other chapters.

Chapter 2 focuses on how identity is constructed, showing how novels allow the processes of narrative construction, its problematic aspects, and the effects of that construction, the social and political interactions involved, by way of a reading of E.L. Doctorow's *The Book of Daniel*. The significance of narrator, narrative voice and point of view is discussed: the novel's protagonist, Daniel, needs to find a voice in which to speak and he has to work out the point of view from which to tell a story that will incorporate an identity that is his own. Daniel's characterization shows that identity may be expressed multivocally, and may be fluid or slippery.

That idea is developed in Chapter 3: Philip Roth's *Operation Shylock* shows the slipperiness of identity and the possibility of splitting, of multiplicity.

The novel's depiction of the difficult idea that one could have a double raises the issue of recognition as necessary for identity, which in turn speaks to the public, potentially political, nature of identity.

Chapter 4 takes up two issues derived from particular narrative techniques. Nadine Gordimer's *A Sport of Nature* shows that narrative gaps add to the possibility that narrative identity will be disunified. Not all about a life is known or shown in the telling. This novel also directs attention to a highly debatable aspect of identity, that of the extent of choice involved in identity construction. Virginia Woolf's *Mrs Dalloway* exemplifies the fragmentation of self and identity as a typically modern theme, presented by means of fragmented plot and structure.

The theme of uncertain identity which has been developed by these readings is focused in Chapter 5 on the content *and* structure of novels as showing how contingency – chance and coincidence – affect the person and their attempt to construct identity. Contingency represents a further threat – more fragmentation – to the self, and to the possibility of a certain identity. This is well displayed in Paul Auster's *Leviathan*, where it is also made clear that there are limits to authorial control of identity construction. This novel is also an exemplary instance of narrative form as capable, through emplotment, of assimilating disruptive effects within an overall coherence. This reading also presents the idea that a developed sense of identity, albeit uncertain or disunified, is a necessary prerequisite for agency and action.

In some respects *Leviathan* is a key novel for this study, not least in the connotation of its title. The exploration of several dimensions of 'that great multitude', echoing the recurring theme of multiplicity in the other novels, contrasts sharply with the association of narrative identity with the unity of a life. Chapter 6 takes up that issue. Assertions about narrative unity, linked with the idea of the unity of a life, are called into question by Thomas Pynchon's *The Crying of Lot 49*. The narrative issue raised by the novel is that closure is not a feature of modern novels, and that coherence does not have to be underwritten by movement towards closure. The significance of emplotment as discussed in Chapter 5 is reiterated here.

The political implications of the overall argument of this study concerning narrative identity are developed in Chapter 7, indicating how this basis can be built on with regard to the application of narrative elements to political argument, the narrativization of political identity, the relationship of the person to the political sphere, and the implications of narrative for political agency and action.

The characters encountered in these literary readings are people who face certain difficulties in narrating their identity. There is not necessarily *a* story to be told: then the questions proliferate: Which story is to be told? Which story will be believed? Whose story is to predominate? More specifically, if political identity is (also) narrative identity, what does narrative suggest about the characteristics of such an identity? If narrative identity carries connotations of identity as being disparate, multiple, characterized by gaps and fragments, liable to chance, incomplete – disordered and disunified – how does this relate to the political identity not only of the person but also of the group, the nation, the state, or extra-state political entities? What is the meaning of narrative identity as that is applied – as it is – to citizen identity, identity politics, national identity, the identity of the state? What of the contradiction that narrative identity may be taken to indicate pattern, a movement towards closure, whereas, if the term is unpacked, narrative may indicate just the opposite? In the political realm it is argued or assumed that – to put it crudely – order is good and disorder is bad: how then could the political encompass political identity, at any level, which is narratively construed or characterized as uncertain, split, multiple, fragmented?

These are the questions surrounding narrative identity as it might be used in political theorizing which this study addresses.

2   The narrative construction of identity

Identity requires the telling of stories both by and about the self: stories the person tells others about themself, or stories others tell about the person, or stories in which the person is included. Narrative identity construed as storytelling entails identity as the public presentation of the self. The fundamental question entailed by this characterization of identity is *how* to represent one's own or another's public self – life or behaviour. Mere description is not sufficient – there is also a need to explain, to account for, to justify. To talk of narrative identity entails attention to how the story is told, the mode of construction, structures and techniques, and why the story – '*this* story' – is being told, and whether it is convincing.

Narrative construction of identity

Narrative identity entails construction; the process of the construction of identity takes a narrative turn. That is, if narrative then narration – a process of construction; or, conversely, if construction, then narrative.

The idea of narrative construction of the self is well recognized – for instance, in the assertion that 'the self is a kind of aesthetic construct, recollected in and with the life of experience in narrative fashion' (Crites 1986: 162). That process – in Alford's terms, of appropriation, reappropriation, organization, rearranging (Alford 1991) – equates to the construction of the self, and the typical mode of such a process is narrative construction.

The strongest claim for narrative construction of the self is made in William Lowell Randall's *The Stories We Are* (1995). Randall suggests that we author ourselves into being, and that 'pure unstoried action, pure unstoried existence in the present is impossible'. Our life ('character') is 'formed, revealed, and re-created by the exigencies of an unfolding "plot"'. It is a case of not just having but being a story:

> A life has a beginning, a middle, and end, like a story. A life is about someone doing something, as is a story. A life has a main person in the middle of it, as a story often has. A life can be fraught with conflict, can be seen as manifesting a set of recurrent themes, and can even be divided

into certain chapters – again, as can a story. A life is a sort of world within itself, as is a story.

(Randall 1995: 93, 205, 110–11)

Somewhat similarly, Schechtman claims that, '[t]he sense of one's life as unfolding according to the logic of a narrative is not just an idea we have, it is an organizing principle of our lives' (Schechtman 1996: 113).

However, narrative identity requires a rather different emphasis than that focus on self-creation: it is not confined to self-narration. Attention to narrative identity has therefore to be wider than specification of the narrative self. For example, there are discrepancies between how we present our own character and what it looks like from the outside – 'our life and the genre by which we story it do not always jibe' (Randall 1995: 165). Just as the self and identity are, analytically, both separate and related, so too the narrative construction of identity must be distinguished from, while linked to, the narrative construction of the self. The construction of narrative identity includes response to others and their stories.

It is clearly not just the stories I tell about myself that affect the shape and direction of my self-creation but the stories others tell about me as well . . . [t]hese stories help to create the social climate in which my life is lived and to determine the range of options and opportunities by which it is bound.

(Randall 1995: 44)

To adopt the idea of narrative identity, and certainly to draw out the implications of so doing, necessitates some understanding of narrative construction – the narrative process, the way in which narratives are put together, how they achieve their effects. Jerome Bruner asserts that, '[I]t is only in the narrative mode that one can find an identity and find a place in one's culture' (Bruner 1996: x, 121, 42; cf. Bruner 1987; Cave 1995: 112). However, despite emphasis on the naturalness of the storytelling habit, the act of narrating involves selection, patterning, fitting events, characters and episodes into a story. If narrative construction, then it follows that certain rules are imposed: the construction of identity by narrative means need not necessarily be determined – by plot or closure for instance – but in order to be a narrative, certain guidelines have to be followed. What is significant in this context is not construction(ism) as such but the process of narrative construction. Narrative structures and techniques indicate, among other things, that the process of narrative construction of identity is a matter of showing and of placing ourselves and others in the public realm.

Narrative identity is both embodied and embedded. The person, as a biological entity, a human being, has originally 'no identity at all', but moves from that state to recognition of the self (as object of knowledge) through experience and passion to an awareness of identity that is inherently political in that identity entails seeing – being aware of – the self as part of a collective, achieving identity through sexuality, matters of taste and morality, and property (Norton 1988: 11, 39); and the story told about the embodied self is located in relation to the past and to its context.

Separate lives can be recounted as episodes in a containing and continuing narrative, or narratives. Critique of liberal theory focused on the individual has emphasized the setting in which the person is located – thus MacIntyre's 'tradition', or insistence on the significance both of local settings (or traditions) and interaction with others (the Other). In fact, even the autonomous self needs a setting: '[a]utonomy is not a totally personal creation but only flourishes within a community which provides the requisite social forms to sustain it' (Bellamy 1992: 247; cf. Crittenden 1992). The person has to exist, to tell their story, in a social world – they are a situated, located self. Persons construct identity 'by locating themselves or being located within a repertoire of emplotted stories' and 'make sense of what has happened and is happening to them by attempting to assemble or in some way integrate these happenings within one or more narratives'. Action is guided by narratives 'on the basis of the projections, expectations, and memories derived from a multiplicity but ultimately limited repertoire of available social, public and cultural narratives' (Somers 1994: 614).

'Construction' may be objected to as too mechanical; alternatively, constructed identity can be said to be analogous to performance, 'constituting ourselves as works of art' (Love 1993; cf. Siegle 1986: 105; Randall 1995: 37, 39; Ezrahi 1995) – including writing or telling. The narrative construction of identity tends to blur the lines between 'construction' with mechanical connotations and 'creation' with artistic overtones – somewhat in line with the dictionary definition of constructionism as 'artistic expression by means of mechanical structures'.

The inclusion in this study of readings of novels proceeds from the fact that identity construction can be observed in narrative fictions. This recourse to novels acknowledges their autonomy as literary constructs; and it is 'construct' that affords at least one link to theoretical concerns. Observation of how identities are constructed within the novel (to reiterate, as a matter of form *and* content) may assist understanding of how narrative identity is constructed – building an identity by telling stories – and the implications of that process of construction for the usage of the term in a political context.

I have suggested that narrative construction can be studied by attention to narratives; it is time, then, to look at a narrative fiction, E.L. Doctorow's *The Book of Daniel*.

The Book of Daniel

This novel is clearly about the construction of identity: narration and plot make this plain. The process of construction is foregrounded throughout the novel at two levels: the fictional process whereby the character, Daniel, puts together the story of his life, and the authorial process whereby the writer, Doctorow, utilizes narrative structure and technique for fictional characterization of the process.

This is a novel where form and content are noticeably strongly interconnected. The construction of identity depends on certain narrative techniques and is expressed by narrative elements – voice and point of view. So, for instance, multiplicity of voice and point of view both stem from and represent ambiguities or confusions in Daniel's identity, including his own awareness of that identity (Fowler, D. 1992: 48–9). Such features effectively direct the reading of this novel because form and content combine to produce the effect of instability.

The novel begins as Daniel, ostensibly writing his thesis in the university library, records the events of Memorial Day earlier in the year, 1967. His sister Susan has been admitted to a mental hospital having attempted suicide. Daniel goes with his wife and baby to join his foster parents, the Lewins, at the hospital to try to get Susan discharged. This event and Susan's subsequent death structurally frame the narrative in which, in order to find out why she attempted suicide, Daniel has to think back to their childhood, the arrest and trial of their parents, Paul and Rochelle Isaacson, executed for treason (based on the true story of the Rosenbergs), and how those events affected their children. Daniel tells two interlocking stories: that of the Isaacson family, and that of Susan and himself since their parents' death. In each case, the narrative structure is such as to 'explain' the execution of the Isaacsons, Susan's hospitalization and death, and, implicitly deriving from these, his own situation.

Daniel's book

In several senses this novel is 'Daniel's book', his thesis, an attempt at analysis. At the beginning of the novel, he is in the library, 'roaming through the stacks, searching, too late, for a thesis' (17).[1] The thesis which Daniel purports to be writing is another framing device for the novel; what he writes – the book of Daniel – has at times the appearance of notes for, or sections of, that work. As a thesis, his book is to be presented: so narrative construction of identity is not merely a personal matter, for the protagonist's own satisfaction, but a public narrative. However, his thesis is not his academic work but rather the explanation he seeks for the immediate event of his sister Susan's attempted suicide and, behind that, their family history, the events of their childhood which have brought them to positions of cynicism and despair. The analysis required is of the Isaacsons' arrests and executions – and consequently of the state of America. Daniel's attempt to find a thesis – to analyse and explain – reveals not only that there was more to his and Susan's lives than would be apparent to their political friends or enemies, but also tells *his* story, which he needs to write – 'I, Daniel, was grieved, and the visions of my head troubled me and I do not want to keep the matter in my heart' (170). His book focuses on his life, despite the fact that he thinks that he is writing Susan's life.

A thesis requires the accumulation of evidence; Daniel accumulates evidence; but what the narrative presents is more than just factual or objective evidence. This narrative telling is neither innocent nor objective. Alternations between telling the story and narrative description, narratorial harangues and historical discourse combine to present a picture of Daniel as well as of his sister and parents. Non-fictional passages interspersed throughout the novel appear, at first reading, to break up the narrative. However, there are connections between the narrative and non-narrative sections. For example, in a passage on Bukharin, a comment on his behaviour during the 1938 trials – 'And what good did it do him except that he became a hero in a novel and an image of sorrowful nobility to Sovietologists' (54) – could be a comment on Paul Isaacson. Furthermore the whole passage, with its reference to differing historical interpretations of events, suggests the unreliability of historical narratives – of the kind that Daniel purports to want to write. Daniel's book shows how ambiguous may be the materials – the evidence – available for the process of narrative construction.

If this is a thesis, one might expect conclusions. These are presented as provisional in that Daniel offers three endings, each of which offers a comment on the story(ies) he has told. In one ending Daniel returns to his childhood home to find poor black inhabitants, worse off than the Isaacsons had been – and hence a reminder of the continuity of suffering. His sister's funeral forms another ending. In yet another ending, he is back in the library, writing his dissertation/novel/journal/confession. The choice of endings indicates a certain circularity, a return to the 'now' of the novel specified at its beginning, which of itself belies the supposed linearity of narrative and, thence, of narrative identity. Daniel has moved on, but he also has had to go back. In the 'present time' of the novel he is finally told to 'Close the book, man . . . don't you know you're liberated' (309). The revolution has begun, and its locus is life, not books. The novel closes with a quotation from the Biblical Book of Daniel. The book ends – on the page – but Daniel's story is obviously not finished. According to Levine, '[the] multiplicity of endings suggests both the process of self-realization and the continuity of history' (Levine 1985: 47); and the absence of a 'determinate ending' to the novel is 'less important than that Daniel has taken control of the narrative. A space of action seems open to him for the first time' (King 1988: 53).

There is certainly no closure in this novel – not only multiple endings, but also no end to the uncertainty indicated by an incident towards the end of the novel when Daniel visits his parents' betrayer, Selig Mindish. An episode in Disneyland provides a sudden twist to the story he has been recounting, by way of the understanding that there are alternative versions of what his parents may have been and done, of their innocence or guilt. If that is the case, then his thesis may be false. As with Susan's life and death, so the

Isaacsons' guilt or innocence is never resolved. (Daniel's comment on Susan's death is 'She died of a failure of analysis' (307).)

Reactions to *The Book of Daniel*, especially immediately after its publication in 1971, have often been expressed in terms of its assumed political stance, in particular that it depicts the 'failure' of the New Left (cf. Fowler, D. 1992: 44). Such judgements fall into the trap of presuming that the novel is some kind of a historical chronicle, with direct parallels to be drawn with historical events, particularly the Rosenberg trial. The narrative 'taken as read' strongly works against that kind of reading: there is uncertainty, and, for a thesis, a disturbing amount of doubt about every bit of evidence. As Daniel remarks early in the book: 'Everything is elusive. God is elusive. Revolutionary morality is elusive. Justice is elusive. Human character' (44). That remark comes when Daniel supposes that 'the couple on the poster' (representing Susan's idea of her parents) are not the Isaacsons, but the real spies for whom the Isaacsons were stand-ins – a possibility that was current at the time. 'That couple got away. Well-funded, and supplied with false passports, they went either to New Zealand or Australia. Or Heaven' (43). The text within the text is inconclusive; indeed, the identity of the text as such is debatable, given the several ways that it is possible to read this novel – a 'generic mixture of journal form, history, thesis and fiction' (Hutcheon 1988: 137).

Daniel as author

What narrative does Daniel want to construct? How is he to construct that narrative? How does Daniel, as writer of his book, construct his own identity and that of the other characters? *The Book of Daniel* supports, and demonstrates, the contention that identity *does* have to be constructed – told or written. Daniel strives for autonomy and self-authoring, from the simplest, most basic level, of what name he is to be known by, through his persona as son, stepson, brother, husband, father, by way of the movement from thesis-writing as a graduate student to writing his book, the 'thesis' of his parents' innocence or guilt. Daniel's attempt to do that brings out what is involved, albeit negatively at times: remembrance, reflection, collection of evidence, comparison with historical or cultural analogues; and selection, amendment, rethinking – any and all of the stages in writing or telling. Remembrance and evidence allow Daniel to move towards a future where he and others will be able to recognize his identity.

The overt narrative construction evident in this novel draws attention both to how identity is 'written' and to the non-certainty of that construction. Daniel discusses his book *as* a construction, what a critic calls 'an artistic endeavor and hope for more than just historical accuracy', attempting to 'invent and give expression to symbols and images that unite history and fiction, the general and the particular, the world of external pain and oppression and the world inside himself' (Girgus 1988: 84, 76). 'How does one, the story asks, tell oneself without losing oneself?' (Newton 1995: 16): what *The Book of Daniel* (like others of the novels read here) makes clear is how much is given away in the process of narrative construction; the very act of narrating carries the risk that more can be read into the account of identity than was intended. This novel seems to show that self-narrating does not – cannot – guarantee control of the identity so constructed.[2]

Daniel's legacies

Daniel ostensibly explores the confusions of Susan's identity, but in practice has to come to terms with his own need to cope with the legacies of his family, culture and historical and socio-political background, in order to move towards self-understanding and identity. Family, the Old and New Left, America itself, constitute the legacy which Daniel has to negotiate in order to find himself (Levine 1988: 67). These are no gift to him. For instance, as he says,

> [a]ll my life I have been trying to escape from my relatives and I have been intricate in my run, but one way or another they are what you come upon around the corner, and the Lord God who is so frantic for recognition says you have to ask how they are and would they like something cool to drink, and what is it you can do for them this time.
>
> (31)

Doctorow says that the idea of a radical family – 'all the paradoxes and contradictions of that family against whom the entire antagonistic force of society is directed' – was one of the core ideas for the book (Trenner 1983: 46). But this novel is not 'the story of the Isaacsons as seen retrospectively through the eyes of their child' – as a more straightforward, conventional novel or narrative history might have it. Rather, it is an attempt to show how that story – of the Isaacsons' family life, of the arrests and executions – shaped the identity of their children.

The Isaacsons are the focus of much of Daniel's anger. From his present perspective he is scornful of their naivety, attacking both his mother's realism and his father's idealism (Schulz 1988: 14). But Daniel has two sets of parents: he is either Daniel Isaacson or Daniel Lewin, either the son of Paul and Rochelle Isaacson or the son of Robert and Lise Lewin, taken in by them after the Isaacsons' execution – and thence a very practical problem of identity, naming, together with the deeper issue of deciding which are truly his parents. The corresponding problem in political terms is that he cannot figure out whether he is a radical or a liberal – or whether he even has the choice (King 1988: 49).

The Lewins are parodied as typical bourgeois liberals for whom 'civility is the essence of being human. It is what makes communication possible. The absence of civility disturbs them because it can mean anything from rudeness at a table to suicide. Or genocide' (28). And they are incapable of regretting taking the children in, even '[A]s cruel as we are. And we are really terrible low down people' (14). One critic suggests that Daniel represents 'a politicized version of Freud's family romance', in which different parents, 'usually prominent and powerful', are fantasized. If this is so, romance is overcome by nightmare for Daniel because of the Isaacsons' notoriety as traitors. The children felt betrayed by their parents, but they cannot escape the problem of being who they are:

> [i]f in their proud, snotty, tormented adolescence he and his sister tacitly came to the conclusion that Paul and Rochelle Isaacson were not worth their loyalty, there was, however, nothing they could do to squander it . . . They were like figures in a myth who suffer the same fate whatever version is told; who remain in eternal relationship no matter how their names are spelled.
>
> (65)

Daniel rejects the family name, but also recognizes the value of both his grandmother's religion and his mother's politics as '[S]ome purchase on the future against the terrible life of the present' (43). His family legacy includes the curse from his grandmother, through his mother, 'let our death be his bar mitzvah', which is compounded by Susan's belief that he repeats their killing by his lack of radicalism. But his father's Jewishness becomes real to him, re-realized in one of the book's endings, when he has prayers for the dead said for his sister.

Family identity is a major theme of this novel, not least because of the centrality of the Isaacsons and Daniel's remembrances of them. In its treatment of the identity of the family, this novel breaks down any supposed division between the family as private and the political. It well demonstrates that there are both personal and social aspects to identity, despite the fact that because this is Daniel's book the subjects of the novel relate always to him, to his self-awareness at the 'present' stage of his life. He presents himself as cold and cynical, overtly detached from relationships. For example, his immediate reaction to Susan's condition is that he is grateful to her 'for relieving the dangerous tedium of his graduate life. She would be all right. In the meantime there was drama, a sweet fatality, a recharging of the weak diffused impulses of giving a shit' (15).

By showing the circumstances surrounding the formation of a person's identity as a process that involves self-awareness, consciousness of the possibility of self-shaping, but within a particular historical and political context, the novel shows how necessary the social context is, positively or negatively, and the intersections with wider, extra-personal identities. Doctorow has explained that he was interested in 'what happens when all the antagonistic force of society is brought to bear and focussed on one or possibly two individuals', and what kind of 'anthropological ritual' that is (Trenner 1983: 61). Identity is not only a matter of social construction; but identity construction has to be social – the self, the personal, is not enough. Daniel 'comes to see his subjectivity not in terms of any humanist notion of unique-ness and individuality, but as the result of processes which appear to be outside him (politics)'. He cannot produce 'the realist novel's conventions of ordered and meaningful identity'; his 'I' is 'social and political, as well as fragmented and discontinuous' (Hutcheon 1988: 84).

Daniel, Susan and their contemporaries are said to be legatees of the Cold War attack on the Old Left, which left a 'complex legacy of idealism and betrayal, self-righteousness and self-deception' – a comment on what they are as well as what they have inherited. Fowler sees Daniel as

> the essence of his campus generation's dismay and distrust . . . alienated from the American WASP establishment because the establishment had one summer's midnight strapped each of his parents into the chair at Sing Sing penitentiary and killed them with bolts of electricity. Daniel does not *play* at alienation and radical campus theatrics, and his disquiet with the American national myth is desperately real.
>
> (Fowler, D. 1992: 43)

Given 'the radical choice' entailed by his political legacy, 'the twin inheri-tance of repression and radicalism that haunts post-war America', then 'it is understandable why Daniel feels ambivalent about this dubious inheritance' (Levine 1988: 67; cf. Levine 1985: 41, 43).

This novel might be said to be 'about' American identity – conceived, for instance, 'in terms of a collective enterprise involving religious, moral, and political principles', the meaning of which 'has variously been defined by such phrases as the New Jerusalem, the inalienable rights of man, and democ-racy' (Schulz 1988: 14). Schulz is particularly helpful in suggesting the inter-play between form and content as a way of showing 'the idea of America' as dynamic. The particular value of Schulz's commentary on Doctorow's work is that it suggests the simultaneous existence of, and the parallels between, national and personal identity – 'America' existing as a collective ideal as well as an internalized quest. Levine, speaking of Doctorow's novels as political in that they address 'Freud's judgment that "America is a gigantic mistake"', says that, 'By this I do not mean that Doctorow shares Freud's judgment but rather that his fiction describes the gap in America's life between its ideals and its reality' (Levine 1985: 19). Schulz appears to agree with this judgement, speaking of 'the gap that separates ideal vision from reality'. American heroism 'turns out to be fragile and problematic': 'Precisely because of his orientation toward a goal that presumably can be realized on this earth, the American hero emerges as a radical quester, rest-lessly driven and more often than not deeply alienated' (Schulz 1988: 15).

Doctorow himself claims that because:

there is so little a country this size has in the way of cohesive, identifying marks that we can all refer to and recognize each other from . . . [there is] enormous pressure on us all to become as faceless and peculiarly indistinct and compliant as possible. In that case . . . the need to find color or definition becomes very, very strong.

(Trenner 1983: 58–9)

Hence the characterization of Daniel as fighting to realize an identity in part dependent on, but also needing to be independent of, his personal and political inheritance.

Daniel as victim or survivor

Critics have accounted for Daniel's identity in terms of victim; but he is also survivor, both of his family and of their politics, struggling to find his place in the society that killed his parents. Daniel had thought that 'we were important people. I thought the world really revolved around my family. We had this way of understanding everything' (96). But what happened to the Isaacsons became something neither they nor he had any control over, participating in without making decisions (Levine 1988: 61). So Daniel appears constrained by the trauma that took his parents from him and redefined his own identity. However, Doctorow asserts that what is of interest in this novel is Daniel's position as 'survivor of his own holocaust'.

The Book of Daniel shows how difficult it is to break free of one's inherited past, but also shows that this can be done. 'Daniel's problem is how to escape the narratives imposed on him by others': Cold War narratives of dangerous communists; left-wing stories of heroic parents and suffering children; Susan's (and the New Left's) story of rich but pitiable children of martyred radicals; and even the possible story offered by Disneyland – corporate America's version of the past and future. His only way of escape is 'by seizing the narrative and telling his own story, which implies undermining the other narratives that have tried to incorporate his experience. Thus he writes himself into existence and becomes . . . his own progenitor' (King 1988: 53). Daniel becomes the writer of his own book *as* a survivor, 'a writer, a student of history who imaginatively reconstructs the events he has survived' (Levine 1985: 65).

Daniel needs to write that history to gain a life. As Philip Roth says:

You search your past with certain questions on your mind – indeed, you search out your past to discover which events have led you to asking those specific questions. It isn't that you subordinate your ideas to the force of the facts in autobiography but that you construct a sequence of stories to bind up the facts with a persuasive *hypothesis* that unravels your history's meaning.

(Roth 1989: 8)

For Daniel, writing his book represents a process of organizing himself, of maturing. Levine associates this with a process of mourning, only completed 'when Daniel has closed his book and re-entered the world of the living. Writing is the activity by which he comes to terms with the legacy of the dead and his responsibilities as a survivor' (Levine 1988: 70; cf. Girgus 1988: 77).

The extent of choice involved is a debatable aspect of identity construction, as is the way that aspect of identity is worked out narratively. 'Throughout the novel Daniel is urged to choose', and '[F]inally he makes the radical choice but only after he has learnt to do it without rejecting his heart' (Levine 1985: 46). The legacies of family, political and cultural history and national identity constitute givens of Daniel's identity – but what this and other novels strongly suggest is that givens are not determinant: the process of construction includes the affirmation or rejection of what is given.

Narration

Daniel's book, his telling, precisely and vividly, even shockingly at times, is an exercise in recording a struggle for identity. But this *is* a fiction: the actual process of construction is that of the writer, Doctorow. How then does he show Daniel constructing his identity?

The reader gets to know what is happening, who the characters are, why they act as they do and what motivates them, as one might in real life, by a combination of direct telling, reported events, hints, clues and connections. Passages in the book are written in free indirect speech – a literary technique frequently employed in post-realist narratives whereby thoughts are reported as spoken, although they have never, in fact, been voiced. This is a narrative technique which presents 'a character's thoughts with an honesty and eloquence that character would not have been capable of without the aid of the author'. For example, in this novel the reader is taken by Daniel/ Doctorow into the mind of the ghost of Daniel's grandmother, who 'whispers to him from beyond the grave' (Fowler, D. 1992: 36–7). Although long sections of the book appear as conventional realist[ic] accounts of actual happenings, at times passages of stream of consciousness interrupt the narrative flow, even in mid-sentence. The non-chronological narrative prevents the reader from going with the story unthinkingly, as do the frequent switches between narrative and non-narrative.

Doctorow explains that 'beginning with *Daniel*, I gave up trying to write with the concern for transition characteristic of the nineteenth-century novel . . . I can't accept the conventions of realism any more' (Trenner 1983 40). For example, the device of having Daniel appeal directly to the reader, as in 'A NOTE TO THE READER/Reader, this is a note to you' (56), allows for comment on the narrative; but there is a further narrative twist when 'Daniel' questions the reader's identity: 'Do you believe it? Shall I continue? . . . Who are you anyway? Who told you you could read this?

Is nothing sacred?' (62). These direct appeals to the reader are among the Brechtian distancing devices prominent in this novel, reinforcing the impression of a book in the process of being written.

Daniel, as the novel cleverly shows, is confused. That confusion is represented by structural features such as non-chronological narrative: obvious disjunctions in the narrative flow, cuts and transpositions, reflect Daniel's state of mind (King 1988: 49, 50). The depiction of identity construction in progress is achieved by narrative technique: multivocality, recurring images and symbols, lack of closure – the trappings of '"rhetorical" literary presentation' used 'to point to the humanly constructed character of these trappings – their arbitrariness and their conventionality' (Hutcheon 1988: 45). Three interrelated aspects of narrative technique are particularly noteworthy in this novel: narrator, narrative voice and point of view.

Narrator

My proposition that identity be regarded as a matter of storytelling, as the public expression and acknowledgement of the self, implies the involvement of a narrator. A narrative is not presented directly to an audience: it is mediated by a narrator – whether or not the narrative voice is 'audible'. 'The narrator's presence derives from the audience's sense of some demonstrable communication. If it feels it is being told something, it presumes a teller. The alternative is a direct witnessing of the action' (Chatman 1978: 157). This is an important aspect of narrative identity. What is presented is not pure fact but a mediated version of what is to be shown (though paradoxically, the narrator is ostensibly responsible for the narration, and tells the story as 'true fact').

Two features of narration especially prominent in this novel, unreliable narration and self-revealing narration, are important for narrative identity. Narrators may, in general, be perceptive or obtuse, reliable or unreliable. Do we then, 'believe everything that the narrator tells us, or suspect that either deceit or obtuseness on his/her part requires us to see more than he or she does?' (Hawthorn 1992: 117; and see Randall 1995: 172–3). There is a technical sense of unreliable narration whereby '[w]hat makes a narrator unreliable is that his values diverge strikingly from . . . the rest of the narrative': that is, the norm of the work 'conflicts with the narrator's presentation, and we become suspicious of his sincerity or competence to tell the "true version"' (Chatman 1978: 149). Unreliability may also be a result of irony on the part of the narrator, and thus 'potential deception', or of 'inconscience' – 'the narrator is mistaken, or he believes himself to have qualities which the author denies him' (Booth 1983: 158–9). (This latter sense is typical of Daniel, and of the narrators that follow.)

Can the 'I' who tells the story be trusted? First-person narrators may be considered particularly authentic, but they may also be particularly unreliable because they do not know as much as other characters – or the reader. Even where Daniel is clearly the storyteller, there are challenges to his narrative – as, for example, when Susan objects to his characterization of their mother, or when he himself, reporting an outing to hear Robeson sing, details his father's behaviour and then says 'How do I know this? If I was crouched behind a seat, how do I remember this?' (52). He corrects his own story from time to time – for instance, having described his father as not understanding his young son, Daniel comments, 'But this describes just a moment's oversensitive perception by the little criminal of perception. He was warm and affectionate' (34); or, more subtly, on his parents' deaths 'for crimes they did not commit. Or maybe they did committ them. Or maybe my mother and father got away with false passports for crimes they didn't committ. How do you spell comit?' (43).

Narrative identity is as vulnerable to unreliable narration as any other form of narrative. That this is so is one of the more important understandings to be gained from a movement away from dependence on realist novels as the model for (understandings of) narrative: post-realist novels call into question the nature of authorship and narration in a way that the omniscient narration of high realism hardly allows.

Daniel is, almost parodically, even comically so, the figure of the omni-present, directive author. This is, in several senses, his book. He corresponds to Randall's 'dramatized' narrators 'who are very aware of themselves as conveyors of the story' (as distinct from 'undramatized' narrators, who 'rarely if ever discuss their writing chores', who 'seem unaware that they are writing, thinking, or speaking, at all') (Randall 1995: 172). However, despite the surface self-awareness, narrator's interjections and management of narrative flow, the 'authorial' presence in the novel is counteracted by at least two factors. One, already noted, is content – the ambiguity surrounding the Isaacsons' political activity and death, despite Daniel's intention to tell 'the Truth'; the other is structural – by way of his narratorial presence as 'author', Daniel gives away more than he may mean to.

Emotional outbursts frequently interrupt the otherwise casual, familiar tone of the narrative: 'Ah Susy, my Susyanna, what have you done' (16), or 'OH PAULY, OH MY POP, IT'S ALL RIGHT, IT REALLY IS ALL RIGHT. BUT WHY DID YOU HAVE TO GIVE YOUR GLASSES TO MINDISH?' (114). There is inconsistency between Daniel's high-minded judgements on his parents and foster-parents, and his straightforward but rather naïve accounts of his own immaturity, as for example when he describes deliberately burning his wife, but then works on their relationship: 'In these talks she looked for a rationale to forgive me and I was able to help her find one. We tried to share responsibility for my actions. We considered me as our mutual problem. I was shameless' (103). Such an evasion, typical of Daniel's narration throughout, points up the possible unreliability of self-narration – and the difference between narrative and description and chronicle.

Voice

Telling identity involves the choice of voice in which to speak. Doctorow has said that 'Each book comes in its own voice, not mine . . . The problem is in *finding* that voice.' When asked why he chose Daniel as narrator, he explains that he began writing the novel 'in the third person, more or less standard past tense . . . very chronologically scrupulous'. Then he became bored and discarded 150 pages, and then, 'I became reckless enough to find the voice of the book which was Daniel's' and 'to speak through Daniel and to have Daniel speak through other sensibilities' (Fowler 1992: 31–2, 38).

As with many other aspects of this novel, there is a complication. Daniel 'speaks' as the 'I' of the story that is being told, but also as 'author' he comments from time to time on how the story is being told (as a real-life teller would). There are two Daniels, the character *in* the story and the author *of* that same story. Daniel as 'author' also has to find a voice. Girgus points out that while one of Daniel's clear themes is his anger at Susan's self-destructive fate, even that 'is complicated and confused by his search for his own moral identity and authenticity – his voice'. And he remarks that Doctorow created 'not one voice in the sense of a clear pristine tone and identity for his main character' but rather 'a process by which Daniel attempts to find that voice as part of a much wider effort at growth and maturity . . . the voice becomes an instrument for exploring different attitudes, ideas and experiences' (Girgus 1988: 76, 75).

As 'author', Daniel frequently seems to stand back from the story he is telling: this is, it must be remembered, a thesis, so facts are to be objectively reported. At times the narrative voice is detached, approximating to the omniscient author of a realist novel. At the beginning of the novel third-person omniscient narration quickly changes as 'an intrusive, nervous "I" speaks directly to the reader, and this "I" is also a Daniel' (Fowler, D. 1992: 33, 34). Shifts between first- and third-person narration continue throughout. There are also anonymous interruptions and occasions where a voice 'behind' Daniel intervenes in the narrative. This technique is used to confirm facts: for example, on the Lewins' treatment of the children, 'Share and share alike, the cardinal point of justice for children driven home to them with vicious exactitude. (Do not strike, this is rhetorical but true. Only a son of Rochelle's could say this line)' (63).

The device of direct 'authorial' intervention in the narrative can be evasive – and thence draws attention to the effect of construction. For example, when Daniel is describing his wife's parents, and her father's questions about his daughter's bruises, there is a sudden shift to a new paragraph: 'This is no day to be in the library. It is too beautiful and warm . . . I will go back and take them to the park' (59). This is too obviously 'Daniel the good husband and father', out of line with the immediately preceding narrative and with the picture of him in those roles elsewhere in the novel (though, confusingly, *that* picture is also ostensibly presented by himself).

Shifts in narrative voice are further complicated by changes in tense or person, either indicating change of narrator or emphasizing Daniel's continuing management of the narrative. For example, when he goes to examine Susan's abandoned car after her suicide attempt, there is a section of third-person narration, describing what Daniel does, and then:

> This describes the picture the moment before Daniel got the picture. To be just, he had started something in the restaurant so as to get to Susan's car. He had needed to see the car. The feeling that crept upon me was of being summoned. They're still fucking us.
>
> (30)

It is as though, given that this *is* all the book that he is writing, Daniel switches from first to third person to become the author not the subject.

Despite the fact that Daniel is apparently telling the story, this is a multi-vocal narrative,[3] and so voice is connected to the multiplicity of identity which literary theorists account a feature of modern(ist) identity (O'Donnell 1992: 6). The narrative voice – who is speaking – apparently shifts from time to time, and Daniel himself speaks in more than one voice. Such multi-vocality conveys an impression – or the reality – of instability, uncertainty about identity.

Point of view

Doctorow's novels are characterized as carrying 'an almost Jamesian multi-plicity of perspectives, observers and observations' and 'a great variety of narrative strategies, striking differences in point of view' (Friedl 1988: 19), an observation that is certainly true of *The Book of Daniel*. Indeed, Doctorow is said to have found himself

> imagining the story being told via a narrative of images that simply appeared and accumulated before the mind's eye like photographs without captions, or video clips without any sort of voice-over commentary that would help the reader place the material in time, place or consciousness.
>
> The novel that resulted is a sort of prose video that takes place inside several consciousnesses, skipping at will from mind to mind, tone to tone, point of view to point of view.
>
> (Fowler, D. 1992: 32)

Just as Daniel's is the narrative voice, so the novel is ostensibly narrated from his point of view. First-person narration usually ties the narrative to a fixed point of view. However, although it might appear that actually occurring events are multi-perspectival, whereas stories are told from one point of view at a time (Lodge 1992: 26), narrative point of view may also be shifting and multiple. In this novel there is not a single point of view. A particularly obvious instance of shifting point of view is apparent in Daniel himself, between his stance as serious writer of history and his narration as from a child's consciousness, showing the effect of events on a child. For example, the Isaacsons' arrests, which constitute a major section of the narrative, are told as Daniel remembers the events from the perspective of his childhood. That this novel is, in part, narrated as from a child's point of view is appropriate both in respect of the extent to which his narrative is retrospective, remembering in detail and trying to get the sense of episodes in his childhood, and as a reminder of Daniel's continuing immaturity. (Such retrospection, (re)patterning the events of the past in order to account for the present, is a major feature of narrative construction: but it is problematic, as I show below.)

The Book of Daniel parodies or takes to extremes features such as the assumption of omniscience, the ability to see into the motives or intentions of others, as against questioning and uncertainty which, according to critics like Martin, 'contribute to the total perspective from which a narrative account is presented to the listener/reader/viewer' (Martin, W. 1986: 51). Yet the novel does show how the process of identity construction is accompanied by the development of a distinct point of view so there's an overall impression of Daniel's confusion, anger and search for resolution.

Point of view is shifting and multiple – Daniel's, obviously, as child and as young man, but also Susan's, their parents', and even, eventually, the Mindishes', expressed as a realization of the similarity between Daniel and the Mindishes's daughter, 'the identity of their situation . . . locked in family truths' (Levine 1988: 67). Again, the concept of embedment implies, among other things, that there will be different possible points of view. As with voice, so multiple, or shifting, points of view suggest the potential instability of identity – as many stories as points of view? Narrative voice and point of view, often interrelated if not indistinguishable (Siegle 1986: 240), both relate to identity at least in terms of clarity of narration. The crucial question is whether a distinct – clearly voiced – identity is possible. In this novel both are closely related to Daniel's confusions about identity. Daniel's is nowhere near a 'finished' life. As depicted he is only getting to the point where he has an identity at all, where he knows who he is: all else is to come?

Generally speaking, point of view constitutes a perspective or stance: 'Point of view is the physical place or ideological situation or practical life-orientation to which narrative events stand in relation' (Chatman 1978: 153, 154). Voice, on the other hand, is the expression of that point of view. Various technical devices, such as tense, grammatical person, focus, or the complicity inherent in the use of 'we', may contribute to a total point of view, directing the reader/listener along certain lines. However, it is also held that '[P]oint of view does *not* mean expression: it only means the perspective in terms of which the expression is made' (Chatman 1978: 153); it is 'a set of attitudes, opinions, and personal concerns that constitute someone's stance in relation to the world' (Martin, W. 1986: 147). But as with voice, so here the question is whose – or what – perspective?

Issues in narrative construction

The Book of Daniel makes it plain that the narrative construction of identity is not unproblematical: issues raised by that idea form a major part of this study. An understanding of identity and identity structure as 'fluid and responsive to its social context' entails thinking of identities as 'dynamic processes' and understanding that we are 'constructing our reality and our selves in a constant movement', rather than the traditional perception of identity as the result of a developmental process, 'found' and, however fragilely, static in adulthood. 'Narrative identity, being at the same time fictitious and real, leaves room for variations on the past – a "plot" can always be revised – and also for initiatives in the future. It is an open-ended identity' (Martin, W. 1986: 8). All of this is evident from Daniel's story.

The very element of construction as characteristic of narrative allows that different stories may be told – different points of view adopted – about the same events concerning the same person. 'Our life, it turns out, is not one story but many, a plethora of stories in fact, both stories within us and stories we are, in turn, within' (Randall 1995: 185). Certainly 'the stories we tell' and 'the stories that are told about us' may vary according to time and circumstance. A classic political case is the hero of the people, revolutionary leader, guerrilla insurgent, become (elected) head of state and world statesman.

Identities – especially externally ascribed identities – may be contestable, changing, for instance, in response to exterior political conditions. 'Identities, whether racial or other, are not permanently fixed. Rather, they are socially constructed and inscribed with particular meanings within the context of existing power relations' (Kellner 1995). For instance, Cornel West remarks that the 'common condition' of 'Blackness' is 'stretched too far when viewed in a *homogenizing* way that overlooks how racist treatment vastly differs owing to class, gender, sexual orientation, nation, region, hue and age' (West 1995: 159). Crude 'black and white' distinctions are not supportable: Dorothy West's *The Wedding* (1995) presents a vivid portrayal of the conflict of understandings and values involved in 'passing'; Toni Morrison's *Tar Baby* depicts variations within 'black identity' (cf. Gubar 1997).

Narrative structuring allows that narratives may be revised, reinterpreted – to incorporate other(s) stories; unexpected events can be assimilated; stories can be reconstructed – on the basis of remembrance, memory or invention; and identities can be retold in reaction to previous narratives of identity. Recollection and memory are essential to the narrative process – remembering the past in order to tell and retell and revise narrative identity. Because narrative is processual, there is constant revision and editing, allowing the assimilation of untoward events, the unexpected: the story is shaped and reshaped as it is being told. Cave speaks of 'the practical sense of positioning and repositioning which ordinary individuals go through in order to find a name and a place that they can consider their own' – as against notions of either an authentic self or a deconstructed self (Cave 1995: 109; cf. McCormick 1988: 224 ff.; Bernstein 1994: 65).

While 'human subjects develop (and inherit) the identity of a character in the gradually unfolding narrative that is lived time', 'the script is not entirely prewritten; only certain backdrops are preset', and 'we interrupt the ongoing drama with retrospective assessments and refigurations'. 'It is as such a narrator that we make sense of our lives, delineate the character(s) that we are and have been' (Kerby 1991: 109, 110). This raises the question as to whether identities can be *re*-constructed. Remembering is a problematic facet of narrative construction. 'History' – attempting to tell a story, to go back into the past – is, as Susan Stephenson shows Graham Swift's *Waterland* (1992) to epitomize, a tricky concept: 'Historical data, common knowledge and myth become difficult to separate'. Stephenson points out that Swift's novels 'render problematic the relation between what is lived and what is told': the problem is that of the attempt at recovering 'certain meaning'. The antidote to the possibility of disabling uncertainty is then remembrance, 'the constant process of recalling imagining, judging what has past [*sic*] in the light of a possible future' (Stephenson 1998).

Narrative may also – and, it may be claimed, justifiably – not merely remember but invent. J.M. Coetzee has said:

> You tell the story of your life by selecting from a reservoir of memories, and in the process of selecting you leave things out. To omit to say that you tortured flies as a child is, logically speaking, as much an infraction of truth to fact as to say that you tortured flies when in fact you didn't.
> (Coetzee cited in Banville 1997: 24; and cf. Cave 1995: 110–11)

Cave suggests, in a remark that could well be speaking of Daniel, that the stories told to establish identity are not 'strictly fictional', but neither do they relate securely to the real world: 'They may indeed seem more fluid and ingeniously inventive than fiction, especially as they have to be continuously reassessed and updated to take account of shifting circumstances and new evidence' (Cave 1995: 112).

Identity may be formed in reaction to a previously-held identity, or to givens, or to other constraints on free construction. For example, for the young women, Sula and Nel in Toni Morrison's *Sula*: '[B]ecause each had discovered years before that they were neither white, nor male, and that all freedom was forbidden them, they had to set about creating something else to be (Morrison 1982: 52)'. In extreme circumstances at least, it can be necessary to (re)create a new identity. Miller points out that 'national identities are continually being rebuilt', for instance 'when imperialism gives way to post-imperial retrenchment, or when previously excluded groups demand and are granted recognition within the boundaries of what is taken to constitute the nation' (Miller, D. 1995: 155).

Politically speaking, interpretation is significant, as linked to the understanding that 'identity' is not a fixed term. The stories that constitute narrative political identity may be interpreted differently by tellers and listeners, and among listeners (cf. Siegle 1986: 133–6, 185). Persons are collectively and individually embedded in an ongoing history which in turn requires a process of interpretation; but that need for interpretation opens up further possibilities for identity narratives. 'If we were to revise that story by interpreting its events from a different point of view, much might change' (Martin, W. 1986: 8). The question of interpretation also arises in connection with the perceptions of others, their recognition of the person's stories, and the negotiations by which stories by and about the self are combined in the construction of an identity.

That stories of identity may be interpreted differently is indicated by Rancière's comment on identification as 'worker', which takes on a double meaning: 'against those who treated them as "workers" – "their" workers – they took on this label': the 'workers' understood the label not as associated with 'a definite technical and social activity, but with a certain way of being at one and the same time inside and outside the symbolic order of the distribution of social identities' (Rancière 1995: 88). However, that identity is constructed – not constituted by a random selection, or telling, of characteristics or events where interpretation would predominate over telling – entails that context limits the range of interpretations that can be given to any story (cf. Siegle 1986: 129).

Because narrative identity is constructed, it may appear that the person is free to tell any story they like, or, indeed, that several – many? – stories can be told. Cave's account of narrative construction well summarizes the position: '[i]t is both possible and normal to give more than one account of the same segment of life and of the identity of the character or characters who figure in it': different people may 'give different accounts of my behaviour and of what kind of person I am' and also I am 'perfectly capable of telling my own story in different ways' (Cave 1995: 112, cf. 110–11). But as he also says quite plainly, 'we are not free . . . to construct any identity at all'. 'Narrative identity' rules out essentialist views of the person and identity, but that does not allow *any* story to be told, *any* identity to be constructed.

Most generally, for any one person there is one set of facts/events/ characteristics from which a story can be constructed; but there is a limit to what stories, how many stories, can be told dependent on that set and feasible combinations to be constituted from it. As Randall points out, different versions of a life-story 'might actually interact with one another to produce the peculiar blend of story-lines that constitute my identity as a person and thus "load" the process of my self-creation in a particular direction' (Randall 1995: 201).

'One of the ways human beings assess and interpret the events of their life is through the construction of plausible narratives' (Bernstein 1994: 55). Because my conception of narrative identity as a matter of storytelling entails construction in public, a particular constraint is the formal requirement of intelligibility. The possibility that any story can be told, or any revision made, is ruled out by the necessity that the stories are to be understood – not necessarily agreed with, found acceptable, but at least falling within the range of the possible, and minimally intelligible (Polonoff 1982: 50).

Narrative identity is neither completely given nor completely freely constructed. It is to be distinguished from those understandings of identity that involve, explicitly or implicitly, a kind of essentialism. That notion of identity is particularly obvious in discussions of what constitutes identity, common in philosophy, which stipulate the need for some element consistent over time which would define an identity, such as memory: 'some sense of self-identity – some sense of the same self being present to itself in its remembered past, its engaged present, and its projected future' (Schrag 1997: 17). Construction entails that identity, or the characteristics that make it up, cannot be solely given(s), so that whereas the essentialist position conventionally rests on the assumption of a preconstituted identity, narratively constructed identity is, at any particular time, provisional (cf. Aronowitz 1995: 114–15).

Narrative construction, the process of narrating, is carried out by reference to events and experiences encountered or recalled. 'Narration into some form of story gives both a structure and a degree of understanding to the ongoing content of our lives' (Kerby 1991: 33). My understanding of narrative identity is that it is a product of self *and* context, combining what is given *and* what is made. Whereas a strictly constructivist position would imply that identity cannot be pre-given at all, the characteristics that make up identity – including narrative identity – do include givens.

The major constraint on what story(ies) can be told is that the self is situated, embedded. This relates to the linguistic – and hence political – aspect of identity and identity construction. Anne Norton refers to a (Hegelian) process of identity-making, which is both individual and political, the latter because it is 'embedded in language, a collective endeavor between two or more who take upon themselves . . . the constraints of a common form' (Norton 1988: 189–90). 'How others story us' has a 'direct effect on the range of social, professional, and economic options' that are open to one, 'an effect on the people who are drawn to me and the company I come to keep', and consequently an effect on 'the nature and direction, the scope and shape, of my self-creation'. This, in turn, 'has an effect on how I story myself in the future, the versions of my own story towards which I gravitate in times to come' (Randall 1995: 44).

Identities are not context-free: the self is embedded in a culture and a history – narratives lived in, in which one is a character. Narrative identity is constructed by reference to, if not in conjunction with, pre-existing and surrounding stories: 'all of us come to *be* who we *are* (however ephemeral, multiple and changing) by being located or locating ourselves (usually unconsciously) in social narratives rarely of our own making' (Somers 1994: 606). Separate lives can be recounted as episodes in a containing and continuing narrative, or narratives, one of which is the political story – hence the stories of person, group, regime interlock. As Kerby has it, much narrative construction of identity is 'a matter of becoming conscious of the narratives that we already live with and in' – he instances family roles. 'Such external narratives will understandably set up expectations and constraints on our personal self-descriptions, and they significantly contribute to the material from which our own narratives are derived' (Kerby 1991: 1, 6; cf. Parker 1994: 17). Kerby refers to MacIntyre's formulation: 'I inherit from the past of my family, my city, my tribe, my nation, a variety of debts, inheritances, rightful expectations and obligations', and, 'the story of my life is always embedded in the story of those communities from which I derive my identity' (MacIntyre 220, 221), an observation confirmed by Daniel's inheritance of legacies ranging from family to nation.

This reading of *The Book of Daniel* emphasizes the *process* of construction. Narrative identity equates to 'a work-in-progress' in which as narrator, protagonist and reader all at once we are squarely 'in the middest', making it up as we go, while 'our "character" is being revealed and re-created by the exigencies of an unfolding "plot" of which we ourselves are partly the author' but which, in turn, 'is continually being shaped by those of the many larger stories in which it is set' (Randall 1995; 205–6). If narrative identity is processual, the telling is important: hence my interest here, and in reading the novels that follow, in narration, narrator, voice and point of view. My reading of this novel directs attention to the mode of narration, elements of narrative suggestive for politics such as the non-intrusive commentary of the novel, achieved by such techniques as shifting point of view or multiple voice. Subsequent chapters take up in more detail other narrative elements relevant to narrative identity, such as emplotment narrative gaps and closure.

I have indicated already that identity is not necessarily fixed or stable. The problem of the maintenance of identity, and the possibility that identity is – or can become – multiple and/or disunified is examined in the next chapter.

3   Uncertain identity

In *The Book of Daniel*, Daniel's narrative construction of identity is a shaky process but he is a very immature person; and the book ends at the point where a stable, adult life could be said to be beginning, when he does appear to be finding a voice in which to narrate identity. But what of identity for an established personality? Philip Roth's *Operation Shylock* shows the uncertainty even of a mature identity, calling into question the characteristics which go to make up identity, and emphasizing the part recognition plays in establishing identity.

Operation Shylock

The Book of Daniel is clearly a fictional construct, albeit with historical references. Narrative voice, and authorial presence behind that voice, is distinct – the narrator is self-consciously writing a life. Whereas Daniel constructs, because the plot of *Operation Shylock* is apparently driven by events, the protagonist, 'Philip Roth' reacts. In both cases though there is ambiguity: questionable evidence available from the text; 'real' facts which may or may not be relevant to the narration; authorial or narratorial manipulation. This novel raises fundamental questions about identity in a case where the process of construction can be presumed to have already been undertaken – and where the story is not unarguably fictional. Whose voice is speaking is unclear; and while the crucial relationship in the plot is with the protagonist's other self, there is also a complex relationship between author and narrator, both of whom are, ostensibly, Philip Roth.

The novel centres on the American Jewish novelist, 'Philip Roth', who is recovering from a breakdown probably brought on by the effects of sleeping pills, Halcion, prescribed after major surgery. He is on his way to Israel on business when he is informed that someone using his name is already there. In Israel, he meets friends and relatives who confuse him with his double – Pipik (the name 'Roth' gives this creature). He eventually confronts the impostor: this double is dying of cancer, but together with his ex-nurse and now lady friend, Jinx, he takes 'Roth' on, both on the subject of the impostoring and on Diasporism – Pipik's plan to avoid a second Holocaust, consequent on Arab destruction of Israel, by returning Jews to their countries of origin in Europe. Pipik has been using 'Roth's' identity to propagate this idea.

One of the friends 'Roth' meets, by chance, is an ex-Columbia colleague, the Palestinian George Ziad. Ziad has returned to Israel to fight the Palestinian cause and is instrumental in involving 'Roth' in argument about, and some understanding of, that problem. This is achieved by way of visits to Ziad's family in the Palestinian sector and observation of the military trial of a young Palestinian accused of terrorism. This trial contrasts with another trial which 'Roth' attends, that of John Demjanjuk, being tried in Jerusalem for war crimes. The major plot theme concerning 'Roth's' identity is mirrored by, commented on, and further complicated by, two sub-plots, or thematic strands, the 'true' identity of Demjanjuk, and the battle of ideas between 'Roth' and Ziad; and the plot becomes increasingly involved with questions of Jewish and Palestinian nationalism.

'Roth' becomes involved with an elderly American, Smilesburger, who mistakenly gives him a large amount of money for Pipik's Diasporist cause. Towards the end of the book, Smilesburger reappears when 'Roth' has been kidnapped, and attempts to involve 'Roth' in a Mossad intelligence operation – Operation Shylock. The story ostensibly ends when 'Roth' refuses and is freed.

The plot moves between issues of personal and political identity – and in places gives way to programmatic statements on these subjects voiced by characters in the course of interactions within the plot: for example, both Ziad and Smilesburger lecture 'Roth' at length about the Jewish situation and his duty to it. The extent to which identity is dependent on the perceptions of others is well brought out: the novel highlights the extent to which identity may be conditional on recognition through its depiction of the crisis of identity consequent upon 'Roth's' attempts to understand his double.

The novel opens with a concern for self-recognition. Description of 'Roth's' breakdown and recovery sets the action of the plot within the context of his own state at the time, including not only his illness and recovery but plans for work in Jerusalem already under way. This substantiates 'Roth's' claim to be in command of himself; but simultaneously he worries that his breakdown is not solely drug-induced. His 'transformation' might be due to 'something concealed, obscured, masked, suppressed, or maybe simply untreated in me until I was fifty-four but as much me and mine as my prose style' (27):[1] he might have been permanently affected by the effects of the drug.

Confidence in his own identity is confused by news of his double. However, 'Roth' is initially decisive: the Roth in Jerusalem 'most certainly was not me', and he decides that he will let the imposture continue. The logic of the situation is that Pipik will be unmasked because 'he manufactures . . . a version of me so absolutely not-me that it will require nothing, neither judicial intervention nor newspaper retractions, to clear everyone's mind of confusion and expose him as whatever he is' (36). For, 'he was not my but *his* hallucination' and,

> up against reality I had at my disposal the strongest weapon in anyone's arsenal: my own reality. It wasn't I who was in danger of being displaced by him but he who had *without question* to be effaced by me – exposed, effaced and extinguished.
>
> (36)

'Roth' phones the impostor, adopting a false identity, but is met with laughter: so, 'He knows, I thought, hanging up. He knows perfectly well who I am' (43). The question that frames the narrative is 'Who *is* "Philip Roth?"'. Similar questions persist throughout: 'How many Roths are there?', or 'Are all the Roths one person?'. Does Roth, author *or* narrator, know who he is – 'Does the reader?'

Uncertainty of identity

> Even when he was in familiar company (his immediate family, for instance) it sometimes seemed to Richard that those gathered in the room were not quite authentic selves – that they had gone away and then come back not quite right, half remade or reborn by some blasphemous, cackhanded and above all inexpensive process. In a circus, in a funhouse. All flaky and carny. Not quite themselves. Himself very much included.
>
> (Amis, *The Information*, 1995: 29)

Roth's novel confirms in practice – through plot and characterization, by narrative techniques such as unreliable narration, evasions and misjudgements and narrative gaps – that identity is not set. Identity is liable to questioning, to doubling, splitting or multiplicity: then even an apparently entrenched identity such as that of 'Philip Roth the well-known author' can be put in doubt. For example, the tension in 'Roth' between being an assimilated American Jew and his potential for Israeli citizenship comes to the fore in Jerusalem. Not only is he forced by Pipik's Diasporism to (re)consider his attitude to the state of Israel, but his chance meeting with Ziad involves him in arguments on his own level as to where his duty lies.

Narratives such as this support and extend an understanding of the contemporary experience of identity as uncertain or unstable. Identity can be precarious, and inasmuch as identity can be established through story-telling, it depends on certain narrative features, including a clearly articulated narrative voice.

However, narration is complicated in this novel by the device of a double – an alternative characterization and voice which is and is not that of the narrator. 'Roth's' perception of himself and recognition by others are threatened by the existence of another bearing identical defining characteristics. This, in turn, makes the requirement of recognition inherent in *narrative* identity problematic at the same time as it emphasizes the public aspect of identity. My reading of the novel suggests that the establishment of identity is not altogether simple for selves (actually existing or fictional), for groups, or for nations. Although it is possible to cite definitions and theories of identity, as I have done in the Introduction, accepting what is in the narrative immediately destabilizes those findings.

Narrative and narration

The understanding that it is necessary to narrate in order to establish identity is complicated in *Operation Shylock* by the conspicuous confusion between 'real' author and fictional narrator – 'Philip Roth the novelist' is apparently both author of, and character in, this text – and between the narrator and his double. Much critical study has been directed at this ambiguity. Roth the writer is quoted as admitting the possibility that his novels constitute: 'the ever-recurring story that's at once your invention and the invention of you', that is, '"mock autobiography"' (Hilfer 1992: 158). His straight-faced explanation of the double is that,

> A man of my age and bearing an uncanny resemblance to me and calling himself Philip Roth turned up in Jerusalem shortly before I did and set about proselytizing for 'Diasporism' . . . Inasmuch as his imposturing constituted a crisis I was living rather than writing, it embodied a form of self-denunciation that I could not sanction, a satirizing of me so bizarre and unrealistic as to exceed by far the boundaries of amusing mischief I may myself have playfully perpetuated on my own existence in fiction.
>
> (Roth 1994: 1, 20)[2]

'Philip Roth the character' remarks early in the story that characters from his – Roth's? – novels are 'broken free of print and mockingly reconstituted as a single satirical facsimile of me' (34); and this duality might explain the double – 'if it's not Halcion and it's no dream, then it's got to be literature' (34).

Narrative voice

Narrative voice in this novel is of more than usual interest; but its identification is of more than usual difficulty. *Who* is telling this story of a life? At times 'Roth' the narrator seems to become confused with Roth the author as, for example, when narration gives way to commentary:

Pipik's being as an antagonist, his being *altogether*, is wholly dependent on the writer, from whom he parasitically pirates what meager selfhood he is able to make even faintly credible.

But why, in exchange, does the writer pirate from him? This is the question plaguing the writer as his taxi carries him safely through Jerusalem's western hills.

(245)

This is the voice of an omniscient narrator – or of the 'real author' – the writer. However, later in the same passage:

It would be comforting to think that, within the confines of a plot over which he's had no authorial control, he has not demeaned or disgraced himself unduly . . . It would be comforting, it would be only natural, to assume that in a narrative contest (in the realistic mode) with this impostor, the real writer would easily emerge as inventive champion . . . but instead the Jerusalem Gold Medal for Vivid Realism has gone to a narrative klutz who takes the cake for wholesale indifference to the traditional criteria for judgment in every category of the competition.

(246)

The attribution of voice is difficult in such passages – is author in dialogue with character, or is narrator reporting a reverie in the mind of author/character? Is the writer speaking, within his narrative, or is the narrator speaking for the author? Or is it all fiction, internal to the narrative, what the narrator would have been thinking as the character he is describing? Harold Bloom talks of Roth's experimentation in 'shifting the boundaries between his life and his work', so that Roth may have succeeded 'in inventing a new kind of disciplined bewilderment for the reader, since it becomes difficult to hold in one's head at every moment all of the permutations of the Rothian persona' (Bloom 1994: 45). Bloom's difficulty is suggestive for a general understanding of narrative identity: if narrative voice is plural, if the listener cannot identify who is speaking, what then of recognition and mutual intelligibility?

Doubling

Confusion as to the identity of the Roth persona – author, narrator, character, or all three – is compounded by the narrative device of doubling. Doubling in plot and characterization is matched by narrative structure, so that the depiction of doubling is linked, structurally, with 'Roth's' sounding like Pipik while simultaneously maintaining the confusion as to who this 'Roth' is. The treatment of doubling as a central element of this narrative contributes to an understanding of the extent to which identity is constructed not given. This is apparent in Pipik's ability to construct the self-same identity as 'Roth' from scratch, and to take on that identity for himself – in effect parodying 'Roth's' sense of identity.

'Roth' has to deal with the co-presence in Jerusalem of the other 'Philip Roth'. One strange effect of this is that 'Roth' begins to think his way into the 'Diasporism' that his double is preaching, and even to impersonate Pipik, in an act of redoubling. His visit to Ziad and Ziad's tirade against 'Roth's' refusal to espouse Zionism occasions the plot turn by which Ziad's reminder of the rich Jewish life 'in their true homeland Manhattan' encourages 'Roth' to hold forth in the same terms as Pipik. The voices of 'Roth' and Pipik seem to 'fuse together', as they do in a tirade to Ziad's wife, outshining Pipik 'in a Diasporism even more extreme than his' – which may be "Philip Roth" disengaging from Roth while surpassing Moishe Pipik' (Bloom 1994: 46). 'Roth' finds himself able to put across Diasporist views in what starts as parody but becomes a convincing enough version of the case. This comes to a head when 'Roth' repeats the performance to a young Israeli soldier, until he realizes that

> something was running away with me again and there seemed to be nothing I had more strength for than this playing-at-Pipik. That lubricious sensation that is fluency took over, my eloquence grew, and on I went calling for the de-Israelization of the Jews, on and on once again, obeying an intoxicating urge that did not leave me feeling quite so sure of myself as I may have sounded . . .
>
> (71)

As he later explains to Ziad, apologizing for his earlier masquerading as Pipik, 'I don't know these days what I am' (283). The (re)doubling reinforces this presentation of the difficulty of expressing even to oneself a unified or coherent identity.

Doubling could explain divergences within the person, voiced within the text by characterization or, more subtly, by shifts in narrative voice. It also enables the presentation of opposed points of view; in this sense the imitation may be taken to suggest that Pipik is a manifestation of Roth's consciousness – 'one of the disputatious inhabitants of the mind of the actual Roth who creates at interesting length the *faux*, but not altogether *faux*, debate on the present position of Israel in the world' (Hardwick 1997: 12). But Pipik cannot be taken as representing Roth's conscious performance of one aspect of himself unless Roth the author is intentionally presenting a character who has severe doubts about his Jewish identity. (This could explain the references to Pipik as 'not real', not to be treated as another *person*, as when 'Roth' describes Pipik as 'a terrifying incubus insufficiently existent who manufactures his being cannibalistically' (247). It would also account for the somewhat puzzling plotting which allows 'Roth' to neglect obvious moves against a real impostor such as calling in the lawyers.)

The exaggerated circumstances of being confronted by a double, together with the problematic identification of Roth/'Roth', show how difficult it can be to establish *an* identity. One of the aspects of narrative identity construction already identified is that it is possible to construct different stories from one set of facts. Doubling could be categorized as a paradoxical case of that problem. The process whereby the person can be identified in relation to another by reference to what one is, what one is not – it being normal to define by negatives, as in 'I am not that other person' (Norton 1988: 7) – is upset by the presence of a double. Such possibilities opened up by the central theme of 'Roth's' encounters with his double are emphasized by the parallel plot-line whereby 'Roth' becomes interested in the trial of John Demjanjuk, elderly American immigrant, who may or may not be Ivan the Terrible, concentration camp guard – 'a reflection of the thematic doubling carried over into terrible reality' (Bloom 1994: 46).

Splitting

The persistent question encountered in reading this novel is whether the double exists or is a projection of Roth's own alternative consciousness. There is a point in the plot where the narrative voice becomes – not for the first time – apparently that of the writer, complaining that the story is 'frivolously plotted, overplotted, for his taste altogether too freakishly plotted, with outlandish events so wildly careening around every corner that there is nowhere for intelligence to establish a foothold' (245). (What provokes this is a visit from Jinx to his hotel room, at which point 'Roth' finds himself 'half in love with her'.) Then 'Roth' begins to think about the double – 'what, if anything, is there of consequence' about him? All that he knows of Pipik adds up to

> someone *trying* to be real without any idea of how to go about it, someone who knows neither how to be fictitious – and persuasively pass himself off as someone he is not – nor how to actualize himself in life as he is. He can no more portray himself as a whole, harmonious character or establish himself as a perplexing, indecipherable puzzle or even simply exist as an unpredictable satiric force than he can generate a plot of sequential integrity that an adult reader can contemplate seriously.
>
> (245)

The 'competing versions' of Roth who appear in the novel, and the 'Roth'/Pipik relationship have led one critic to assert that 'the entire structure of *Operation Shylock* – its permutations in tone, its dialectical strategies, its warring doubles' in effect 'mirror the interplay of the unconscious and conscious realms' (Kauvar 1995: 433, 431).

This novel can be read in terms of the psychoanalytical idea of bipolarity and 'splitting'. Splitting is technically defined as a defence mechanism 'by which a mental structure loses its integrity and becomes replaced by two or more part-structures' – the ego splits, and 'typically only one resulting part-ego is experienced as "self"'. This process can be dysfunctional, for example, again typically, where the emotional attitude following splitting is to regard one as good, the other as bad; but the term can also be used to describe 'reflexive self-awareness' (Rycroft 1968: 156).

Alford includes an account of this process in his discussion of the self in social theory. Against conceptualizations of the choosing, valuing self familiar to political theory – for example, Taylor's 'agents' (Taylor 1985) – Alford asserts that fear and desire divide the self against itself. The self is 'never as whole, never as coherent' as some theorists want to suggest: and so the 'decentering' of 'a certain philosophical utopianism' in accounts of 'the autonomy and cohesion of the normal healthy self', and the acknowledgement of 'a fluidity and instability to the self even in the best of circumstances'. Thus, for instance, Alford refers to the Rawlsian concept of the rational self as splitting off and ignoring 'the fears and desires that fragment and motivate the self, even in the well-ordered society' (Alford 1991: 8–9, 154). As Di Stefano has it, 'Autonomy as consistent self-identity over time seems to require a splitting within that, nevertheless, secures the integrity of the autonomous self by means of privileging its "higher-order" reflections over "lower-order" desires' (Di Stefano, 1993: 11).

This process may be objected to, as in Barron's discussion of citizenship, where 'the person insofar as s/he appears in the public realm of politics', is detached from the 'real person' in that, in the 'non-public dimension', the individual 'may well be consumed and defined by experience, lacking a sense of self beyond the roles contingently inhabited and the ends pursued', as against the political ascription of (and an *entitlement* to) an identity independent of such contingencies (Barron 1993: 85, 93). What is excluded in the process of the construction of citizen identity is the 'imaginary', and so the subject is divided against itself (Barron 1993: 91). MacIntyre associates the phenomenon specifically (though not exclusively) with the problem of the liberal self, arising from the fact that

> each individual is required to formulate and to express, both to him or herself and to others, an ordered schedule of preferences. Each individual is to present him or herself as a single well-ordered will. But what if such a form of presentation always requires that schism and conflict within the self be disguised and repressed and that a false and psychologically disabling unity of presentation is therefore required by a liberal order?
>
> (MacIntyre 1988: 346)

Modern novels are said to struggle with a 'contradictory construction of identity', whereby acknowledgement of 'the multiplicity of consciousness' and of identity goes along with efforts to voice that multiplicity, to synthesize it in narrative form (O'Donnell 1992: 6–7). In *Operation Shylock* 'Roth's partitioning confirms the existence of a multiform self', whereby the 'competing variations create the tension of perpetual self-contradiction and continual uncertainty' (Kauvar 1995: 422, 433). One of the more interesting suggestions as to the doubling and splitting he is seen to be subject to is that, as already suggested, Pipik, his double, might be 'the one who seeks to be his public self' (Hagen 1995: 143).

When 'we put part of ourselves into others . . . they are not really opposites at all but different ways of looking at the same process' (Alford 1991: 31–3). The strange relationship between 'Roth' and Pipik could be explained as a fictional depiction, a characterization, of the process of 'selfobject transference', which can split the self 'in order to mitigate internal conflict by projecting bad parts of the self into others', making the other 'a holder, or container, of parts of ourselves'. Alford refers to the Freudian idea that 'the ego itself could hold two conscious contradictory beliefs at the same time' hence, 'not repression, but a decision of the ego, so that the parts holding the conflicting beliefs never touch'. This occurs because 'the unempathetically responded to part of the self goes underground'. However, the split-off part does not 'wait silently' but 'frequently operates on its own, independently of the rest of the self'. Such a 'nonintegrated selfobject' – which may contain all the good or all the bad aspects of the self – may reinforce splitting by 'holding the good and bad even further apart' (Alford 1991: 31–2). Both Daniel and 'Roth' would appear to be such selves.

One identity or many

Doubling and splitting pose an obvious query as to the singularity or plurality of identity – one identity or many for any given body – a question that relates to multiplicity as an observable feature of narrative identity, to multivocality, and to the possibility of different stories from the same set of facts or characteristics. Is the formula one person having one identity with multiple facets (and the person capable of adopting different roles); or does one person have a number of identities – as recognized by themself and others? In *The Book of Daniel*, Daniel appears as child, graduate student, husband and sexual 'tormentor', grieving brother, father, social theorist, and 'other Daniels besides' (Fowler, D. 1992: 36). A nice example is provided by the Nicaraguan guerrilla, Tomas Borge, who 'assumed new identities at will' with 'whims, or the exigencies of the moment' reflected in different uniforms: 'specially designed military uniform . . . Soviet-style tunic and matching cap . . . guerrilla fatigues . . . police uniform and a full firefighting outfit':

> Nicaraguans never knew which uniform, or which Borge, would turn up on any given day. The only element of continuity was his own awareness that he was always playing one role or another, his seeming sense that he was moving through life like a character in a yet-unwritten novel.
>
> (Kinzer 1992: 17–18)

Are these, and Daniel's, different manifestations of the self, merely roles, different aspects of one identity, or different identities?

It is outside the scope of this study to deal adequately with this question, which is properly an enquiry for philosophy and/or psychology. I only note the problem inasmuch as it is pertinent for a political understanding of narrative identity – as for instance in consideration of citizenship. I have already alluded to some of the possibilities: for example, that it appears normal that one presents oneself differently in different contexts. A person may use the technique of multivocality in telling their story – *The Book of Daniel* makes this point clear; and Daniel's construction of identity is taken to show, among other things, that there may be several stories about a life. *Operation Shylock* takes up the issue in terms of the exaggerated case of doubling but also, more prosaically, by way of suggesting the different identities that are open to any one person, as both Roth and Ziad demonstrate.[3]

This is a particularly relevant topic for politics and political theory in connection with the ascription of political identity, in practice and in theory. In particular, what weight should be attached to the distinction of *political* identity: is political identity a facet of an identity overall, or a separate (and dominant) identity? Mouffe would appear to solve the problem, at least in relation to one aspect of political identity, in her reference to 'the multiplicity of relations of subordination' whereby '[A] single individual can be the bearer of this multiplicity and be dominant in one relation while subordinated in another'. Such a 'multiple and contradictory' subject's identity 'is therefore always contingent and precarious, temporarily fixed at the intersection of those subject positions and dependency on specific forms of identification'. She also alludes to 'different subject positions' rather than 'one identity among many', in respect of political identity as citizenship (Mouffe 1995b: 318, 323; cf. Mouffe 1995a: 38).

There is little difficulty with the idea that identity changes over time, though philosophers debate the element of continuity, what constitutes 'the same person', in that case. A solution to that problem is suggested by the unremarkable claim that '[T]he bounds of the self are given at the outset, but its identity changes over the course of its experience and is subject to revision' (Gill 1986: 123–4) – a possibility already allowed for in terms of construction and *re*-construction. Beyond that understanding, however, the openness of the question as to singular or multiple identity constitutes one component part of the understanding that identity is liable to be fluid, fragmented, various. Cave notes that according to 'recent philosophers', identity may be 'in some sense an amalgam, a singular concept with a composite character' (Cave 1995: 115). At the least, narrative identity directs attention to the form and nature of the composite(ing).

Multiplicity

Reflecting on Ziad, 'Roth' thinks that he

was out to settle the issue of self-division once and for all . . . he wanted a life that merged with that of others, first as Zee in Chicago, with ours and now all over again here with theirs. . . . [But h]is life couldn't seem to merge with anyone's anywhere no matter what drastic experiment in remodeling he tried. Amazing that something as tiny, really, as a self should contain contending subselves – and that these subselves should themselves be constructed of subselves, and on and on and on . . .

Multiple selves had been on my mind for months now, beginning with my Halcion breakdown and fomented anew by the appearance of Moishe Pipik . . .

(151)

Randall makes the claim that we *are* stories; but he cautions that, '[T]o suggest that we *are* stories, as opposed to merely *have* or can *tell* stories, may unsettle us with the suggestion that [we are un-grounded, or that] . . . our "identity" is not a single reality but a multiple one' (Randall 1995: 11). Although 'multiple identity' may, in its most technical sense and as an adverse condition, belong to the realm of psychiatry and psychoanalysis, in a wider sense it has implications for an understanding of narrative identity. 'I do not story my life in a narrative vacuum': because identity draws from other narratives, including the community story, the culture of institutions, or national stories, 'a variety of versions of my life-story' might interact to produce 'the peculiar blend of story-lines that constitute my identity as a person' (Randall 1995: 193–201). There may be 'no one "authorized version" of my story at all', no "true story" of my life that is capable of identification apart from one limited version of it after another' (Randall 1995: 204), though there may be a 'dominant version'. This is matched in the political context by the suggestion that 'subjects are produced through multiple identifications, some of which become politically salient for a time in certain contexts'. Identity is 'an ongoing process of differentiation', an 'ambiguous' process, even though, as in the ascription of group identity, it may be that 'it works precisely and necessarily by imposing a false clarity' (Scott 1995: 3–12, 11).

Laclau notes 'a new and widespread interest in the multiple identities that are emerging and proliferating in our contemporary world' (Laclau 1995: 93). Various dimensions of multiplicity are recognized in recent political theory: for example, with reference to the modern conditions of multi-cultural, multi-ethnic and multi-religious societies, 'The collective identity of a plural state then is differently textured from that of the culturally homo-geneous nation State. It is complex and nuanced, and necessarily multi-stranded and multi-layered' (Parekh 1995a: 150). Assumption of identity as 'single and fixed . . . may be more a convenient philosophic fiction than a reflection of the realities of people's lives', given changing attitudes to racial and national identifications (Mendus 1995; cf. Jackson 1994). John Rex claims that ideas of both the autonomous subject and socially created identity

have been replaced by 'the notion of multiple identities and a de-centred subject defining his/her selfhood only through a belief in a personal narrative',
in the context of the erosion of nation-state boundaries and consequent
changes in the individual–society relationship (Rex 1995: 21; cf. Laclau
1995). In connection with multiculturalist debate, and objection to the
ascription of group identity by reference to one dominant characteristic, it
is pointed out that 'identities are complex and multiple and grow out of a
history of changing responses to economic, political and cultural forces'
(Appiah 1995: 110).

Such recognitions of multiplicity may convey the impression that this is a
condition which does not present any particular problem for many theorists;
indeed, it is either taken as a given of modern societies or positively welcomed
(cf. Smith 1995: 130). However, general acceptance of multiplicity as a
feature of the modern political world not only neglects potential problems,
such as the adverse effects of splitting or subordination of certain identities
in favour of others, but may of itself reflect the separation out of different
strands of theorizing about the political subject which narrative identity
counteracts.

O'Sullivan's 'civic association' model of the political (referred to in
Chapter 1) would incorporate a political version of multiple identity in
terms of affinity to different causes in situations of social and cultural diversity. Aspects of plot and characterization in *Operation Shylock* address this
idea by showing how ethnic, cultural and national identities may overlap,
diverge or conflict for given individuals in specific cases. For instance, Ziad's
wife complains about his nationalism: 'In America . . . I thought I had
married a man who had left all this victimization behind, a man of cultivation who knew what made life rich and full', not a man who 'can't start
being a human being until the occupation is over' (160). She puts against
this the possibility of a dominant cultural – in this case, intellectual – identity.
As she says to 'Roth':

> Why aren't you loyal . . . to your *intellect*? Why aren't you loyal to
> *literature*? . . . You ran, you were *right* to run, both of you, as far as you
> could from the provincialism and the egocentricity and the xenophobia
> and the lamentations . . . you plunged into a big new free world with
> all your intellect and all your energy . . . devoted to art, books, reason,
> scholarship, to *seriousness*.
>
> (160–1)

The obvious case of multiplicity in this regard is Roth/'Roth's' contentious
political identity. As author, narrator, or character(s) he is American – a
citizen of the USA. His ethnic/cultural designation is Jewish American academic and intellectual (cf. Kauvar 1993: 369), though as a Jewish American
he may choose whether or not to identify himself as such (cf. Brettschneider
1996). He is potentially Israeli, entitled to settle there by the Law of

Return, and subject to diatribes insisting that that is where he 'belongs'. He is also, at least potentially and possibly actually, an Israeli agent. The multiplicity and difficulty of that set of identities contrast with, and are emphasized by, the corresponding set attached to George Ziad.

Ziad's is another striking characterization of multiple and enigmatic identity whose political affiliations, like 'Roth's', are in doubt. Ziad is ostensibly American intellectual turned Palestinian loyalist. In his role as Arab zealot, he turns out to be as much a Diasporist as is Pipik, though for a different reason (wishing to get the Jews out of Israel in order to restore it to Palestinian rule). However, these political affiliations are in doubt – he may be loyal Palestinian or he may be a Israeli spy. This latter is structurally significant in that it serves to reinforce the openness of the narrative. As the plot ostensibly progresses towards conclusion, that movement is disturbed when Smilesburger speaks to Roth of 'the enterprising Ziad', and offers another question about identity: 'Who is George Ziad, what is *his* game?'

Ethnic, cultural and national identities may overlap, diverge or conflict for given individuals in specific cases. The concept of multiple identity carries a double meaning in *Operation Shylock*. It can refer to the different identities located in one person: thus Roth is both Jewish and American and both together, as another category, Jewish American. It can also mean the various identities ascribed to a person: Roth is either assimilated Jewish American or failed Israeli patriot; Ziad is either fellow Jewish American or Palestinian zealot or Israeli spy.

Political identity

This novel has a precise political significance in its reminder that personal identity is formed and recognized within a public, political sphere. The setting in Israel, and dissent among its characters on the question of national identity, allow the book to be read as contributing to debates on the identity of both nations and persons, and the interactions between the two – as in the understanding that national identity is one aspect of the placing of self in the public sphere.

The novel raises acute questions of national identity, including the extent to which political affiliation is to be expressed in terms of nationalism and nationality. There is an interplay of personal and political – Jews may be Zionists, Israelis, Diasporic Jews, American Jews; the novel is 'about' Israeli Jews and Palestinian Arabs in the context of the problematic issues concerning the identity of Israel as a state, as Jewish homeland, and as occupied Palestinian territory. The identity of the Israeli state is called into question by episodes such as the trial of Palestinian children, or 'Roth's' encounter with a young Israeli officer who questions Israel's acting 'out of self interest', to 'preserve its existence', and who knows the politics of the Arab–Israeli situation but still can hardly survive his existence as a soldier.

National identity is also a matter of self-definition, and an instance of 'who am I' becoming linked with 'who are we', in yet another form of multiplicity.[4] As with the identity of the state as such, the novel depicts an especially hard case. Israeli nationality represents a problematic instance of national identity, as 'Roth's' characterization makes clear. By nationality, 'Roth' is American, but his Jewishness subverts that apparent certainty – as a Jew, he may become an Israeli. Crudely speaking, the novel presents an alternative for any modern Jew – assimilation or Zionism. That would hardly be a pressing question for Roth, who is – as author *or* character – apparently fully integrated into American society, were it not for his double's fanatical pressing of the case for Diasporism. 'The time has come to return to the Europe that was for centuries, and remains to this day, the most authentic Jewish homeland there has ever been . . .' And so to a 'problem' which, according to Turner, 'motivates' Roth's fiction, that

> [i]t is not easy these days for liberal Diaspora Jews to figure out where exactly their ancestral fold belongs. Back in southern Poland, perhaps, in a nice little condo within easy reach of the Auschwitz railway junction? In a suburb of the new Jerusalem, seized from Egypt in 1967 and kept out of Arab hands only by force? In one of the Jewish retirement enclaves in Florida or someplace, where a sense of communal identity can be kept up only by clinging to an ill-remembered past?
>
> (Turner 1993: 21)

It is not only 'liberal Diaspora Jews' who have difficulty figuring out where their roots are: for example, modern conditions produce such figures as the immigrant, the refugee, or the global businessman with several passports. An actual example is that outlined by Doris Somer, born in 'something called a displaced persons' camp', unable to fill in the 'nationality' slot on her college application form, wrongly assuming that she had become American when her parents became citizens, so that America is only a 'contractual artifice', and then a 'double positionality as a would-be American and a European has-been' (Somer 1991: x).

The most common expression of national identity is by way of citizenship. However, the Israeli setting of *Operation Shylock*, and the interaction of characters with that state, challenges those theoretical conceptions of citizenship which would make it the predominant political identity, necessarily taking precedence over other identities, or claims on the person, features of their lives which would go towards other constructions of identity. The ambiguous ending to this novel only reinforces the relative ambiguity of 'Roth's' characterization. But whatever political decisions he makes, it seems obvious that citizenship alone would not constitute a sufficient definition of identity. The extent to which 'one identity or many' is an open question is given concrete expression in the possibilities open to 'Roth' or Ziad.

National identity is linked with the moral identity of both persons and the state: thus a critic's remarks about 'the backdrop in the novel of a volatile West Bank where the Israeli moral being seems under threat constantly', 'Roth's skeptical vision of the Israeli moral ledger' and 'the moral rigorousness of Roth's fictional approach' which implicates 'both stone-throwing Arabs and gun-wielding Israeli soldiers' (Furman 1995: 648, 649). Those moral identities interact in the political realm, resulting in a further twist to the understanding that identity may be multiple. For example, when 'Roth' takes on Pipik's identity, he makes the Diasporist case in terms of a moral argument. The line is that if threatened with a second, Arab-generated Holocaust, Israel would use nuclear weapons; but then

> [T]he Israelis will have saved their state by destroying their people. They will never survive morally after that; and if they don't, why survive as Jews at all? They barely have the wherewithal to survive morally now. To put all these Jews in this tiny place, surrounded on all sides by tremendous hostility – how *can* you survive morally? Better to be marginal neurotics, anxious assimilationists . . . better to *lose* the state than to lose your moral being by unleashing a nuclear war.
>
> (158)

In the context of the general suggestion that states have a moral identity, this is also a clear indication of the understanding that the identity of the nation is coterminous with the identity of its peoples.

Ascription and identification

Against Ziad's arguments for engaging in the politics of Israel, 'Roth' asserts his American-ness – like Roth, 'growing up Jewish as I did and growing up American seemed to me indistinguishable' (Roth 1989). However, his dilemma(s) stem from a situation corresponding to the remark that 'identity is not fixed, nor is it self-evident, and it becomes meaningfully different in different contexts' (Scott 1995: 27): his Jewishness *matters* in Jerusalem. The distinction between 'Roth's' 'Jewish' and 'American Jewish' identities may be analysed in terms of the theoretical idea of 'nesting', whereby particular entities – in this case identities – are contained in more general ones. In 'Roth's' normal context Jewishness is 'nested', contained, within his American-ness; but in Israel it becomes more centrally significant: '[s]election of the appropriate level may involve strategic advantage for the kinds of issues which are joined'. Either the larger or the less inclusive identity may be prioritized (Cook 1997: 7, and *passim*). 'Roth' is challenged as to which to identify with.

His identity as a Jew is called into question, directly by way of Ziad's attacks on him, and by contrast with his cousin Apter, a good man who lives simply in Jerusalem. His encounters with Pipik entail exposure to anti-Semitism voiced – and 'legitimated' – as part of Pipik's AA-type programme for curing anti-Semitism), placed alongside a debate on what a Jew – a 'good Jew' – should be. If the former has any effect on 'Roth', it is only inasmuch as it makes the latter question more pressing – in one interpretation of the ambiguous plot, although 'Roth' is himself dubious as to his motives for agreeing to undertake the Mossad mission, Bloom suggests that 'by accepting . . . he leaves the reader free, I think, to decide that, for him, it may also be a mission against Jewish self-hatred' (Bloom 1994: 48).

Roth/'Roth' can be denoted assimilated Jewish American, failed Israeli patriot, just as Ziad can be fellow American intellectual, Palestinian zealot, Israeli counter-agent; but such a labelling process is not straightforward. Labelling may derive from political expediency (Buj 1996: 415), which directs attention to the fact that ascription is not all imposed – groups and members of groups may themselves adopt a (politically) convenient label: self-ascribed identity affirms certain characteristics as collectively and politically useful. For instance, the adoption of 'ethnic' identities in the USA by groups such as Italian-Americans may serve (simply), 'as a part of their *strategic* political and social arsenal without confusing this with anything but a relatively small part of the "self"' (Aronowitz 1995: 113). Another instance is that of New York dock-workers adopting a Puerto Rican 'national' formation initially in response to employment issues but subsequently involving location, language and culture as well. Such cases are also examples of shifting identities: from class ('worker') to political identity ('oppressed minority'), for instance; and 'since these identities were intimately linked to "personal" identity, these activists in some respects assumed new identities as their networks of group associations were radically altered' (Aronowitz 1995: 116).

Although political identity is often ascribed, by reference to characteristics taken to distinguish a group, there may well be a discrepancy between the person's self-recognition and the identity they are deemed to have for political purposes. The potential for discrepancy is evident in the positions understood by and ascribed to characters in *Operation Shylock*, for example in the case of Ziad's arguments with 'Roth' about his Jewish identity. Why should he, as both Ziad and Smilesburger argue he should, feel an obligation to, or any responsibility for, the state of Israel? Both 'Roth' and Ziad variously accept or reject the ascription of various identities, and in so doing making plain the interconnection of identity and identification:

> [t]o identify someone is not just to distinguish them from others; it is also to identify them with others. Identity is a matter of standing with as well as standing apart, of community as well as individuality. 'Who' we are is disclosed by our singularity amidst a condition of plurality; it involves describing what makes us different and the shared life in which those differences can be noted and understood.
>
> (Euben 1990: 96)

Identity is then 'a matter of describing the community to which one belongs and the characteristics that distinguish one within it' (Euben 1990: 46). Ethnic and national identities 'operate in the lives of individuals by connecting them with some people, dividing them from others. Such identities are often deeply integral to a person's sense of self, defining an "I" by placing it against a background of "we"' (Appiah and Gates 1996: 30).

Ascription entails that the person as author of their identity gives way to the person as character – a figure in the story being told by or about a political collectivity. But even then the potential dichotomy between ascription and the experience of members of the designated group is a factor to be considered in the construction of identity. Identity entails acceptance of, identification with, a specific characteristic and/or collective identity, or rejection and re-identification. In either case it is necessary to arrive at an identity which is recognized by the self and in public.

Recognition

This novel takes the matter of identity beyond 'Roth's' initial commonsense assurance that Pipik 'most certainly was not me' – and what is to be gathered from the novel in this respect is not necessarily invalidated by the possibility that Pipik is a creation of 'Roth's' own imagination. Among the consequences of the uncertainty of identity – that it may be fluid and shifting, split, multiple – is that recognition becomes an important factor (Taylor 1991: chapter 5, 'The need for recognition').

In what does identity consist: the person's own account, or affirmation, of themselves, their own understanding, or recognition of who they are, the stories they tell about themself; or does it consist in recognition by others? Clearly, both are necessary. The characterization of 'Roth' in this novel is a reminder that self-recognition is basic to a sense of identity. The narrative construction of the self entails internal consistency – we are intelligible to, we persuade or satisfy, ourselves. The narrative construction of identity requires a further, more stringent level of intelligibility or coherence. We must persuade others of our stories and be persuaded by theirs, be willing to incorporate theirs into our own, to adjust our own to fit with theirs or at least be able to accept – live with – theirs with no completely destructive effects on our own (Taylor 1991: 45–9).

Alford says that '[A]t the heart of the concept of the social self is the ability to see oneself as one sees others', and 'the central means through which a person sees himself is the reaction of others' (Alford 1991: 5). Euben makes the point very clearly: 'To identify someone is to "place" them in a location or story, to recognize and name them, to "remember" who they are as where they fit in some larger scheme', claiming to have 'knowledge of who they are (as recognize implies) and where they come from', and 'where they come from and now belong, and where they stand in the world' (Euben 1990: 39–40). In relation to the politics of areas such as Israel, and in terms which relate to my understanding of identity, Jacqueline Rose points out the difficulty of national entitlement where the assertion of national entitlement is '*self*-affirmation', rhetorically and ritually blind to 'the other on whose recognition its claim finally depends'. 'National belonging' has a 'subjective, imaginative component', that of recognition: 'The viability of a nation does not rest with its own self-imagining, but on whether the other can (chooses, wants) to recognise *me*' (Rose 1996: 84–5).

The question of recognition is a major strand in my reading of *Operation Shylock* alongside that of the multiplicity of identity. This is evident in the most straightforward reading of the novel 'for the plot'. The sub-plot of the trial centres on the question as to whether John Demjanjuk is recognizably Ivan the Terrible. More importantly, politically speaking, the uncertainty surrounding both 'Roth's' and Ziad's identities, and the interaction between these two within the context of Israeli politics suggests fundamental questions as to the place of recognition in identity. Most centrally, 'Roth' is confused with Pipik by people on whom he should be able to rely to recognize him, and to recognize the impostor for what he is.

The novel sets out the difficulties incurred when the conventional markers of self or identity are put in doubt. This is depicted in an exaggerated fashion by the device of the double. Pipik resembles 'Roth' in every detail, can tell his life story, and convince his close friends that he, Pipik, *is* 'Philip Roth'. But if 'Roth's' friends are taken in by Pipik, in what consists 'Roth's' 'true' identity? This is especially troubling when Ziad, formerly associated with 'Roth's' stable American identity, mistakes him for Pipik, with the confusing consequence that 'Roth' then takes Pipik's identity in asserting the Diasporist thesis which Pipik has been using 'Roth's' name and identity to propagate.

In trying to fix identity, 'Roth' places some emphasis on personal charac-teristics – name, appearance, even handwriting. This of itself suggests that identity is largely, under normal circumstances, a matter of what other people recognize. Certainly, these kinds of personal features serve to validate identity if it is in question – as, for example, in the case of a passport photo-graph. Personal characteristics – or at least some combination of them – are just that, personal in the strong sense of being distinct to, unique for, a given person. They are not shared by anyone else. 'Roth's' dilemma in the face of the threat to his identity posed by Pipik is that this does not seem to hold – it is not a sufficient basis for identity. 'Roth's' own sense of identity becomes insufficient: regaining his identity demands the recognition of others.

If identity is definable in terms of 'what the self shows the world' and/or 'how the self is shown to the world', on recognition, then there is an inherently political aspect to identity, as in Wendy Brown's reference to 'politicized identity' – the presentation inherent in 'I am' – as against the 'unpoliticized "I"' of liberalism (Brown 1993: 390); or, as Kerby puts it, 'I' implies 'you' (Kerby 1991: 28). Identity is formed and recognizable, recog-nized, within the public, political sphere (cf. *Constellations* 1996). Narrative identity is intrinsically public identity, because its propositions are worked out in a public way: it presents the self to an audience – the reader, the listener – and has to be verified by them.

Identity defined as a public matter carries with it an understanding of the self among others, and thence identity constituted, in part, by membership of groups. In this respect, and for larger entities than the person as well – for group identity and national identities, for instance – ascription, identification and recognition interconnect, as do cultural and moral identity with political identity. These complex relationships are depicted in this novel by way of the dilemmas of identity recognition experienced by major characters caught up in a complex political situation.

The matter of recognition is a prominent feature of narratives: as content, recognition – especially as dealt with in terms of mistaken identity – is a familiar theme; and structurally, difficulties of narration such as unreliable narrators demonstrate the problems involved in establishing identity in this sense. One implication of recognition as an element of narrative identity is that others are necessary, as listeners and as endorsers of the story of identity being told. This has some added significance where theory takes the other to be oppositional: narrative identity is relational, and the telling of stories of identity is marked by reciprocity (Guaraldo 1998: 263–5). Narratively speaking, recognition is linked to 'reader-response' but while that response is necessary to identity, it is not guaranteed and cannot be defined as a right. 'Narrative' identity implies that recognition depends on acceptance of the story that is told which must therefore be intelligible, if not conventionally coherent: the story must to some extent be persuasive.

The requirement of recognition for the construction of identity carries with it a new set of problems and issues. While 'the fact that I feature in other people's stories and they in mine is crucial to the continuous narrative con-struction of identity', that fact also 'necessarily makes identity problematic, a site of many crossings over and displacements' (Cave 1995: 117). The stories one tells oneself may not coincide with those others tell – which, as expressions of recognition, may also vary between themselves. In his helpful discussion of recognition as an aspect of identities, Cave instances the real-life case of Demjanjuk, suggesting that the problem of his identification 'cannot be separated from the enormous ethical and historical questions which his case raises'. The possibility that he was wrongly identified might be because 'the desire to identify that truly terrible and terrifying figure had become so intense'. The general point to be made is that 'the need or desire for recognition may . . . construct its own object, making it difficult to separate "identity" from the values, desires, legal conventions, and so forth that are channeled through the recognition' (Cave 1995: 115).

Operation Shylock adds the strand of recognition to the understanding of narrative political identity: and this can be further extended in terms of the link between identity and agency. The public presentation of identity is both a requirement for and precursor of agency. Personal identity is developed within the public realm and unless an identity is recognized there, there is no basis for effective action. The person needs recognition by others for the achievement of identity; in a political context, this translates as a need for recognition by others in order to act. If others – their fellows or their rulers – do not know who they are, if they are not recognizable, they will not be given the opportunity to act. Or, they will be inhibited, prevented from acting by misrecognition: '[a] person or group of people can suffer real damage, real distortion, if the people or society around them mirror back to them a confining or demeaning or contemptible picture of themselves' (Taylor 1994: 25).

'Roth's' capacity for meaningful activity depends on who he is as understood by others. Conversely, as he well demonstrates, a person's capacity for political agency, their membership of groups, their cultural preferences and predispositions, their national allegiances, all impact on their identity as a person. A consequence of that can be that identity may not be fixed, may be expressed differently in different contexts, may not in fact be singular at all – which, re-turning, has repercussions for recognition. Recognitions may vary – as stories of identity may vary (yet another facet of the multiplicity of identity).

Roth puts in narrative, fictional form, what amount to polemical arguments about identity, including issues of national and cultural identity. Those fictional 'arguments' are personified: and the text presents not only what the characters *say* but what they *are* – their identities indeed. And emplotment shows the strengths and weaknesses, the anomalies, of ideas presented directly, even didactically, by characters. The novel thus opens up major themes and issues for this study – primarily those I have dealt with at some length here, but also some that can only be alluded to or taken up briefly in this discussion, such as the responsibility incumbent upon both tellers and listeners inherent in narrative identity, or interpretation as implicit in the reception of identity stories, and bound up with recognition.

Operation Shylock is a complex novel and is somewhat difficult to unravel. In a sense one shouldn't try to unravel it but, as Newton suggests, 'see the picture whole' (though it is legitimate to observe how narrative techniques produce the total effect). At the least, this novel reinforces the understanding that persons are as complex as contemporary novels can be, suggesting that doubling, splitting and multiplicity might be considered significant features of identity.

The fundamental problem presented is how to establish identity when faced with a major threat to its stability – a problem personified in the intrusion on 'Roth's' life of the double Pipik. 'Roth's' dilemma, together with the complicating sub-plots of this novel, destabilizes the concept of identity to an extent that makes it much easier to think about the possibility of multiple identity. In its depiction of Roth/'Roth', *Operation Shylock* corresponds somewhat to remarks made by Italo Calvino, who argues that the novel should be a net that trawls in as much as possible, reflecting the multiplicities and complexities of the world:

> Some might object that the more the work tends towards the multiplica-
> tion of possibilities the further it departs from the unicum which is the
> *self* of the writer, his inner sincerity and the discovery of his own truth.
> But I would answer: Who are we, who is each one of us, if not a combina-
> tion of experiences, information, books we have read, things imagined?
> Each life is an encyclopedia, a library, an inventory of objects, a series
> of styles, and everything can constantly be shuffled and reordered in
> every way conceivable.
>
> (Calvino 1996: 24)

As for authors, so also for characters (and the self who is the subject of narrative identity may be either). The result can be disturbing: modern novels tend to show the modern self as fragmented. However, the modern self is also capable of exercising choice in what to affirm and what to deny, what to include and what to omit in the construction of identity. These facets of narrative identity are taken up in the next chapter.

4 Gaps and fragments

Modern political theory has worked with a variety of selves – the autonomous rational chooser, the encumbered self, the self submerged in the larger political identity of the group, the self as citizen. Simultaneously, modern novels have tended to present modern selves as either the surviving realist protagonist (akin to the autonomous rational chooser) or the interiorized, fragmented, inherently disunified modern self (akin to the alienated loner of social theory). How do these figures tell their stories? How are they depicted? What stories are told about them?

These questions suggest attention to the way in which different types of narratives have dealt with identity and imply a supposition that modern novels will be of most relevance to modern theory. The type of novel likely to offer most help to current attempts to theorize the political will be that which represents an attempt to push at the limits of the genre. Hence my contention that it is post-realist and/or experimental novels – taken to mean other than classic realism, and to include modernist and late-modernist work – which can offer more than realist novels to modern political thought. That category includes experiments in realism, including 'non-innocent realism', characterized by awareness of 'the suspect nature of language, the manipulative power of art, the fragility of character, and the relativity of value and perception'. Such writing incorporates 'parodic, shifting tenses, multiple narrative possibilities and fictive games'; but also, importantly for an interest in identity, it is 'committed to an assertion of the significance if no longer quite the centrality of the individual located against a history whose logic cannot be easily evaded' (Ziegler and Bigsby 1982: 10).

A Sport of Nature

Nadine Gordimer's *A Sport of Nature* well exemplifies these comments on 'non-innocent realism'. Even in this accessible novel there is multivocality, and shifting point of view; and narrative gaps problematize the presentation of identity. It raises the important issue of the extent to which persons may modify or adapt their identity may respond in various ways to aspects of given or inherited identity, and the effects of so doing. The novel also: it shows how a person's identity is in part a matter of the stories other people tell about them, and hence the possibility of problems caused by ascription of identity; how selectivity can also be self-imposed – by choice of what to include and what to leave out; how the presentation of the person in the public realm is constructed in part by choice as to what to deny and what to affirm of given characteristics.

The novel is set in southern Africa. As a child Hillela, deserted by her mother, had been sent away to school, spending the holidays alternately with her aunts – Olga, a rich socialite, and Pauline, a committed liberal. She is expelled from school because of association with a coloured boy and is sent to live with Pauline, but leaves there after being found in bed with her cousin. She then drifts into various jobs and eventually meets a journalist with whom she flees South Africa. He deserts her, leaving her among but not part of a colony of political refugees. As the narrative has it, this man should be given credit, 'for having been the one who, however reluctantly, moved her on' (140).[1] 'Moving on' – a recurring phrase in the novel – takes her through a series of affairs until she meets and marries Whaila Kgomani, a black South African political activist in exile. With Whaila she hopes for 'the rainbow family', believing that colour can be transcended. He completes her: 'When we are together, when you're inside me, nothing is missing . . . everything broken off, unanswered, abandoned, is made whole' (207). And their child will be, '[O]ur colour. A category that doesn't exist. She would invent it' (208). However, their baby is born 'perfectly black', and Whaila is killed by the South African security forces; but his death politicizes Hillela. She had found, 'a sign in her marriage, a sure and certain instruction to which one could attach oneself and feel the tug of history' (232). So when Whaila is shot, 'even if she had not been hit, the little beach girl was buried'; 'Mrs. Kgomani had gained an equilibrium that discarded girlish fantasies . . . She was no longer a distraction to catch the eye. She was part of the pre-occupation she had once disrupted so naturally'(253–4).

Hillela's newly acquired political consciousness leads her first to America, where she works on behalf of African aid agencies, and then back to Africa. There she again forms a personal relationship with a black politician, Reuel, the General, President of his country exiled after a coup. She assists him in his return to power, and the book concludes with the couple's attendance as visitors at the ceremony when the new South African flag is raised.

Identity

Hillela's identity is naturally dependent on self-perception but is also in part a matter of ascription, dependent on the perception of observers. The understanding which she reaches about herself does not necessarily clarify her identity as perceived by others. She is

[T]o some a problem child; to others, the beloved; an opportunist; an adventuress – is she an innocent, grasping survival, or a determined seeker after power finding her own particular way out of the deadly 'advantages' of being born a white South African?

(Gordimer 1987: dustjacket)

Before Whaila's death, 'As a white South African actually married to a black South African, she remained for her hosts at these same gatherings an embodiment of their political and ethical credo, non-racial unity against the oppression of one race' (229). After it, apparently working hard for the cause, 'She had – she made – all the right connections'; and a black leader for whom she worked 'always admitted that he never anywhere had anyone more energetic (even if she was a woman, even if she was white)' (261). But as in the early part of her life, there were causes for mistrust: 'never mind "Whaila Kgomani's widow", she had her life in her own hands . . . the young widow had intimate friendships, it was said; she would never lack admirers, or the means of communicating with them' (273).

The specific, peculiar process of her politicization both clarifies Hillela's understanding of race and colour and allows for the construction of an identity that is not stereotyped by assumptions about those or other elements. From Whaila's killing onwards, whatever the confusions, misunderstandings and ellipses in Hillela's story, she always came 'straight from the kitchen where Whaila died on the floor. It was all of her they needed to know. She began there. It was the signature of her life; what she had been, what she was, and would be' (277). Hillela discovers from Whaila's death the possibility of an identity that does not deny her race, gender or sexuality, which does not deny her own version of commitment to her country, expressed, as she had come to understand it, through the personal matter of her relationships. Fundamentally, it is the expression of her intense devotion to Whaila that becomes her identity; and that intensity expresses itself as political commitment, against expectations generated by her previous life or by her continuing aberrant inclinations or behaviour. The novel shows how she uses a new identity as Whaila's widow to operate politically – but in her own way, by continuing sexual relationships which allow her increasing political influence:

Everyone has some cache of trust, while everything else – family, lover, love of fellow men – takes on suspect interpretations. In her, it seemed to be sexuality. However devious she might have to be . . . and however she had to accept deviousness in others, in herself – she drew upon the surety of her sexuality as the bread of her being.

(330)

Although overtly promiscuous – Hillela appears to be a type of sexual adventurer more often encountered as the male protagonist of a 'picaresque novel' (the dustjacket categorization of the book) – sexuality is intrinsic to Hillela's identity (cf. Ettin 1992: 21–2, 69, 72, 85; Cooper 1990: 71–2 and *passim*). The foregrounding of gender and sexuality in this novel makes clear the importance of insisting on the embodiment of identity, in parallel with the comments that 'Racial identities, like those along the dimensions of gender and sexuality, are defined in a peculiarly corporeal way', so that 'the significance of the body may sometimes be as profound as it is in our gendered identities' and 'it is not surprising that important events occur in the land-scape of identity when race and gender compete for and combine in a single body' (Appiah and Gates 1996: 3–4; cf. Bordo 1993). It is her sexuality, initially a danger and the cause of disruption or suspicion, which becomes what grounds her, gives her a 'place' and, thence, a secure identity.

Choice

Hillela could have grown up to be like either of the aunts who had taken care of her. But rejecting both models of what a white South African woman might be, by leaving, moving on, she is able to attempt something new. Remarks about Gordimer's identity relate well to Hillela:

> [a]t each stage there is an opening out to new possibilities, a willingness to be exposed to new demands, no matter how difficult these may be for the inner life. . . .
> And that identity includes assertion, the obligation of an equal among equals. In making this assertion is the finding of a place, and in finding a place the formation of an identity.
>
> (Gordimer 1988: 5, 9)

'Finding a place' can be read as a question of ethnicity – the choice is to be South African, with all that that implies, especially for middle-class white women, or to be (as Gordimer herself has wanted to be) African. But that necessitates a distinctive perception of race, where the choice is clearly a political choice.

What this novel suggests, most interestingly, is the way in which being a woman actually enables this. The question of gender is significant not only because Hillela is always regarded as potentially her mother's daughter – feckless, promiscuous, unreliable, apolitical – but also because it is her sexuality which prevents her fitting into conventional categories and struc-tures from an early stage, and which then shapes her (political) identity. Although in one sense she *changes* identity after Whaila's death, in another sense Hillela *realizes* her identity then, and becomes increasingly free to make political use of her sexuality. Attribution of gender identity in her case is too crude a characterization: going beyond that typification allows her the expression of herself.

The possibility of choice recurs throughout the novel – and what one makes of oneself is shown as enabling political agency. Fictional accounts of identity suggest that there is choice as to what is made of such given components of identity as race, gender and ethnicity, elements which are not commonly thought of as matters of choice.[2] Novels show how presumably fixed categories can be breached, the extent to which they are social or cultural constructs, the relative instability of the social and institutional props which support those categories, and, as a consequence, the scope for exercising choice. *A Sport of Nature* shows that even a strong combination of given factors – being a woman, being white, and being South African – need not inhibit, indeed may even serve as potential for, the construction of identity. The novel emphasizes not so much any one of these components in particular but the interrelationships between them *and* the possibilities of choice as constrained or enhanced by those complex interconnections. The element of choice involved allows for affirmation – or denial – of given factors, or affirmation of unusual, unconventional aspects of an identity.

One contribution of narrative to theoretical debates is to help to counter the excessive emphasis in liberal theory on the choosing agent. Narrative refines this not by an equally exaggerated emphasis on community, but by some refinement to the understanding of choice in connection with identity. John Gray accounts choice a major factor in autonomy which includes the requirement that we are at least 'part authors of our lives', that various aspects of our lives are not 'assigned' to us (Gray, J. 1993: 307, and see 322–3). The most basic question here is whether the political agent is an encumbered or unencumbered self (Ball 1995: 295–6). Charles Taylor points out that people

> may feel they have it in them to do something significant; or alterna-
> tively, they may come to feel one day that they just haven't got what it
> takes . . . [or] that some external limitations stand in the way: that
> people of their class, or race, or sex, or poverty will never be able to
> develop themselves in the relevant ways.
>
> (Taylor 1989: 46)

And so to a question of 'the outer limits of relevant possibilities for us, and hence the direction our lives were moving in or could move in' (Taylor 1989: 46). How far is the person free to affirm or deny the constitutive components of identity? If all or most is fixed, what is the possibility of choice; if all or most is chosen, what is the possibility of constructing a certain identity?

The further more complicated question is: how much choice does the political agent have in the construction of their own story as against the effects of contingency or chance as well as the limitations of given characteristics? Is it the case that,

I am indebted in a complex variety of ways for the constitution of my identity – to parents, family, city, tribe, class, nation, culture, historical epoch, possibly God, Nature, and maybe chance – and I can therefore claim little or no credit (or for that matter, blame) for having turned out the way I have.

(Sandel 1982: 142)

Connolly holds that identity is 'deep in its contingency', because 'happenstances of genetics, family life, historically specific traditions, personal anxieties, demands, and aspirations, surprising events' make it up, and 'some of these elements become impressed into me as second nature . . . and entrenched' (Connolly 1991: 119–20 and see 171–81).[3]

Connolly is concerned with the way in which the modern, emotivist, self is able to 'evade any necessary identification with any particular contingent state of affairs' having 'lost its traditional boundaries provided by a social identity and a view of human life as ordered to a given end' (Connolly 1991: 31, 32, 34). Hillela would appear to be, by this formulation, the type of the modern self. However, what she makes of herself, the identity she eventually acquires, largely through the exercise of choice, is, conversely, more rooted than Connolly's argument would allow. This is despite the circuitous route she takes – and some of her wandering is certainly the result not of intention but of contingency – what she becomes is not 'any role' or expression of 'any point of view' but a response to her political context.

All Hillela's adventures move her, albeit accidentally or contingently, towards a certain identity, that of the white woman who consorts with black political leaders, who assists them, from her position as a white woman, in their struggles for black power, using gender as a basis for political commitment. As Hillela shows, and as I go on to argue more fully, even where contingency intervenes, the person may be – in crucial circumstances for the development of identity – free to choose and to respond. While contingency suggests a certain arbitrariness in the make-up of any identity, choice allows that there is a certain degree of freedom in how to react.

While one is not absolutely free to choose, neither is all completely given; and the boundaries are not fixed, in either direction. The negotiability of identity can be gathered from the ambiguities and complexities embodied by characters in novels, combining in single lives what are differentiated strands of theoretical analysis; by the upsetting of simple categorizations like black/white, man/woman; by relationships which mediate these categorizations in unexpected ways, as for instance with (the political effects of) relationships between white women and black men. The complexity of the narrative depiction informs the theoretical discussion of choice, not least by subverting assumptions about the categories which are taken to distinguish identities.

Structuring identity

To what extent is Hillela – the 'sport of nature'[4] – author of her own identity and to what extent a character, always defined by other people's descriptions and expectations of her? Does she construct her own story: what is the process of narrative construction?

This novel is open enough about its own narrative form. The narrative is presented as a conventional third-person recounting of the events of Hillela's life, narrated in a notably dry, detached tone; but this is interspersed with passages apart from the main narrative which appear to be voiced by Hillela herself, reflecting retrospectively on those events, and with commentary as from an omniscient author. There are 'authorial' contradictions to the 'biographical voice', as well as neutral historical reporting.

The narrative thread of Hillela's story is discontinuous. The narrator reports from time to time that she has been lost sight of; little is known about certain periods of her life – for instance, immediately after she left South Africa, 'there is little to attach in a contiguous, concrete identity'; some things have to be inferred; and

> This is not a period well-documented in anyone's memory, even, it seems, Hillela's own. For others, one passes into a half-presence (alive somewhere in the city, or in the world) because of lack of objective evidence and information; for oneself, the lack of documentation is deliberate. And if, later, no one is sure you are really the same person, what that is certainly relevant is there to document? . . . In the lives of the greatest there are such lacunae – Christ and Shakespeare disappear from and then reappear in the chronicles that documentation and human memory provide. It is not difficult for a girl of seventeen (out of sight of the witness of family and friends) to be absent from the focuses of a woman's own mnemonic attention in later life: to be abandoned, to disappear.
>
> (119)

And as Hillela herself points out:

> If it is true that the voice of a life is always addressing someone . . . there is a stage in middle life, if that life is fully engaged with the world and the present, when there is no space or need for reflection.
>
> (396)

Key events are left unreported or vague, as though detail has been forgotten by Hillela herself or never known by observers of her life. For instance, the exact circumstances of Hillela's marriage to Whaila are typically obscured by the narrative: Hillela is first aware of Whaila as a political figure when he interrupts her conversation on the beach with another man; later there is only a detached and circumstantial reporting of their marriage:

> [a] line in the *curriculum vitae* devoted to Whaila Kgomani in a *Who's Who* of black twentieth-century political figures. *In 1965 he married in Ghana, and had a daughter* . . . when asked about her early life: – I was very young, working at the embassy in Accra when I met Whaila at a reception given by the late Kwame Nkruma. – . . . Though in conversation with Madame Sadat after the assassination of President Sadat . . . it was recalled differently:- You always remember the beginning, not the end. Fortunately. It was in Accra, a man passed me in the street and then turned round – Whaila: we recognized each other.
>
> (198–9)

Overall, the effect is that of watching Hillela create her identity. It may be necessary to lose parts of one's life-history in order to construct a particular identity. Certainly it suits Hillela to be lost from sight from time to time: and the effect of these gaps in the narrative is to enhance the impression that the 'Hillela' who emerges is a deliberate construction.

Narrative gaps

A Sport of Nature not only draws attention by its content to the range and expression of choice possible to selves constructing identities – and the political outcomes that may result – but the structural feature of narrative gaps represents a further potential destabilizing of identity inasmuch as they make the narrative account of that identity uncertain or incomplete. Gaps, parts of the story which would seem necessary to full understanding yet are omitted in the narration, would appear to affect the coherence of the narrative. To recognize gaps in the narrative is to cast some doubt on the simple view of story progressing continuously from beginning to middle to end and on the connection of story so understood with the conception of a unity of a life.

The narrative construction of identity involves selection and representation *and* omission and non-representation, and the resulting account may be ambiguous. Such ambiguity is expressed in different ways in the novels read in this study. Daniel has the problem of what legacy to affirm, what of his family to incorporate into his own identity. A major gap in Daniel's narrative, impossible for the narrator to fill, is a full exploration of the possibility that his parents' 'true' identity was as cover for the real spies, for whom the Isaacsons/Rosenbergs were executed to allow their escape. Yet the matter of their guilt or innocence has a formative effect on Daniel and his sister. 'Philip Roth' represents ambiguity of authorship and self. As 'author' he struggles to piece together a whole life, but his narrative omits the information necessary to clarify both his own fictionality – or not – and his relationship with the Israeli state, especially in respect of the Mossad operation. A certain foreknowledge of that, offered by the Preface (though readers may either ignore a Preface, or only return to it after finishing the book, or, if they do read it, forget it once they are embarked on the narrative proper) somewhat distracts from recognition of another, connected, gap. This is the unnarrated period one between Roth's 'final' conversation with Smilesburger and his return to the United States – the period in which the operation presumably took place, represented structurally by a gap 'on the page', located between the end of the final chapter and the beginning of the Epilogue. The gaps in Hillela's stories occur both in her story as the novel tells it, and in the mode of that telling. There is uncertainty about the actual details, or the significance, of certain events in her life. The question as to *why* she chooses certain directions is left unanswered, at best to be deduced from the narrative history that is (partially) presented. Hillela forgets part of her story; others cannot remember or misrepresent parts of her history.

Gaps occur when a person chooses to forget parts of their story; when it is convenient – not least politically – to alter, to re-tell their story; when others do not, or cannot, know the full story; when versions of events vary as between observers – a frequent occurrence, and one that tends to suggest that there cannot be a 'true' narrative identity. All of these possibilities are characteristic of Hillela's story; and all of these eventualities are recognizably realistic, 'life-like', and should cause no surprise when encountered in a narrative. In this sense, gaps do not really matter. For Hillela, it is what she becomes that is noteworthy, not that she 'disappears' from view from time to time.

Identity is not synonymous with life-story, not least because the identity constructed for presentation to the world may contain gaps compared to a chronological account of life-events. In that sense it could be claimed that fiction is more 'realistic' – or truthful – than 'real life', where the latter is presented as a chronicle, where all is accounted for, with no gaps. The non-realist novel, not aspiring to verisimilitude, does not aspire to provide full information. Kundera accounts narrative gaps essential to the novel: 'Encompassing the complexity of the modern world demands a technique of ellipsis, of condensation': the alternative is 'endless length'. He regards 'the art of ellipsis as crucial. It insists that we go directly to the heart of things' (Kundera 1988: 71–3).

In the case of narrative identity, an element of the choice involved is the choice of what to tell and what not to tell. Stories are constructed: narrative identity does not record or register each and every fact, but rather presents a picture, a selective description 'drawn from life' – in more senses than one. What the person wants to tell, or have told, about themselves may well emphasize the good and interesting, and skip over the bad or boring. Conversely, problems with ascribed identity are immediately obvious – what is omitted, judged to be irrelevant, depends on the intentions of the ascriber, the reason for the ascription.[5]

Breaks in the continuity of a story represent what is not displayed – but that tautology requires some elaboration. (The kind of gap I refer to is not the normal, and necessary, structural gap in narratives as for instance between chapters, of the kind which causes the reader no problem (Chatman 1978: 29; Randall 1995: 124).) Is what is not displayed irrelevant? Is it being concealed for purposes of narrative suspense or surprise? Is the missing information *in principle* recoverable, or is it lost altogether? What sense can be given to narrative identity when the very process of narrative (narrating) includes elements that detract from, or confuse, recognition of who the self is; what to make of the manipulation possible in narrating identity – a problem familiar to students of autobiography and life-stories. The questions are relevant to the idea of narrative identity.

Peter Johnson's discussion of narrative gaps suggests that they leave narrative open to the charge of slackness (Johnson, P. 1996). Alternatively, they may indicate that the particularity and detail which characterize fictional narratives does not entail chronicling each and every event or action or providing explanations for them. Selection is a basic characteristic of narrative, and narrative coherence does not necessarily depend on chains of (causal) explanation being maintained but consists of something much more like the plausibility or possibility of a position – an identity – arrived at. (Inasmuch as storytelling is a way of giving account of oneself, or attempting to account for others, of telling an identity, it should be theoretically sufficient that reasons, the explanation, could be given – that the story could be told. 'And then what happened?' should in principle be answerable, but need not actually be recounted.)

There might be a requirement on the narratee to fill the gap; or that requirement might be met by incorporating acceptable, plausible explanation for the gaps, or the potential challenge avoided altogether by telling an intelligible, coherent story such that the gaps are accepted or not even noticed. Such ways of coping with gaps are evident in *A Sport of Nature*; and the novel also touches on the associated problems of memory and continuity which are associated with philosophical or psychological work on identity. Gaps can be significant of themselves in the story being told. This marks an important difference between narratives and theoretical texts: not surprisingly, theory aspires to telling a complete story, working towards eliminating gaps. One advantage of turning to narrative would be to acknowledge narrative gaps as an aspect of narrative and, thence, of narrative identity.

Narrative identity has to combine the understanding that there is a choice of what to tell and what not to tell with some account of how to cope with gaps – how to arrive at a coherent story. The feature of narrative gaps in stories of identity suggests that coherence does not depend on causal chains of description or explanation. Gaps tend to exclude strictly causal explanations – in that connection Johnson cites Gallie's acknowledgement that 'there are contingencies in life – unforeseeable disaster, accidents, windfalls, losses and so on – which create discontinuities in sequences of events and in the development of character' (Johnson, P. 1996). Rajchman talks of gaps – or 'intervals' – in the 'web' of history, gaps in official memory where minorities emerge to problematize traditions. Then history is 'not linear or progressive, any more than it is circular or cyclical'; and 'if history is a 'web', it is one with many gaps and holes which allow it to be constantly rewoven in other ways' (Rajchman 1995: ix).

Modernism

Commenting on *A Sport of Nature*, Brenda Cooper refers to experiments with voice and point of view as typical of modern literary practice, noting the 'jigsaw of fictional points of view – a fragmentation of viewpoint' in the novel, and its 'contradictory authorial voice – both know-nothing and all-knowing' (Cooper 1990: 84–5). This draws attention to two elements common to the modern novel, self-reflexivity and fragmentation. The former is that process whereby, as Giddens puts it, in the setting of 'high' or 'late' modernity, 'our present-day world', and 'against the backdrop of new forms of mediated experience', the self, 'like the broader institutional contexts in which it exists, has to be reflexively made': 'The reflexive project of the self, which consists in the sustaining of coherent, yet continuously revised, biographical narratives, takes place in the context of multiple choice as filtered through abstract systems' (Giddens 1991: 3, 5). In narrative terms, the idea of self as narrator entails such reflection on oneself. The characters whose construction of identity is referred to in this study well exemplify this process.

Cooper's reference to fragmentation suggests that some attention to literary modernism and the modernist novel – a genre not usually associated with political analysis – would be a helpful move.[6] Modernism is often associated with high or elite art, apoliticism, a concentration on the inner consciousness apparently unhelpful to my concerns. However, as 'the movement which has expressed our modern consciousness, created in its works the nature of modern experience at its fullest', it is prima facie likely to speak to the modern condition (Bradbury and McFarlane 1976: 28). The depiction of characters in modern novels represents an attempt to present the modern self, including fragmentation as an aspect of narrative identity.

Mrs Dalloway

One of the most frequently alluded to works of modernist fiction is Virginia Woolf's *Mrs Dalloway*. In this novel Clarissa Dalloway goes about preparations for her party on a day when the return of her old friend Peter Walsh from India causes her to reflect on her youth and her present life. Peter too remembers what he had thought was Clarissa's early promise – radical and energetic – and how that has been wasted. That might be attributed to her marriage; her MP husband, Richard, is seen going about his daily business, including lunch with Lady Bruton who, as a political mover and shaker, is the antithesis of his wife. However, Richard finds time to call in on Clarissa after lunch, to bring her roses, and to tell her that Lady Bruton had asked after her warmly. A parallel sub-plot concerns Septimus Smith, suffering from shell-shock, and the efforts of his wife to persuade him to continue with medical treatment, and the failure of the doctors to understand his misery, resulting in his suicide. Clarissa's party takes place: it includes an unwelcome guest, an inadequate woman who depresses Clarissa; the unexpected arrival of Sally, the friend with whom she had shared her youthful ambition to make a difference to the world, now settled in a rich but provincial marriage; and the arrival of the Prime Minister, which endorses the success of her party. Peter Walsh and Sally still regret Clarissa's departure from what she could have been, but Clarissa herself is finally satisfied with what she has achieved – that day at least.

'In *Mrs Dalloway*, a fashionable lady gives a party, a man who has been in love with her comes back from India, a young man suffering from war neurosis commits suicide.' The story is easily accounted for: but this is not primarily a novel of plot and action. In noting the few 'events' of the novel, Walter Allen observes that '[W]hat happens on the surface is relatively unimportant', but that it is enough to enable Woolf to show life as in 'a state of constant creation, changing endlessly from moment to moment' (Allen 1964: 41). Much political discussion is concerned with process and progress to the extent that such a concentration on moments of time would seem inappropriate in that context. Conversely, though, the theoretical tendency to treat persons as static, caught at a particular moment, deprives them of the depth, the range of association at any one moment, that Woolf conveys and the advance of the narrative by these moments gives a sense of immediacy which is lacking in more detached theory.

As is common in modern fiction, the use of image or symbol conveys meaning, and a kind of structure (cf. Gath 1989). The 'moments' of the novel are connected in part by the use of images which 'form patterns apart from character and plot' (Bradbrook 1963: 264). For instance, there is a recurring image of time, made concrete by the clocks that are noticeable all through the day that this novel recounts (Jones 1992: 9; cf. Stevenson 1986: 50). In the context of this study, the crucial image is that of Clarissa's self 'coming together as a diamond'. One of the 'moments' recorded in the novel is when she looks into the glass and sees

> the delicate pink face of the woman who was that very night to give a party; of Clarissa Dalloway; of herself . . . That was her self when some effort, some call on her to be her self, drew the parts together, she alone

knew how different, how incompatible and composed so for the world only into one centre, one diamond, one woman who sat in her drawing-room and made a meeting-point, a radiancy no doubt in some dull lives, a refuge for the lonely to come to, perhaps; she had helped young people, who were grateful to her.

(40)[7]

And as she passes from her private room into the public sphere, the sight of others, she is depicted as 'pausing on the landing and assembling that diamond shape, that single person' (41).

Mrs Dalloway is not ordered in conventional form: it exemplifies the comment on modernist novels that

> [t]hough experience can be organized into historical order for narrative purposes, it does not always exist in the mind in that way. Memory can precipitate various disordered, distant events into present consciousness, mixing past and present. . . . [and from this] intermingling of past consciousness with present awareness, an extensive history of the previous life of each character can be assembled.
>
> (Stevenson 1986: 20, 21)

And this even when only a single day is presented in the novel.

Woolf's abandonment of linear structure and adoption of stream of consciousness

> was related to her personal concern with testing the meaning of life against the fact of death; for the privileged moment she was to offer as a kind of answer to the problem could only be given proper emphasis in a novel of the new kind, in which the causal or chronological ordering of events was subordinated to rendering the impression they made on the individual consciousness.
>
> (Lodge 1977: 185)

This is not a political novel by any commonly held understanding of that sub-genre, but in both form and content it does have some considerable political significance. Woolf's best work is said to demonstrate 'how richly the immediacy of experience engages also what is substantial in experience'. She combines an aesthetic or impressionistic perspective with an interest in human values so that 'the "stream of consciousness" which her writing endeavours to capture . . . reflects a genuine humanity, a real and compassionate concern for what makes life rich and what dries it up' (Holloway 1963: 73; see also Stevenson 1986: 16; Stevenson 1992: 5, and Chapter 1 *passim*).

Politics and party-giving

Clarissa Dalloway gives parties.

> Defined by her love of life, by her capacity to preserve this attitude in the
> face of war, death, sickness, age, and the limiting demands of her own
> personal ego, Clarissa sees her parties as a prism, a medium through
> which the lives of others may pass unobstructed and be combined.
>
> (Edwards 1977: 172)

The novel works around this idea: and I suggest that this has some political
relevance.

Lee Edwards suggests that we might 'create an alternative emotion and set
of social patterns based neither on systems nor on power but deriving instead
more directly from individuals'. While it is 'difficult to have any faith in the
efficacy of individual belief or action, simpler to die or to work for a cause or
to locate reality somewhere else than one's own life', Edwards also asserts
that the old ways 'do not seem to have done the hypothetical Armenians
much lasting good either', whereas 'the way of the hostess has been confined
to the private house' – not tried or tested.[8] Her reading of *Mrs Dalloway*
suggests that there is – or could be – an alternative politics: 'Virginia Woolf
is suggesting that we damn ourselves if, in constructing a view of the world
we deny a connection between politics and feelings or values, and so create a
politics lacking both beauty and joy' (Edwards 1977: 176, 177). It is an
unusual, but significant, contribution to political understanding to suppose
that feelings could, or should, be expressed politically, that enjoyment of life
has a contribution to make. But such an expression of the place of pleasure
and beauty in personal and social life speaks directly to Jane Flax's comment
on 'the poverty of the public sphere' in the course of her discussion of the
Enlightenment and modernity:

> The privileging of speech and rational argument over other qualities
> such as nurturance and caretaking (traditionally female activities) or a
> commitment to beauty or pleasure remains unquestioned within these
> theories. All individuals are to value a certain kind of rationality as the
> superordinate public virtue. One may not speak out or make public
> demands out of desire or aesthetic commitments. . . . The importance of
> spectacle, drama, rhetoric, painting, sculpture, or music in constructing
> a rich public life . . . is nowhere acknowledged or incorporated.
>
> (Flax 1994: 89)[9]

However, as Edwards points out, most people 'are not predisposed to take
seriously the notion that giving parties and celebrating life provide viable
social or political alternatives' to public concern with, for example, war
and the prevention of war. The student of politics may well echo Edwards'

question: 'How could Clarissa's life bring pressure to bear against harsher realities' not included in her kind of vision of what was important in life – as in the reiterated 'she loved her roses (didn't that help the Armenians?)' (132). The novel certainly acknowledges the more usual forms of 'helping the Armenians' – letters to *The Times*, parliamentary action, meetings and committees – but implicitly questions the efficacy of such activity, especially in the light of specific human problems.

Peter Walsh recalls that Clarissa had had, in their youth, a theory:

> It was to explain the feeling they had of dissatisfaction; not knowing people; not being known. . . . It was unsatisfactory, they agreed, how little one knew people. But she said, sitting on the bus going up Shaftes- bury Avenue, she felt herself everywhere; not 'here, here, here'; and she tapped on the back of the seat; but everywhere. She waved her hand, going up Shaftesbury Avenue. She was all that. So that to know her, or any one, one must seek out the people who completed them; even the places.
>
> (167)

Edwards believes Woolf in this novel to have been trying 'to focus our attention . . . not simply with the topics of individual isolation and interaction commonly counted as her subjects, but with a larger framework depicting and examining modes of social organization' (Edwards 1977: 161). She reads the novel through the understanding that characters are 'embedded in a social structure containing possibilities for both limitation and liberation'. Woolf's focus is, she says, 'always on the social, on the ways in which indi- viduals respond to the roles assigned them by the world and on the nature and significance of the roles themselves' (Edwards 1977: 174).

Modernism may include, as *Mrs Dalloway* suggests, some sense of com- munity – individual characters 'brought into relationship with others by shared experiences' (Allen 1964: 41). Clarissa has a strong sense of the other and hence her need for parties, to bring those others together:

> But to go deeper, beneath what people said (and these judgments, how superficial, how fragmentary they are!) in her own mind now, what did it mean to her, this thing called life? Oh it was very queer. Here was So-and-so in South Kensington; some one up in Bayswater; and some- body else, say, in Mayfair. And she felt quite continuously a sense of their existence; and she felt what a waste; and she felt what a pity; and she felt if only they could be brought together; so she did it.
>
> (133)

Parties are part of the social world – people come and go, meet and part, at parties; even at the simplest level, a politics concerned with the social order might reasonably be interested in parties. Again Flax has a relevant comment: 'Many social aspects of public life, for example, the contributions of personal/political associations in building and sustaining political interest and loyalty, are also ignored' (Flax 1994: 8). And individuals who value roses are the same individuals who are political agents. (A point made by the roses that Richard Dalloway, albeit busy with politics, buys and takes home for his wife?)

The interconnections are suggested at the very beginning of the novel, when Mrs Dalloway goes out to buy flowers for her party: 'What a lark! What a plunge' – but that plunge is immediately into the social world, awareness of the dispossessed, the warning toll of Big Ben and the awareness that social ills 'can't be dealt with . . . by Acts of Parliament'. And then, revolving again, the war was 'over; thank Heaven – over', and 'she too [like the King and Queen] was going that very night to kindle and illuminate; to give her party' (3–5). It is the extent to which her party-giving can 'kindle and illuminate' – fulfil a social function – that justifies Edwards' argument and its wider implications.

However, as Clarissa Dalloway herself ponders,

> suppose Peter said to her, 'Yes, yes, but your parties – what's the sense of your parties?' all she could say was . . . They're an offering; which sounded horribly vague. . . . But could any man understand what she meant either? about life? She could not imagine Peter or Richard taking the trouble to give a party for no reason whatsoever.
>
> (133)

Clarissa Dalloway affirms life, and not just in a generalized, Lawrentian-Leavisite, way – as in 'the Laurentian maxim that "nothing matters but life"' (Leavis 1972: 53), for example – but also in a way that can be accounted political. The point is made, implicitly, in response to Peter Walsh's reflection that Clarissa 'had a sense of comedy that was really exquisite, but she needed people, always people, to bring it out, with the inevitable result that she frittered her time away, lunching, dining, giving these incessant parties of hers' (86). When Clarissa becomes aware of this criticism, the affirmation of life is strongly put.

> Well, how was she going to defend herself? . . . They thought . . . that she enjoyed imposing herself; liked to have famous people about her; great names; was simply a snob in short. Well, Peter might think so. Richard merely thought it foolish of her to like excitement when she knew it was bad for her heart. It was childish, he thought. And both were quite wrong. What she liked was simply life.
> 'That's what I do it for,' she said, speaking aloud, to life.
>
> (132)

It is not surprising, given the stress on the individual in the modernist novel, that 'the politics of *Mrs Dalloway*' should be a matter of personal consciousness, of happiness, of noticing the natural world, rather than a politics of meetings and process. (Though that kind of politics underlies the novel, characterized by Richard Dalloway, whose activity as an MP occupies the day that Clarissa Dalloway spends in preparing for her party.) *Mrs Dalloway* presents a public identity issuing from a concentration on inner consciousness. In the reading I have given the novel, following Edwards, agency is as central an issue as in the other more overtly political novels read here. In this novel the matter is presented by way of the variety of possibilities represented by its characters: effective withdrawal, personified by Peter; active political life for Richard Dalloway and Lady Bruton; political activity of a distinctive kind as I have ascribed that identity to Clarissa. Even Septimus Smith, ironically, a casualty of political agency: his consultant, Dr Bradshaw, stands as the civilian equivalent of the military officers who failed to protect Smith.

Septimus Smith is accounted Clarissa Dalloway's 'mad double', functioning as a kind of other self to the main character of the novel. The effect of this is to make death a central feature of a novel apparently celebrating life. Clarissa Dalloway represents life, as contrasted with the actual death of Septimus Smith and with what that death represents – war, the misuse of power.

War is a present factor in the lives of characters in this novel. 'This late age of world's experience had bred in them all, all men and women, a well of tears. Tears and sorrows; courage and endurance; a perfectly upright and stoical bearing' (10). Marching soldiers are, as for Peter Walsh, a sign of order. But these impressions are belied by Smith's centrality in the novel, in the account of whose experience the war is summarized:

> He went to France to save an England which consisted almost entirely of Shakespeare's plays and Miss Isabel Pole in a green dress walking in a square. There in the trenches the change which Mr Brewer desired when he advised football was produced instantly; he developed manliness; he was promoted; he drew the attention, indeed the affection of his officer, Evans by name.
>
> (94)

It was this latter attachment – 'a case of two dogs playing on a hearthrug . . . They had to be together, share with each other, fight with each other, quarrel with each other' (94) – analogous to Clarissa's attachment to people, that becomes Smith's problem, for when Evans is killed he stifles his pain, a repression which issues in his madness and suicide in the post-war world. Developing 'manliness' entails a panic 'that he could not feel' (95). As he returns to England, Smith considers that '[I]t might be possible . . . it might be possible that the world itself is without meaning' (96). And he apparently purposefully removes himself from the real world – 'with a melodramatic gesture which he assumed mechanically, and with complete consciousness of insincerity, he dropped his head on his hands. Now he had surrendered; now other people must help him. People must be sent for. He gave in' (99).

His death intrudes into the party itself. 'What business had the Bradshaws to talk of death at her party? A young man had killed himself. And they talked of it at her party – the Bradshaws talked of death' (201). But as Clarissa considers this, she acknowledges that

> [A] thing there was that mattered; a thing, wreathed about with chatter, defaced, obscured in her own life, let drop every day in corruption, lies, chatter. This he had preserved. Death was defiance. Death was an attempt to communicate, people feeling the impossibility of reaching the centre which, mystically, evaded them; closeness drew apart; rapture faded; one was alone. There was an embrace in death.
>
> (202)

Septimus Smith might be Clarissa Dalloway's mad double but through his death she is able to reconcile death and parties. One of the final scenes of the novel, uniting death and time in a reflection, and direct connection, of Septimus Smith's association of the two, is that of Clarissa watching an old lady in the house opposite preparing for bed. Then

> [t]he clock began striking. The young man had killed himself; but she did not pity him; with the clock striking the hour, one, two, three, she did not pity him, with all this going on. . . . She felt glad that he had done it; thrown it away while they went on living. The clock was striking. The leaden circles dissolved in the air. But she must go back. She must assemble.
>
> (204)

The striking of the clock, repeating a recurring image in the novel, represents present time, the continuity and the continuation of life, thence reaffirming what had been said at the beginning of the day – that she, Clarissa Dalloway, 'loved . . . this here, now, in front of her' (9).

Recent criticism has recognized certain aspects of the political in Woolf's work. For instance, feminist criticism has represented her as a feminist icon, or dealt with the politics of gender expressed in her work, the tension in her work between her political awareness and her class position. Other criticism has dealt with her use of symbol and imagery as politically significant, or her place in the modernist canon as implicating her in apoliticism. Such readings of Woolf, and of this particular novel, are necessarily limited by the assumptions they bring to the text(s). I suggest that a connection can be made between modernist writing – or, a special narrative style and form, as identified in literary analysis – and the politics of narrative identity. One aspect of this is the tension, conventionally expressed as between 'private' and 'political', but more correctly in this context as between interior and exterior[10] (as between self and identity), as embodied in the single self. Another is the depiction, as in this novel, of fragmentation – a typical characteristic, together with the drawing together of pieces, of modern writing.

Fragmentation

A reviewer comments on Margaret Atwood's uses of quilts as a symbol in her novel, *Alias Grace* (1996):

> [t]he thing about quilts, suggests Grace, the protagonist, is that what you see depends on whether you look at the dark pieces or the light. Grace is an expert quilter, and so is Atwood. Our experience, our very consciousness is fragmented and can be rearranged, she suggests.
>
> (Mantel 1996: 4)

As the novel has moved away from classic realism, with its *unrealistic* habit of omniscient narration, so the depiction of characters becomes more liable to uncertainty. A major difference between realist and non-realist novels is that narrative flow is more disrupted in the latter; so both time and person may be (presented as) fragmented (Lloyd 1993; cf. Schwab 1994: 8). The fragmented self – ostensibly unlikely to be capable of constructing *an* identity, or of exercising political agency on the basis of a coherent account of themselves – is a central figure in the modern novel (Pecora 1989).

Fragmentation is especially characteristic of those novels commonly labelled modernist. O'Donnell refers to modernism in terms of a multiplicity of consciousness, and of voice – voice being taken as a projection of selfhood. He refers to the demise of the 'coherent' self of 'nineteenth-century realism', a figure which becomes 'fragmented, spread out in time and space, multiple in its duplicitous desire for wholeness and variation' (O'Donnell 1992: 9). Through his literary readings, O'Donnell effectively disposes of the typification of the modern self which persists in much political theory. As early as Dickens, the author is forced to give up the unitary subject, 'that idealized and narcissistic embodiment of knowledge, control and desire, in which voice and the body are married in the illusion of presence'. That figure is replaced, in literary terms, by 'a version of the "public" self, split up or spread amongst the novel's characters' (O'Donnell 1992: 30).

Fragmentation is another way in which narrative problematizes assumptions about identity (and *Mrs Dalloway* and other modern novels represent the state of fragmentation which theory describes hypothetically). As Charles Taylor suggests, the modernist 'turn inward, to experience or subjectivity' may 'take us beyond the self as usually understood, to a fragmentation of experience which calls our ordinary notions of identity into question' (Taylor 1989: 462; cf. Baumann 1993: 197–8; Giddens 1991: 4–5, 137, 189–91). Coherence is threatened by fragmentation – the presentation of the person as fragmented reflecting fragmented experience; or, on the extra-personal level, constant political identity in the modern world is threatened by the pressures of globalization, the problematic nature of 'Europe', including factors such as the growth of the European Community, the definition of 'Eastern Europe', the breakdown of the Soviet Union, emergent nationalisms, even devolution in the United Kingdom.

Zygmunt Baumann argues that 'modern humans . . . have been analyzed (split into fragments) and then synthesized in novel ways (as arrangements, or just collections, of fragments' within a context where technology fragments 'life into a succession of problems', and self into 'a set of problem-generating facets, each calling for separate techniques and separate bodies of expertise' (Baumann 1993: 195, 197). The argument extends to collectivities: fragmented selves are likely to commit themselves to collective causes, 'as wants gain in intensity when voiced in company, and interests are served better when shared'. So in the case of 'the now prevalent form of collectivization', new social movements, 'the causes, like the tasks and the actors who pursue them, would be similarly fragmented', and '[S]overeign units also fragment under the pressures of globalization' (Baumann 1993: 198, 232). Similarly, with reference to changing relationships among political identity, government and nation, it is said that '[T]he psychological energy (*cathexis*) people once devoted to the grand political projects of economic integration and nation-building in industrial democracies is now increasingly directed towards personal projects of managing and expressing complex identities in a fragmenting society' (Bennett 1998: 755).

Giddens, though, contends that while it has become 'commonplace to claim that modernity fragments, disassociates', yet 'the unifying features of modern institutions are just as central to modernity . . . as the disaggregating ones'; and indeed 'late modernity produces a situation in which humankind in some respects becomes a "we", facing problems and opportunities where there are no "others"' (Giddens 1991: 27). Such a process may, though, be artificial – thus Baumann's contention about the fragmentation he attributes to modern technology, that expertise is applied to specific aspects of the human condition, with attention to specific wants or needs, but none is applicable to the whole. So fragmentation is compounded: 'Life is a sequence of many disparate approaches, each one being partial' (Baumann 1993: 198; cf. Giddens 1991: 4–5, 137, 189–91). If that is indeed the case, then narrative is even more helpful, in its capacity for incorporating fragmentation into the ongoing narrative telling.

Modern narrative not only represents the problem but also offers some assistance. What fiction has to say to the condition of fragmentation is inherent in what appears to be a contradiction in literary accounts of modernism. Novelists depict the fractured self; but they also (claim to) unite the fragments through the narrative, by way of a narrative framework within which fragments may be gathered together, given some overall coherence, with interconnections which strict theories of causality cannot allow for. Modernist works are said to 'work spatially or through layers of consciousness, working towards a logic of metaphor or form' (Bradbury and McFarlane 1976: 50). While such literature may seem to represent 'chaotic accounts of a twentieth-century situation which was in itself chaotic', in the modernist mode, it is 'not so much that things fall *apart*, but that they fall *together*'. The centre exerts 'not a centrifugal but a centripetal force', so that 'the consequence is not disintegration but (as it were) superintegration' (McFarlane 1976: 92).

This capacity of narrative for a form of containment, or inclusion, is described (in an otherwise contentious comment on the characterization in Erich Auerbach's *Mimesis* of modernist writing) as the 'recontextualization of fragments'. Narrative can provide 'a double context in which an episode can appear both within the fiction, as fragmentary, and simultaneously within the written text . . . as part of a meaningful whole'. The 'discontinuous fragments of experience' are brought together – although such synthesis cannot be realized by conventional ways of expression, literary techniques such as the 'ambiguously located "voice" of free, indirect discourse' charac-teristic of modern writing can connect 'the severed parts' (Smyth 1991: 142–3).

The ability of modern narratives to recontextualize is also evident in their ability to encompass narrative gaps. For example, Carol Shields' novel *The Stone Diaries* (1993) received enthusiastic critical notice for the structural process whereby the story of a life is produced from the bits and pieces that relate to the person depicted, such as photographs of the narrator's friends and family (though never of herself), newspaper cuttings, commentaries on her – all fragments of a real life (which this, of course, is not), a life brought together by narrative telling.

Hutcheon comments that 'modernism's focus was on the self seeking integration among the fragmentation', so that its focus on subjectivity 'was still within the dominant humanist framework'. (Hutcheon supposes that 'the obsessive search for wholeness itself suggests the beginnings of what would be a more radical postmodern questioning' (Hutcheon 1989: 108).) This capacity for (re)contextualization has been accounted a (re)turn to 'the best Enlightenment aspirations of intelligibility, order, synthesis and totality', (re)discovered by their turning inwards. 'Not only do modern aspirations to completeness and intelligibility survive here, the essential presupposition is that axiom of the modern age, the unity, changeable but ultimately coherent, of the self and of a life' (Smyth 1991: 144). I do not intend to contribute to that view: as I go on to argue, narrative identity does not convey unity, though narrative telling does work to include disunity, uncertainty, fragmentation, instability – but not to the end of producing a single unified whole.

The only reason for making distinctions between types of novels in the context of this study is to indicate how an understanding of the complexity of narrative identity can, in part, be derived from the types of self presented and the method of their presentation. Kundera says that '[T]he periods of the novel's history are very long . . . and are characterized by the particular aspect of being on which the novel concentrates' (Kundera 1988: 12). I follow this understanding in suggesting that modern or modernist novels depict a particular understanding of identity. The kind of narrating is related to a kind of identity, where not all is shown: there are gaps, there is fragmentation, of both structure and characterization. Post-realist novels work to question theoretical assumptions about identity, the unity of lives, coherence and order: but, the telling as such conveys a certain coherence, and some of these novels offer alternative models which are politically applicable.

Literary modernism does have some resonance for my argument – as for instance in terms of Bradbury and McFarlane's account of modernism, the 'classic declaration' of which was 'that human nature is not to be contained by vast and exhaustive inventories of naturalistic detail arranged and sorted under prescriptive heads but instead is elusive, indeterminate, multiple, often implausible, infinitely various and essentially irreducible' (McFarlane 1976: 81; cf. 26–8); or in the critical view that it is 'the one art that responds to the scenario of our chaos. . . . the art consequent on the dis-establishing of communal reality and conventional notions of causality, on the destruction of tradition notions of the wholeness of individual character' (Bradbury and McFarlane 1976: 26, 27). However (and to reiterate), these characteristics are not confined to modernist work labelled as such, but to post-realist narratives more generally. Acknowledgement of the move away from strict realism, movement on from the classic realist novel, directs attention to structure and form as an overt feature of modern narratives – and that emphasis on form, narrative structure, style and techniques, reinforces the need to move on from realism. While realism is characterized by (a dependence on) closure, post-realist work is open, incomplete. Non-realist writing is distinguished by a 'sort of self-conscious examination within the novel of the language, problems and practice of writing fiction' – problems of narration and authorship, and 'fictional worlds complexly envisaged through the consciousness of characters, often expressed in diverse linguistic styles and unusual chronological structures' (Stevenson 1986: 25).

At the beginning of this chapter I asked what depiction of identity was available from modern novels: both a modernist and an experimental realist novel have been taken as offering some answers to that question. Post-realist or experimental fiction challenges theorizations of narrative unity – not least by the depiction of partially-narrated or fragmented selves; but, by carrying the story over the gaps, by 'contextualizing the fragments', literary narratives also suggest an antidote to fragmentation, the possibility that narrative is capable of coping with the disunity it presents – and hence that narrative identity is congruent with both disunity and uncertainty and with political identity and agency.

5 Contingency, identity and agency

The emphasis in previous chapters has been on the disunified nature of identity – on multiplicity, doubling, splitting, gaps and fragments. Characters in the novels have been in search of identity against the odds: Daniel's ambiguous parentage and its legacy, 'Philip Roth's' uncertainty when faced with an alternative self, Hillela's need to choose between conflicting givens, Clarissa Dalloway's and Septimus Smith's contrasting negotiations of class, status and appropriate behaviour in the light of acute awareness of life and death. None of these novels is straightforwardly realist in any sense that can guarantee resolution of the dilemmas of identity by tying up loose ends in a definitive act of closure. Literary modernism, exemplified by *Mrs Dalloway*, extends the problem by its attention to the fragmentation of the self *together with* the possibility of 'uniting the fragments' by narrative means. That latter move is not, though, confined to modernist literature as such – the other novels read here, decidedly post-realist, debatably late-modernist or post-modernist, also present a continuing dichotomy between fragmentation and unity. That dichotomy is consonant with political understandings of the conditions of modernity as they are experienced by the self *and* with the possibility that narrative is capable both of depicting that experience and of offering some solution to the potentially disabling disjunctions resulting from it.

If human experience is non-unified, and identity accordingly uncertain or disunified, the political implications are disturbing for any understanding of politics and the political which rests on an underlying sense of, or need for, stability and order. How is agency then possible, if a stable sense of identity is a pre-requisite for agency? But then, if agency is characteristic of political identity, how to achieve a coherent sense of identity? The further problem which literary narratives make only too clear is how to realize identity or agency in the face of contingency – another aspect of the modern condition. I have suggested that narrative is capable of representing fragmentation, disunity, uncertainty and of offering solutions to what would otherwise be disabling disjunctions. Narrative also offers the possibility of coping with the contingent, telling stories that incorporate responses to chance and coincidence into narrative identity.

Leviathan

A writer has borrowed a summer cottage in Vermont. One early evening he takes a walk in the woods, intending to walk for half an hour and then turn back. However, he is distracted by thinking about what he is writing and just goes on walking. Eventually he realizes that the light is fading. He tries to get his bearings but cannot, and decides that he must sleep there. Next morning, lost, he walks on, deciding that the woods must end somewhere – he can find a road, and then a house where someone will tell him where he is. Three or four hours later he comes out on a narrow dirt road with no houses in sight. After ten minutes or so on this road, a pickup truck appears, and the driver gives him a lift. The young man driving the truck tells him that he had wandered about ten miles on foot, but the road journey back to the cottage is well over thirty. The driver then says that he knows a shortcut, reverses, and takes a very narrow dirt trail through the woods. A mile or so down this trail, they come upon a man standing by a car. Thinking he must be in trouble, the driver gets out to offer help. The stranger appears angry; the driver continues to go towards him; the man reaches for a gun in his car and shoots the driver; the writer picks up a metal softball bat, jumps out of the car, hits the stranger's head and kills him; when he moves over to the driver, he too is dead.

This is the central incident in Paul Auster's novel *Leviathan*. It is a turning point for the writer, Ben Sachs, who has expressed dissatisfaction with his life – 'I want to end the life I've been living up to now. I want everything to change' (136)[1] – but has not hitherto altered his life as a writer. His killing of a complete stranger is tied into the narrative by ensuing developments and by past connections. The 'stranger' is in fact Reed Dimaggio, the husband of a friend (Lillian) of a friend (Maria Turner) of Sachs's friend and fellow-writer, Peter Aaron. Sachs discovers this when, by chance, Maria is the only person to whom he can turn when trying to decide what to do about this bizarre occurrence.

Sachs decides to find Lillian in order to recompense her for the death of her husband. As events turn out, he could have settled down with her in Berkeley, to begin a new life; instead he takes on the identity of the dead man. He becomes the Phantom Bomber, travelling America blowing up reproductions of the Statue of Liberty as a form of political action, protesting against the state of America; and he himself dies, apparently as a result of an accident with explosives. The novel is framed by the discovery of his body and the FBI's attempt to discover whose it is. His friend Aaron has guessed from a newspaper report that it is Sachs, and determines to tell the 'true' story – the substantive content of the narrative – before the FBI catch up on his own connection with the dead man, as they do at the end of the novel.

Narration

Leviathan picks up on central issues concerning narrative identity raised in previous chapters, including the way identity is constructed by narrator and mode of narrating, voice, multiplicity and uncertainty, recognition, choice. It is central to this study because it reiterates aspects of narration noted in other readings but also further complicates them: in particular it presents a complex relationship between narrator and narrated identity. That identity is constructed, in part, at least, through interrelationships – the self *and* others – is made absolutely clear here, where Sachs and Aaron are implicated in each other's stories, as characters and authors. Sachs is ostensibly the principal character and as such the subject of Aaron's book. However, such is the narration that the focus is as much on Aaron as 'author' as on the 'character' he presents, not least because Aaron's construction of Sachs's identity reveals his own.

The significance of narration is established from the start. Aaron says that,

> I have to accept the fact that they'll be on my case for a long time to come. They'll ask questions, they'll dig into my life, they'll find out who my friends are . . . In other words, the whole time I'm here in Vermont writing this story, they'll be busy writing their own story. It will be my story, and once they've finished it, they'll know as much about me as I do myself.
>
> (8)

Aaron is in a race with the FBI to reveal the facts before they do, not, he says, because he wants to defend Sachs, 'but since he's no longer in a position to defend himself, the least I can do is explain who he was and give the true story of how he happened to be on that road in northern Wisconsin' (2).

Aaron narrates throughout. Sachs appears only by way of that narration, and other central characters only at third-hand as Aaron tells the reader what Sachs told him. Long sequences, often accounts of action, are presented directly, as in realist style as from an impersonal third person, giving the illusion of seeing or witnessing the events being described, and distracting somewhat from the framing element of *Aaron's* narrative. Aaron builds up his narrative account by accumulating evidence, moving between his own knowledge, facts and suppositions offered by others of Sachs's friends, and corrections to the partial story thus constructed offered by Sachs as he occasionally reappears to talk to Aaron. There is therefore a complicated narrative structure: Sachs's story is contained within the narrative of Aaron's account of writing the story of his friend within the sub-plot of the FBI discovering who Aaron is while Aaron tells who Sachs is.

The authenticity of the narrative is established, prima facie at least, by reference to the narrator's inability to tell the whole story. Aaron is not in that sense an omniscient narrator. He is, and remains, the 'author': but parts of the novel are in the voice of those, including Sachs himself, from whom he hears parts of the story. He hears those others in his own real time and so the events they report are not necessarily in sequence. The pattern of the novel is that of amendment, by correction or addition, of Aaron's account of Sachs's life and recent past. Increasingly Aaron's 'knowledge', gained from what he has been told, is corrected later by the teller and then sometimes verified by double-checking, and/or by re-assessing his impressions. So although this is presented as a report, a 'true' story and a presentation of the facts of a case, there are often retrospective revisions, and the narrator has increasingly to admit that he doesn't know the full story. (In a further twist to this most complex novel, the structural interplay of narrative voices is paralleled in plotting: Aaron's identity sought by the FBI is given away when Sachs is found to have autographed copies of Aaron's books.)

Aaron's report is always presented as an attempt to uncover the truth, so that he must constantly justify his opinions – in asides such as 'I don't feel that I have a right to talk about this, but to the degree that it affected Sachs, it's impossible to avoid mentioning it' (154). Aaron also increasingly appears to be writing the book not so much to tell Sachs's story, to explain a mystery, but to unravel the experiences he has shared with Sachs, to establish what 'really' happened. However, the intention to tell the truth results in a narrative that includes the recognition that there may be several versions of the truth. This novel presents different levels of truth and ways of arriving at it throughout – who knows what, when, who is an authority?

At one point it is reported that Aaron had 'lost his sense of' Sachs; but it is also noticeable how Aaron authors Sachs – giving significance to what happens to him. Aaron can appear exceptionally truthful or dispassionate in his reporting. He may also be naïve. He is liable to misread situations. He is inattentive, at times a reluctant narrator, or an ignorant one. He displays his own ignorance, but thinks that Sachs doesn't know his own mind: and so Aaron interprets him, attributing motives, but often misunderstanding what is 'actually' happening.

At certain stages of the narrative Aaron can claim non-responsibility for that narrative, but the innocence that is thereby imputed to him is false. The narrative voice is such – apparently straightforward, earnest, modestly disclaiming perfect knowledge – that it encourages the reader to assume a wise spectator of the events reported. Aaron calmly explains everything that happens, from his own marriage break-up to Sachs's life-history. If not the conventional omniscient narrator, his frequent authorial intrusions leave little doubt as to who is ostensibly in control of the narrative. But the 'omniscient' yet ignorant report, constantly having to be corrected from hindsight, from fresh evidence, shows how difficult it is to tell the story of a life. Again, there are always different possible versions.

Because Aaron is so obviously constructing his friend's story, and doing so from a combination of a variety of sources and his own suppositions, the narrative voice of the novel is both multiple and unreliable. Despite Aaron's narratorial modesty, there is frequent translation, explanation, commentary. This opens up another sense of multiple identity in that an identity is not necessarily unified or single in any fixed sense because it is liable to interpretation – as is doubly demonstrated here as Aaron mistakes, mis-narrates Sachs and in so doing offers an alternative version of himself.

Such multiplicity is implicit in the title of the novel – as is also the multiplicity in Sachs himself, deriving, in turn, from the Hobbesian metaphor:

> 'By art,' writes Hobbes, 'is created that great LEVIATHAN called a COMMONWEALTH or STATE . . . which is but an artificial man', a 'multitude unified in one person'. United by their 'pacts and covenants', individuals elect to relinquish some personal liberty for mutual peace and defense. In his novels, Paul Auster has repeatedly examined the 'artificial men' generated by contracts and covenants and explores the 'multiplicity of the singular', the multitude unified in every human identity. In . . . *Leviathan*, Auster and his alter-ego, Peter Aaron, investigate the multiple selves of Benjamin Sachs.
>
> (Osteen 1994: 87)

When they had first met, Aaron observed that Sachs 'managed to combine a multitude of contradictions into a single presence' (19); and his initial drunken impression proved remarkably prescient – not only 'I was actually seeing double . . . Whenever I looked at Sachs, there were two of him', but 'there were so many of him that afternoon' (24). Accordingly, the 'very quality of Sachs that has defied forensic assaults . . . also inhibits Aaron's attempts to "book" him'. Aaron portrays Sachs 'as an embodiment of the difficult balance between unpredictability and pattern' (Saltzman 1995: 164).

Auster, it is said, has 'an intellectual preoccupation with the possibilities of *telling*, of making a de facto "reality" which can meld with the reality we otherwise know'. This is achieved through 'rhetorical agencies of address', such as using a narrator 'who can serve the double function of protagonist and witness, so that he is both fact of initial proposal and also its verification' (Creeley 1994: 35). In *Leviathan* the narrator is in collusion with the subject: Aaron is, for much of the narrative, reporting on what his friend, Sachs, tells him, and he himself is a character in the story he is telling. But his manifest unreliability as a narrator leads to doubt rather than verification.

Aaron's own doubts support his categorization as unreliable narrator – there is a self-conscious, explicit establishment of that unreliability. In what serves as a general comment on his narration, he says:

> Knowing what I know now, I can see how little I really understood. I was drawing conclusions from what amounted to partial evidence, basing my response on a cluster of random, observable facts that told

only a small piece of the story. If more information had been available to me, I might have had a different picture of what was going on . . .

(141)

The way in which Aaron constructs his narrative, and the development of his status as an unreliable narrator, despite apparent omniscience and/or control, suggest that narrative identity cannot offer a fixed, a final or authoritative account of identity which prompts the question as to how full a picture is needed for that element of recognition necessary for identity.

The narration of *Leviathan* also well demonstrates that the stories told about others reveal much about the teller. Sachs is the protagonist, but the narrative imperative for telling his story entails that Aaron needs to recount parts of his own story in order to get to vital parts of Sachs's. That is, Aaron's story is part of the narrative explanation; he is bound up in the sequence of events that reveals Sachs's identity. In the course of that narration, Aaron gives himself away as, similarly, did Daniel in Doctorow's novel. 'Peter Aaron is both Sachs's mouthpiece and his betrayer. By exploring and authorizing his friend's secret lives, he authorizes his own' (Osteen 1994: 90).

The process of narrative construction in general, and the issue of fictionality in particular, is complicated in this novel – as was the case with *Operation Shylock* – by the extent of the writer's direction of the narrative, and thence of the reader, by way of features of the novel outside of the narrative such as the dedication, 'for Don DeLillo', and the epigraph, 'Every actual state is corrupt'. Furthermore, and again as with *Operation Shylock*, there is uncertainty within the narrative about a strict division between writer/author and narrator. In this case, Peter Aaron, whose initials, most commentators are quick to notice, associate him with the writer, bears certain other similarities to Auster – time spent in Paris, marriage to Iris/Siri, for example – and may be taken to signify or represent Auster, who frequently takes a place in his own fictions. Aaron is like Auster – but so is Sachs: and this produces a further narrative complication.

One feature of this narrative which contributes to the difficulty, if not impossibility, of pinning down characters, or deciding who is narrator or who author, is the element of doubling in the novel. This is a repetition of the Roth/'Roth' problem, but whereas in Roth's novel the matter of doubling is faced directly, in *Leviathan* Auster rather plays with the idea. There is doubling in the structure as well as the plot. Aaron speaks, stands in, or doubles for Sachs. As narrator he insists that '[T]hese stories came straight from Sachs himself', and '[T]hey helped to define my sense of what he had been like before I met him, but as I repeat his comments now, I realize that they could have been entirely false.' Aaron is also himself double in that he is, as Saltzman says, 'both a component of the narrative and its artificer' (Saltzman 1995: 168).

Identity and action

Narrative identity entails accounting for the construction and maintenance of identity within a particular framework – the development of character by way of plotting. The events recounted in this novel have as their outcome changes in Sachs and hence in his identity. In figurative terms, Sachs's life is broken up: with each move he makes towards political action he jumps on to a different path until his life is finally fragmented in a rather literal sense.

Sachs has been, like Aaron, a writer: but his story is that of giving up writing for political action – his identity depends on that shift. Sachs needs to escape from his duty to write in order to act. For Sachs, action is a necessity. Once he had decided to carry on Dimaggio's work,

> All of a sudden, my life seemed to make sense to me. Not just the past few months, but my whole life, all the way back to the beginning. It was a miraculous confluence, a startling conjunction of motives and ambitions. I had found the unifying principle, and this one idea would bring all the broken pieces of myself together. For the first time in my life I would be whole.
>
> (256)

Aaron's search for the truth about his friend's identity mirrors that undertaken by Sachs himself. Aaron's narration of Sachs's move to political action so foregrounds the narrative act that it makes it possible to accept the contention that he too acts, inasmuch as '[W]e create narrative . . . by separating the action from the receiver, who can only learn about it by courtesy of the narrator and thanks to the act of narrating' (Dupriez 1991: 294). Novels direct attention to construction by way of writing; but several of the novels read in this study also suggest a potential conflict between writing and action. This is not, though, a clear-cut division: for example, Daniel needed to author/write in order to establish his own identity, from which political action might follow. Sachs's achievement of identity requires narration, but he entrusts this to Aaron. The interactions are complex. At various points this narrative emphasizes the authorial identity of both Aaron and Sachs.

The construction of identity is shown, for Sachs, in terms of his turn to political action;[2] for Aaron it is disclosed through the narrating. When Sachs reappears for the last time, to tell Aaron of his activity as the Phantom Bomber, he says, with some irony,

> The story needed to be told, and better to you than anyone else. If and when the time comes, you'll know better how to tell it to others, you'll make them understand what this business is all about. Your books prove that . . . You've gone so much farther than I ever did, Peter.

I admire you for your innocence, for the way you've stuck to this one thing for your whole life.

(265)

Sachs could have authored his own story – indeed, he does tell it to Aaron, albeit disjointedly – but that telling is always secondary to his activity. Aaron then writes the story of that identity, but in so doing does more than merely transcribe it.

Sachs moves from self-perceived lack of identity to activity and self-declared 'wholeness' in his move from dissatisfied and powerless writer to fulfilment as the Phantom Bomber. In the course of becoming that figure, he had had to concoct an identity, adopt roles and disguises, create characters by mixing 'a set number of variables . . . into different combinations for each town'. As the Phantom Bomber, he lived out those characters as he moved around the country.[3] This entailed 'constant movement, the pressure of always pretending to be someone else'. Sachs finding himself paradoxically involves a kind of loss of identity, self-negation, invisibility; but this period thus also mirrors the larger sweep of Sachs's life; and both that period and the entire life demonstrate the import of the comment that '[T]heories of the subject, or subjectivity, are abstracted to the extent that they do not allow for the ongoing "growth" of the subject.' What then has to be considered for any 'real life' or political situation is subject plus experience: and thence an 'unappropriated' residue – which systems of political order tend to disregard – which while working against totalizing authoritarian systems 'actually provides the conditions for political activity in that it requires not a given social/political world (into which the subject must fit) but "a world to be made"' (Williams, C. 1998: 8).

Milan Kundera says that '[I]t is through action that man steps forth from the repetitive universe of the everyday where each person resembles every other person; it is through action that he distinguishes himself from others and becomes an individual' (Kundera 1988: 23). Similarly, the Arendtian view is that 'it is only in action, in initiating undertakings and interacting with one another, that men, these unique individuals, reveal what they personally are' (Canovan 1977: 59; cf. Beiner 1983: 13, cf. 125–8). The extent to which (the possibility of) action is necessary in order to realize identity is well brought out in Steve Buckler's discussion of *Hamlet* in relation to Arendt's theory of action:

> Action, then, is a form of conduct which constitutes an insertion of the self into a world of appearances and judgment. . . . One turns from a private being, whose conduct has a correspondingly private meaning, into a public agent, whose identity is indebted to meaning conferred in the light of the public gaze.
>
> (Buckler 1996: 1568)

So for Hamlet it is 'implicating himself in the enactment of a deed which must come to define him . . . a confirmation in action of who he truly is' (Buckler 1996: 1569). Narratives tell of action and action, in the Arendtian formula, is productive of identity (Arendt 1958: 176–84).

Contingency

> Myrtle is an interesting subject – in regard to the question as to whether fate or chance holds the upper hand. The ifs are numerous. If Beatrice had not shown an affection for her, would she not have vanished into the orphanage? What if Pompey Jones's unfortunate arrangement of the tiger's head had not ended Annie's hopes of motherhood? If old Mrs Hardy had woken that morning in a cheerful mood, would Myrtle have been required to follow George down to the town? Then there is the matter of his returning to Blackberry Lane by a different route than was usual. If the woman's screams had echoed unheard in another street, what then? And if Mr Hardy had been confined to the blue room with a cold –
>
> Perhaps chance and destiny are interdependent, in that the latter cannot be fulfilled without the casual intervention of the former.
>
> (Bainbridge, *Master Georgie*, 1998: 168)

At the critical point in *Leviathan* Ben Sachs is alone, in a place he does not know, with two dead men, neither known to him, one of whom he has killed. That killing was unintended: 'It was all a matter of timing and he had been too slow. If he had managed to get to the man a split-second earlier, that last shot would have missed' (172). Now he has to decide what to do. The obvious thing would be to go to the police and tell the complete, strange story; but Sachs is 'a convicted felon' – he has served time for draft-dodging, 'and without any witnesses to corroborate his story, no one was going to believe a word he said' (172). So, panicking, he drives the car away, finds the dead man's possessions inside it, recovers somewhat and decides that he must get back to his wife in New York, despite the fact that they have been separated for some time.

However, when he reaches their apartment, he finds her in bed with another man – though 'he had gone home to Fanny precisely because he assumed there would be no surprises there' (178). He rushes out, and phones his friend Aaron. The line is engaged, because as soon as he rushed off, Fanny had phoned Aaron herself. As this is the middle of the night, Sachs assumes that Aaron has the phone off the hook to avoid being disturbed, and therefore does not ring him again. Instead, needing to go somewhere, he rings Maria Turner. But that turns out to be 'a terrible mistake . . . because she was in possession of the one fact powerful enough to turn an ugly misfortune into a terrible tragedy' (179). That fact is the identity of the man Sachs has killed. Maria's knowledge of *that* stems from her chance finding of an address book dropped in the street. (From Maria's disclosure, all else follows – and note that it 'follows' not only from chance in respect of the immediate events, but also from the apparently random action of Sachs earlier picking up the hardball bat.) It is at this point that Aaron, narrating the story, observes:

> My whole adulthood has been spent writing stories, putting imaginary people into unexpected and often unlikely situations . . . but the real is always ahead of what we can imagine. No matter how wild we think our inventions might be, they can never match the unpredictability of what the real world continually spews forth. This lesson seems inescapable to me now. *Anything can happen.* And one way or another, it always does.
>
> (180)

Barone points out that the phrase 'Anything can happen' occurs in all of Auster's books and he suggests that 'these books are examinations of struggles to find one's way, to make sense of this fact', citing Auster's remark that 'chance is a part of reality' (Barone 1995: 25 n. 3, cf. 15). Bruckner claims that Auster loves 'coincidences that rhyme the most remote, improbable events. He excels at sprinkling his characters' adventures with correlations, which have no a priori meaning, but to which the story gives unexpected consequences' (Bruckner 1995: 27–33, 29). Most critical studies of *Leviathan* comment on the extent to which the action of the plot and the development of character is related to contingent happenings, with instances enough of the 'fortuitous chance and odd, barely credible coincidence' which typifies Auster's work (Wirth 1995: 171–82, 175; Saltzman 1995: 162–70, 164; Kirkegaard 1993: 161–79, 176). The narrative begins on the 4th of July, which is also the date of a party at which Sachs by chance falls from a fire escape but escapes death because his fall breaks a washing line and he lands on the clothes. The party is held on the hundredth anniversary of the Statue of Liberty – the site of a significant occasion in Sachs's childhood, and also the focus of his eventual political activity. And the accident happens because of 'the particular combination of strangers on a Brooklyn fire escape' (*New Yorker*, 1992: 147).

Sachs escaped relatively unharmed from his fall. However, although '[H]is body mended . . . he was never the same after that'. When he talks to Aaron about the incident afterwards, he says that 'something extraordinary had taken place': 'I had put myself in a position to fall, I realized, and I had done it on purpose. . . . I learned that I didn't want to live' (135). 'Furthermore, it happened and it happened for a reason. If I could be caught by surprise like that, it must mean there's something fundamentally wrong with me. It must mean that I don't believe in life anymore'. So he wants 'to end the life I've been living up to now. I want everything to change.'

(135, 136). At 41 he feels that his whole life has been a waste, 'a dismal string of petty failures'. He has to 'step into the real world now and do something' (137). (Aaron makes the nicely misjudged comment that 'I left Sachs's apartment thinking he would pull through the crisis. Not right away, perhaps, but over the long term I found it difficult to imagine that things wouldn't return to normal for him' (137).)

The accident, which has strange effects on Sachs, begins a period of his life which culminates in the random killing and a new life with his victim's wife, Lillian – itself an outcome of the sheer chance that she is Maria's friend. But then, 'with no apparent cause, everything suddenly changed' (229). Firstly Lillian begins behaving erratically. Then Sachs discovers that Dimaggio had become involved with terrorism for political change. He decides to try and continue Dimaggio's work by writing about him; but again 'something strange happened' (254). Diving into a secondhand bookshop to avoid someone who had known him in New York, he immediately notices a copy of his own book, 'The New Colossus', and buys it. Later,

> I sat there on the sofa, staring at the cover of my novel, feeling like someone who's just run into a brick wall. I hadn't done anything with the book about Dimaggio . . . I'd botched every hope for myself. Out of pure wretchedness I kept my eyes fixed on the cover of the book. For a long time I don't think I even saw it, but then, little by little, something began to happen. It must have taken close to an hour, but once the idea took hold of me, I couldn't stop thinking about it.
>
> (255)

That book is 'filled with references to the Statue of Liberty': so Sachs becomes the Phantom Bomber, until his death when, presumably, a bomb he is preparing detonates accidentally.

Aaron's narrative has to incorporate the predominance of chance in Sachs's life (and death): 'like Sachs himself, who takes life's contingencies as cues, Aaron has to accommodate the leakiness, contradiction, and dubious leads that beset his enterprise *within* that enterprise' (Saltzman 1995: x). And so he comes to understand 'that every life is a leviathan, that connections stop nowhere, and that a person's public self is merely the tip of a colossal iceberg shaped by chance, destiny and secrecy' (Osteen 1994: 91). This novel raises in an acute way the issue of contingency as a factor in human lives, as an element which has to be dealt with in the narrative construction of identity, and in the living of a political life.

Contingency may mean several things. It is dictionary-defined as that which is 'neither necessary nor impossible', 'a chance occurrence', a thing that may or may not happen, that is fortuitous, subject to accident(s), is free in the sense of not determined by necessity. Referring to the 'multifaceted character' of the term, Connolly suggests:

By contrast to the necessary and universal, it means that which is changeable and particular; by contrast to the certain and constant, it means
that which is uncertain and variable; by contrast to the self-subsistent
and causal, it means that which is dependent and effect; by contrast to
the expected and regular, it means that which is unexpected and irregu-
lar; and by contrast to the safe and reassuring, it means that which is
dangerous, unruly, and obdurate in its danger.

(Connolly 1991: 28)

'Contingency' directs attention to the unpredictability of politics/political
action. The political is characterized, among other things, by unpredictability of outcomes:

[P]olitics today, as at every previous point in human political history,
consists ultimately in human agency, and the latter, in turn, necessarily
involves both an intentionality which is partially dependent on conscious
human evaluation and a wide range of unenvisaged and potentially
keenly undesired consequences.

(Dunn 1990: 2)

The political chooser – the decision-maker, the policy-maker, for example –
cannot fully envisage what the outcomes will be: 'The final result of political
action often, no, even regularly, stands in completely inadequate and often
paradoxical relation to its original meaning' (Weber 1970 [1948]: 117).
That political action can have unforeseen results, or, more precisely, that
the results of political actions cannot be fully predicted, is a result not necessarily, or not only, of bad judgement or of imperfect knowledge, or even of
the sheer scope, of the range of potential beneficiaries of political decisions
but of the intervention, beyond the knowledge or control of the chooser
(whether free-standing or embedded), of contingency.

The 'constant contingency of politics' is, in Hannah Arendt's view, a consequence of the uniqueness of individuals. Commenting on Arendt, Margaret
Canovan notes that both the tradition of political theory and contemporary
political science tend to generalize in terms such as system, structure,
class and role. While this is 'undoubtedly illuminating', it 'presupposes a
particular view of the human condition' which is 'partial, distorting as well
as illuminating'. Where such terms are emphasized, and 'human individuality and action correspondingly neglected', then 'the natural trend is to a
deterministic picture of life within which events ought in principle to be predictable and forces calculable'. 'And yet', as Canovan adds, 'political events
constantly stagger the onlooker by their unpredictability' (Canovan 1977:
124–5).

However, the capacity of theory to offer a full account of the ubiquity
of contingency, chance and coincidence as factors in human – and thence
political – life is limited by the inclination to treat the contingent as a

problem and therefore to attempt to bring contingency under control. For example, Rawls's intention for a theory of justice is one 'that nullifies the accidents of natural endowment and the contingencies of social circumstance' (though consistently with the main thrust of his theory, the 'contingencies of social circumstance' might be allowed to work for the good of the less fortunate) (Rawls 1972: 15, 102, cf. 72–3, 585). In general, liberal theorists like Rawls are apt to write off contingencies as though they are, as part of a natural and/or un-ordered or irrational world, to be coped with or, preferably, overcome by reasonable principles for orderly arrangements. At best they are to be worked around (cf. Pocock 1975: 166). And theoretical accounts which adopt a relatively deterministic attitude to agents' actions, or which, less rigidly but equally exclusively, rely on the idea of the rational chooser or strong versions of rational choice theory, explicitly or implicitly dismiss the contingent altogether. Modernity's picture of the self is that '[T]he individual subject is conceived of as an isolated mind and will; and his vocation is to get clear about the world, to bring it under the control of reason and thus make it available for human projects' (White 1991: 2).

Even where radical theorists accept the ubiquity of contingency, they quite often regard it as entirely negative – thus reference to such acts of God as floods and famine, or man-made disasters such as environmental pollution or the possibility of nuclear holocaust or the 'globalization of contingency' as involving 'possibilities and potential emergencies that might be resistant to control' (Connolly 1991: 25; Connolly 1987: 141). Dunn is specifically sceptical about the capacity of modern politics to cope with the political choices consequent upon and the hazards facing human kind – economic mismanagement, and environmental and nuclear disasters. He comments on the 'imprudence in the politics of advanced capitalist societies', for example in 'the question of safety in the design of energy installations' (Dunn 1990: 210). Connolly's remarks on the contingency of identity specify 'the death of a parent, the intrusion of war' and that which is 'dangerous, unruly, and obdurate' as the 'surprising events' that might occur to one – he is held to be referring to 'our ultimate human fragility in the face of mortality, disease and disaster' (Young 1992: 512). The implication must be that contingency is to be avoided or, at best, to be negotiated, coped with, as an irritation or handicap if not rather literally a disaster.[4]

The contingent may then, politically speaking, be taken to denote that which is not predictable, which cannot be ordered, that which escapes control, where effect cannot necessarily be derived from cause. However, contingency is not necessary harmful or to be avoided. Alternatively, the contingent might be considered so obviously an aspect of everyday life that a satisfactory account of the political can hardly afford to neglect or disparage it. Indeed, both in so far as the political is defined as 'the art of the possible', as a process of adjustment to the unexpected and unforeseeable, and inasmuch as political society is characterized as secular and timebound, politics itself may be said to be bound up with contingency. Where theory neglects contingency or only treats it as a problem to be coped with, or brought under control, it fails, accordingly, to allow for the effects of contingency in the lives of persons, including their identity as political agents. (But how would it, given that theory frequently fails to make the political agent concrete? Theory deals with types rather than characters, thin rather than thick selves with 'unique modes of human life – whose particular qualities and trajectory in time are, in quite crucial ways, not like others' (Goldberg 1993: xv, cf. 75–6) – including the effects of, and responses to, contingency).

Political theory most often presents agency and action as non-contingent, the result of reasoned decisions followed through by conscious, purposive behaviour. In so far as theory assumes certain regularities or predictabilities, or relies on rules and principles analogous to scientific fact, there is an association with order or control – hence a tendency to assert relationships of cause and effect. For example, while Barber does acknowledge that the 'embedment of politics in action' suggests 'temporality and contingency', along with 'an engagement in the world of ongoing events', he goes on to say that 'politics as a domain of action needs to be characterised by the constraints of necessity and the accompanying logic of necessity' – including the judgement of actions by reference to their location in chains of cause and effect (Barber 1988: 11, see also 206–9; cf. Harrison, R. 1979; Livingston 1991). However, while

> [O]n the one hand . . . chance seems an alogical category that cannot fit our causal lines of explanation . . . when chance *is* the explanation, institutionalized as the operational principle, it is a first cause, a prime mover, and inverts the classic oppositions of reliable/unreliable, truth/fiction, rational discourse/imaginative narrative, order/chaos.
>
> (Siegle 1986: 103)[5]

The challenge for the novelist is to give the unexpected 'The weight of necessity', to convert 'the improbable into the inevitable' (Bruckner 1995: 29); and the trick is to discover the opportunities that chance provides and transform them, through the fervency that the political activist and the novelist share, into a calling' (Saltzman 1995: 168). (That latter remark neatly describes Sachs's journey towards identity as a political agent.) What narrative accounts also show is that less negative occurrences than theorists have tended to emphasize may also – and more often – have their effect; and as *Leviathan* shows, that effect may impinge directly on identity and agency.

Contingency, identity, agency and action

Literary narratives typically show the place of the contingent in 'real lives': plots often hinge on chance or coincidence. Even the direst experiences – death and near-death, for example – turn out to be opportunities for characters to turn to action; and the development of character, and of identity, includes responses to such events. Coincidence and chance lead Sachs towards and into action: *Leviathan* well shows the place of contingency in the achievement of identity through action. This is a particularly good instance of the understanding that purpose can originate from the response to contingency, chance or coincidence; that the acceptance of contingency can free the person to address their identity by re-reading – and thence re-telling – the narrative of their life. Fictional accounts such as this depict characters whose identity is achieved specifically by way of their response to the contingent. Contingencies may act as the impetus for political action, depicting characters whose achievement of political identity is obtained precisely by way of their reaction to the contingent. The question is whether these accounts are merely fictional, or whether they present valid pictures of human behaviour and motivation.

Sachs is not, apparently, a man who considers his options, weighs advantages and disadvantages, to arrive at considered, rational, decisions.[6] In this novel, decisions may stem as much from chance or accident as from rational decision-making; indeed, in actual situations the two become inextricably mixed. For example, it is quite probable that the address book picked up by Maria Turner while walking in one part of New York and not another will contain an address of someone she knows (cf. Feibleman 1968: 8, 12). But that acknowledgement of pattern – people live in relatively small worlds, act by habit, are open only to a limited range of experiences and encounters – cannot explain her behaviour after finding the book; nor does it explain the consequences of her subsequent actions. Action in response to contingency may be within the context of socialization into preferred ways of behaviour – even acting in a conventional manner does not remove the element of chance in provoking the behaviour at a certain time nor the *outcomes* of responses to chance occurrences.

Responses to the contingent might be interpreted as making the best of a certain situation, but may then appear either reasoned or spontaneous. For Sachs, 'the music of chance is paradoxically at once freer and denser than the routine scales of evident cause' (Saltzman 1995: 165). (This observation is followed with a query – 'how then can one be responsible in a mysterious, unpredictable world?' – a relevant political question).

The interesting case for a full consideration of this ambiguity would be Maria's organization of her life as an artist around contrived occasions of chance.[7] Maria represents controlled responses to chance occurrences, responses which are, paradoxically, dependent on those occurrences being pure chance. Spontaneity and control are connected in the sub-plot surrounding the address book which she picks up in the street. She intends to use the address book as a way of constructing an artistic project, building up a picture of its unknown owner by interviewing all his contacts as listed in the book. However, this intention is subverted when one of the addresses turns out to be an old school-friend – Lillian, who becomes a stage in Sachs's movement towards political action.

Maria is an exaggerated example of being driven by chance – she *arranges* contingency. Sachs's behaviour at certain points is clearly unpremeditated. In either case, does making the best of what life throws up negate the element of choice in identity construction which I have already noted, or does it inter- act with it, in the sense of taking up opportunities as they present themselves? The overall impression to be gained from this narrative is that both construc- tion *and* contingency entail choice. Novels show that much of what appears to be a matter of choice is actually subject to arbitrary intervention – contin- gency and coincidence – or that choice, the capacity required for action or agency, takes up, or follows from, chance incidents or occasions. That much might already be evident from Daniel and 'Roth's' experiences; Sachs's characterization confirms the point.

To accept that responses to contingency may form part of political agency and action raises problems concerning intention and motivation. Political agents are defined as having 'capacities for decision-making, for initiating projects, for determining futures, for entering into reciprocal obligations, and for taking responsibility for actions' (Warren 1988: 1, cf. 6, 46, 155). If agency is defined in terms of purposeful action, what then of that sense of purpose in the face of contingency? Where there is an expectation of some measure of intention, clear attribution of motivation, and expectation of and, indeed, primary focus on, outcomes, how does such an understanding sit with the idea that contingency, chance and coincidence have to be accom- modated in the story, and that agency might be based on the response to chance occurrences?

There would seem to be a discrepancy between purposeful action, as understood in political theories of identity and agency, and contingent cause; and the narrative instance appears to subvert the theoretical under- standing. But as the characterization of Sachs suggests, going with the contin- gent does not necessarily hinder action, or adversely affect outcomes. What is more, *Leviathan* offers clear evidence for the proposition that narrative and action, albeit less measured than theoretical accounts may allow, are closely interrelated:

> It is the intentional nature of human action which evokes a narrative account. We act for an end, yet our actions affect a field of forces in ways that may be characteristic yet remain unpredictable . . . [b]y struc- turing a plausible response to the question, 'And what happened next?', narrative offers just the intelligibility we need for acting properly.
>   (Hauerwas and Burrell 1989: 178; see also Bruner 1991: 16)

Auster is quoted as saying that 'there's a widely held notion that novels shouldn't stretch the imagination too far. Anything that appears implausible is necessarily taken to be forced, artificial, "unrealistic"' (Barone 1995: 19). A sense of improbability may stem from the part that chance and coincidence play in these novels: but to find this so may be to deny the extent of chance in real life. *Leviathan* is, as a reviewer put it, an improbable but possible story, where a high degree of chance moves the plot (Horne 1992). In *A Sport of Nature*, *Leviathan* or *The Crying of Lot 49*, as in other novels such as Don DeLillo's *Mao II* (1991), or William Golding's *Rites of Passage* (1980), the characters can be said to be driven by contingency. These novels would appear to bear little similarity to theoretical accounts of action and agency: yet, if they are 'possible stories', then some degree of consonance between the fictional and theoretical (non-narrative) accounts might be expected? That is, political theory might be expected to address how things actually are, or could be, rather than abstractions or idealizations. One task for political theory might be to show how political structures – and political lives – might respond to contingency.

Are the plots of novels like *Leviathan* too contrived – or are they more life-like than many detached theoretical accounts of the possibility of action? In the novel, contingency and ambiguity are inextricable elements of the text. The plots of narratives depend on contingency, as contrasted with the assertion or the programmatic statement in a theoretical text. In the novel the contingent just occurs in the plot – as in real life. Theory might want to resolve it, to explain and explain away; for literature it remains contingent and open. The contrast is well made by Stuart Hampshire's contention that,

> [T]he experience that carries a person beyond the successive routines of experience is initiated suddenly and unpredictably . . . However carefully a person deliberates, in Aristotelian style, about the ends of action, assessing what most makes life worth living, he ought always to be open to surprises, discoveries, and uncertainties.
>
> (Hampshire 1992: 132–3)

Coping with contingency

Explanations of human behaviour need to include contingency (cf. O'Sullivan 1997: 739–54). Novels not only show this to be the case, they also show how it might be done. The question for narrative identity is how to assimilate contingency – how to make it part of the story. The relevant narrative feature is emplotment. Storying, the narrative process as such, allows for such containment.

In terms of content, narrative can accommodate contingency, not in any sense of explaining it away, or of subordinating it to (pseudo-scientific) theories of causality or to (pseudo-psychological) concepts of intention and motivation, but by acknowledging it as a factor in human lives – simply making it part of the storying. Contingencies are assimilated into the story of a life by way of relating them to, 'relating' their place in, an ongoing narrative – as, for instance, in the example of Sachs's understanding of his life 'back to the beginning'.

Novels formally contain contingency by way of emplotment, whereby isolated or chance events are placed within a developing network of further acts. For instance, in *Leviathan*, as the narrative unfolds, events are placed, reported by Sachs and interpreted by Aaron. In that process, the plot – the pattern of these events within the narrative, including the disturbed time sequence consequent upon the combination of Aaron's conjectures and Sachs's occasional appearances and corrections of the story as Aaron understands it – 'explains' the changes in Sachs's identity which are known to have been occasioned by chance occurrences. *Leviathan* makes it clear that narrative identity, as represented in plot, is liable to uncontrollable factors and their effects, and hence quite likely to be fragmented and/or uncertain. But the novel also demonstrates how emplotment serves to 'unite the fragments', showing how Sachs arrives at 'wholeness' – a sense of purpose and the capacity for agency.

Leviathan is especially helpful in this respect in its foregrounding of the narrative process. This is in one sense an exaggeratedly closed narrative: in terms of plot, the end is known from the beginning. However, the 'narrative within a narrative' structure shows the process of construction; and the internal narrative is open. Paradoxically, although Aaron begins at the end, as it were – and in that respect is almost a parody of the omniscient author – it becomes only too evident in the course of the novel that he gets things wrong, does not see connections, does not see what is coming. That Aaron is a confused, unreliable narrator, prone to misunderstandings, to hasty judgements which have later to be revised, and to a continuing inability to decide which versions of events are true, disrupts the initial impression of an over-determined narrative. *Leviathan* is an instance of novels 'which operate by process rather than by overall design' (Morson 1998)[8] – it is such works that I refer to, and which have something to offer political theory.

Randall's exposition of the narrative self includes the comment that it is not 'story' but 'story*ing*' that explains; 'not the noun as much as the verb, not the product as much as the process' (Randall 1995: 206; cf. Alford 1991: 60–2, 138); 'emplotment' emphasizes the *process* of arranging events into a coherent narrative, rather than focusing on plot as overall design with a pre-determining effect on the narrative (Hauerwas and Burrell 1989: 177–80). Thus the presentation of action in the novel is through plotting, ongoing and not moving towards closure. (The emphasis on emplotment serves, incidentally, to reinforce the direction of my turn to narrative. Discussion of narrative identity is often concentrated on attention to life-stories – and hence to biography or autobiography as the relevant genre; historical narratives appeal to the social scientist, but are more often referred to in terms of method than for the story that is told.[9] However, it is in literary narratives that the process of plotting is a central feature, and hence my attention to them.)

Contingency, chance events and their repercussions, are also assimilated into narrative accounts by way of retrospective narration (a feature of narrative connected with memory and remembrance, key elements in studies of identity). Literary narratives most obviously, but narrative *per se*, involve post hoc telling, looking back on what has happened and expressed in some form of the past tense. (This distinguishes narrative accounts from life-plans which are forward-looking, and which might include plans to avoid or side-step the contingent: Giddens talks of 'Reflexively organized life-planning, which normally presumes consideration of risks as filtered through contact with expert knowledge' as 'a central feature of the structuring of identity' (Giddens 1991: 3, 5; cf. Berman 1992: 32–4).) Explanation follows action. Narrative voice may utilize the present tense but always within the context, the framework of a narrative structure, of a story that is past (otherwise it could not be told, but only at best described).

The narrative patterning of events represents a hindsight explanation of how events occurred, and their effects or outcomes, and their meaning – as Johnson says, 'narrative bestows meaning retrospectively; only through the telling of the story can events be identified as significant or trivial, necessary or contingent, permanent or fleeting' (Johnson, P. 1996: 1354). This allows the contingent, disturbing or chance events, apparently unconnected happenings, to be incorporated in a coherent narrative. While the chance occurrence may demand immediate, unmediated response, subsequent telling allows for an element of management. Meaning can be given to the un-expected – some meaning or other, for again, several stories may be possible.

The retrospective character of narrative telling is strongly emphasized in *Leviathan* by the starting point of Sachs's death and the need to account for that death by explaining what led up to it. Sachs's story is told, para-doxically, in terms of – beginning with and returning to – his death; and in more paradoxical twists, Sachs both 'loses' his life by killing Dimaggio and, through that same act, begins a radically new life. There is some indication here of what might constitute continuity – where that is held to be a crucial aspect of identity. Sachs changes his identity to make something of himself; he holds that that requires re-invention and re-identification. However, the narration contains those changes in the life and actions of a character within the narrative, recognized as such by others.

One conclusion to be drawn from this reading of *Leviathan* is that, in addition to the obvious, that life is indeed prone to contingencies and that therefore the fictional is not necessarily as 'fictional' as all that – *political* life is like that. And that being so, the absence from many theoretical accounts of an equivalent to the contingent elements of emplotment present in (fictional) narratives is a hindrance to political understanding. Life is full of contin-gency; and not all contingency is malign. Contingency – chance – is normal. Much political activity, the actions of political agents, originates from responses to contingency – possibly as much as from reasoned judgement? One particular contribution to political understanding to be gained from this novel is the possibility of a positive connection between contingency and agency: a full consideration of political agency requires inclusion of the contingent and its effects. Novels are particularly good at showing how contingency and purpose can be reconciled. Narratives thus violate the systematic nature of theory: they remind theory of the sheer messiness of much lived existence. But they can also – co-incidentally – 'recontextualize' the fragments through emplotment, and explain how contingency has been responded to by retrospective narration, major elements in the process of narrative construction.

6   Coherent identity

To read Paul Auster is to hear a number of his immediate contemporaries echo his preoccupations. Such a quest for *some* coherence in the
chaos of events, be it at the cost of a more or less acute paranoia, such a
quest for an unstable, elusive meaning among resemblances and possible
narratives . . .   How could they not invite one to re-read Pynchon once
more, and more particularly *The Crying of Lot 49*?

(Chénetier 1995: 41–2)

The Crying of Lot 49

The heroine of *The Crying of Lot 49*, Oedipa Maas, is just an ordinary
Californian housewife until she is unexpectedly made the executor of the
will of her late lover Pierce Inverarity, a business tycoon. The framing
device of the narrative is her attempt to find out why Inverarity named her
executor and what that will entail – and to give meaning to unexpected
occurrences which disturb her routine life.

> The death of her ex-lover sets Oedipa on a trail of delirious weird-
> ness which leads from her husband Mucho Maas (who is fond of Sick
> Dick and the Volkswagens, but doesn't believe in them), through
> Dr. Hilarius, Freudian shrink and ex-Buchenwald intern ('If I'd been a
> real Nazi, I'd have chosen Jung, nicht wahr?'), the bizarre postal net-
> work of outcasts called W.A.S.T.E., Genghis Cohen, the most eminent
> philatelist in L.A., Yoyodyne Inc. ('High above the L.A. freeways/And
> the traffic's whine/Stands the well-known Galatronics/Branch of Yoyo-
> dyne'), not to mention Ralph Driblette, and Messrs Warpe, Wistfull,
> Kubitscheck and McMingus, Attorneys . . . [1]

Or, as an American edition of the novel has it,

> As she diligently carries out her duties, Oedipa is enmeshed in what
> would appear to be a world-wide conspiracy, meets some extremely

interesting characters, and attains a not inconsiderable amount of self-knowledge.[2]

As soon as Oedipa begins her duties as executor, she picks up information, in an apparently accidental or contingent way, about the secret postal system. This becomes the central focus of the plot rather than Inverarity's will as such. As she follows up and tries to make sense of signs and clues concerning the mysterious Tristero/Trystero, historical originator of the secret post, she becomes ever more anxious to understand what is happening. She is constantly confronted with signs and symbols which may or may not be evidence of the existence of W.A.S.T.E. Her attempt to understand their meaning involves her in adventures and meetings with a strange set of characters, which only make her more determined to establish what is real.

Oedipa's search for the meaning of public and secret systems produces sub-plots of oddity and confusions, apparently unconnected characters and happenings. These interrelate with her basic need for self-meaning and self-understanding, for identity, and for love. There is a further complexity as plot and sub-plots interrelate with one another and with the three elements of Oedipa's quest – her actual journey around California as Inverarity's executor, her search for the secret of the Tristero, and her quest for love. The latter is related to her affair with Inverarity, which occasions the events of the narrative and which may have been her real love affair. It certainly provides the occasion of her awareness of self and her need to understand.

While holidaying with Inverarity in Mexico City she had seen a painting of a number of girls imprisoned in a tower, embroidering a tapestry

> which spilled out the slit windows and into a void, seeking hopelessly to fill the void: for all the other buildings and creatures, all the waves, ships and forests of the earth were contained in this tapestry, and the tapestry was the world.
>
> (13)

Oedipa had cried, and had

> looked down at her feet and known, then because of a painting, that what she stood on had only been woven together a couple thousand miles away in her own tower, was only by accident known as Mexico, and so Pierce had taken her away from nothing, there'd been no escape.
>
> (13)

Then she asks, 'If the tower is everywhere and the knight of deliverance no proof against its magic, what else?' (13).[3]

The 'what else' could be 'the world of shared meanings', the attempt to discover which is a major theme of the novel. Oedipa's quest is for an alternative to the tower, a 'reality' other than the tapestry she embroiders herself, for a meaning to what she encounters *and* to her self and her identity. Oedipa's 'legacy' could also be the possibility of an understanding of the futility of attempts to construct a romantic, individualist identity and the impossibility of meaning and order in any 'unified' sense.

In following up the will, stranger and stranger things happen to her, which throw into doubt her previous assumptions about the society she had lived in as just another suburban housewife. Who is she – in a fundamental sense; but not only 'who is she' in any personal sense, but where can she locate herself. The identity of the USA itself becomes questionable, and thence her identity as a citizen of that country. Oedipa has her life disrupted by Inverarity's will: she is pushed into the public sphere, but all that she finds is disorder.

This novel offers a readable – and often very funny – story with internal coherence as a narrative structure: but it does not offer any straightforward possibility of constructing a coherent identity for the self, given the amount of coincidence and chance involved in Oedipa's attempt to make sense of her world. Oedipa's search for meaning is also a search for who she is; the narrative is inconclusive on both scores. Pynchon is said to be concerned to parody the 'widespread, if tacit, assumption that meaning is the culmination of an exhaustive series of discoveries, that truth is what everything adds up to' (Hite 1983: 19–20). However, although the world depicted in the novel 'lacks the coherence of a myth that moves towards a projected fulfillment', it is not incoherent. 'It means something that this world lacks unity, purpose and redemptive significance; ironically, it is this meaning that Oedipa discovers during her quest' (Hite 1983: 81). The 'message' or meaning which Oedipa *should* arrive at is that the world and individual lives are to be understood as not subject to order *or* chaos. But that leaves Oedipa with her original problem – who is she; what is the basis for her identity? Her inability to impose meaning on the world, as a way of constructing identity, casts severe doubt on the possibility of the narrative construction of identity.

Neither she herself nor the external world she is offered makes sense. Oedipa's final version of the options open to her is that, as she tells herself:

> Either you have stumbled . . . on to a network by which x number of Americans are truly communicating while reserving their lies, recitations of routine, arid betrayals of spiritual poverty, for the official government delivery system . . . Or you are hallucinating it. Or a plot has been mounted against you . . . involving items like the forging of stamps and ancient books, constant surveillance of your movements, planting of post horn images all over San Francisco, bribing of librarians, hiring of professional actors and Pierce Inverarity only knows what-all besides, all financed out of the estate in a way either too secret or too involved for your non-legal mind to know about . . . Or you are fantasy-ing some such plot, in which case you are a nut, Oedipa, out of your skull.

> Those, now that she was looking at them, she saw to be the alternatives. Those symmetrical four. She didn't like any of them, but hoped she was mentally ill; that that's all it was.
>
> (124)

Oedipa does not find meaning either about the Tristero or in herself – though it could be argued that, like Daniel and Sachs, she becomes different, and to some extent at least she finds herself in the process of the search. By the end of the novel, though, Oedipa is still not reconciled, actually or hypothetically, to what has been revealed to her:

> She had heard about excluded middles; they were bad shit, to be avoided; and how had it ever happened here, with the chances once so good for diversity? For it was now like walking among matrices of a great digital computer, the zeros and ones twinned above, hanging like balanced mobiles right and left, ahead, thick, maybe endless. . . . Ones and zeros. . . . Another mode of meaning behind the obvious, or none. Either Oedipa in the orbiting ecstasy of a true paranoia, or a real Tristero.
>
> (125–6)

Even so, '[N]ext day, with the courage you find you have when there is nothing more to lose', Oedipa follows up her last clue, information about the mysterious bidder for Inverarity's stamp collection, which contains many clues about the Tristero. That bidder might be from the Tristero – or might be Trystero. So she goes to the auction room, the doors are locked, and the narrative ends as 'The auctioneer cleared his throat. Oedipa settled back, to await the crying of lot 49' (127). (Despite the variety of meanings given to both 'lot' and '49' by critics and reviewers, the title phrase and its component parts is, quite simply, derived from the narrative. What might be questioned, given the uncertainty Oedipa is subject to, is what to make of 'settled back' – a phrase usually denoting a certain amount of relaxation and/or satisfaction.)

The solution to the mystery investigated in the plot is withheld and the novel ends with a silence. Hite claims that action needs grounding; narratively, that would require resolution – this is explored thematically in the novel but finally evaded. *The Crying of Lot 49* is characterized by a completely open ending. This novel confounds a simplistic view of narrative by its lack of closure, thematic or structural.

Closure

Theorists voice their arguments in terms like, 'the story I am telling' or 'the story so far'. In doing so, they imply that there will be an ending. And so there is: the last page of the book is reached, the speaker announces conclusion and eventually reaches it – stops talking. Of course there is an end. But, as narratives – including the novels read here – show, endings are not necessarily conclusive as to themes and issues raised.

Narrative texts do have beginnings and ends. A strictly narratological causal process entails that:

> A work begins as it does in its self-appointed place, no matter what may be the state of affairs at that moment in its represented world, because . . . its logic of narrativity depends upon that place as its first term or premise. It ends, similarly, its place of closure being not only concluding but conclusive in terms of this principle, no matter how inconclusive it may be in terms of its characters' experience.
>
> (Sturgess 1992: 45)

Alternatively, though, 'the narratable inherently lacks finality. It may be suspended by a moral or ideological expediency, but it can never properly be brought to term. The tendency of a narrative, then, would be to *keep going*' (Miller, D.A. 1981: x, xi). The contradiction is prima facie confusing; but a helpful distinction can be made between 'ending' and 'closure'. Narratives work towards an ending, but this is a practical consequence of instrumental constraints on time, space, or the capacity of the listener or reader to concentrate, rather than a structural or substantive requirement. Narrative as such does not necessarily entail or imply closure: 'All literary works come to some sort of close or conclusion, but such conclusions do not always provide the same sense of satisfaction or inevitability' (Hawthorn 1992).

In the most general sense, closure is 'a modification of structure that makes *stasis*, or the absence of further continuation, the most probable event' (Hawthorn 1992). More specifically, closure refers to 'the functions of an ending to justify the cessation of narrative and to complete the meaning of what had gone before'; or 'the reduction of a work's meanings to a single and complete sense that excludes the claims of other interpretations', and thus a contrast between 'closed' and 'open' texts (Baldick 1990). The latter, instances of 'process literature', display 'aperture' rather than closure – there are endings but no *final* accounting. The narrative could continue; and 'the story as it has developed is one of many possible stories . . . if it were possible to play the tape over again, there are many points where something else might have happened' (Morson 1998).[4] Dienstag, reading classic political theorists as offering narratives either of reconciliation or redemption, says of the latter, 'Who chooses to attempt a redemption must accept an unreconciled existence, one with loose ends and sharp edges. One gives up the sense of an ending, the good feeling of narrative closure that comes with reconciliation' (Dienstag 1997: 197).

Closure is said by the novelist Joyce Carol Oates to make the narrative intelligible as a totality, 'meaning that when it ends, the attentive reader understands why' (Oates 1993; cf. Miller, D.A. 1981: xi, n. 2; Lodge 1992: 28; Tambling 1991: 73–4, 77–8). Modern novels though – and *The Crying of Lot 49* is a good example – work against such 'totality' and understanding, showing endings – outcomes – as ambiguous or inconclusive. Modern narratives certainly do not necessarily support a view of narrative as inexorably working towards closure. The latter view may have derived from a 'common assumption of an a priori "determination of means by the ends"', and that 'everything in a narrative exists in view of the hidden necessity determined by its final configuration of event and meaning'. The nineteenth-century novel displays closure 'precisely *because* it is a text of abundant restrictions and regulations'. However, the production of narrative 'is possible only within a logic of insufficiency, disequilibrium and deferral, and traditional novelists typically desire worlds of greater stability and wholeness than such a logic can intrinsically provide' (Miller, D.A. 1981: xiii). (Miller equates closure with regulation and control, as against openness and negotiable meanings – hence reference to 'the tyranny of a narrative so thoroughly predestined that it does nothing but produce spurious problems for a solution already in place' (Miller, D.A. 1981: xiii).) In modernism, 'an ultimate signified to which everything in the text eventually speaks' is replaced by 'narratability itself'. Commenting that 'narratability' as such is the 'point' of modern narratives, Miller adds, '[W]e are thus led to confront the possibility, oxymoronic but far from frivolous, of being enclosed in openness' (Miller, D.A. 1981: 265, xiii, 280). So, for example, in Dorothy Richardson's work,

> the lack of a sense of an ending may be due to the fact that she thought of consciousness not as a stream but a pool – 'a sea, an ocean. It has depths and greater depths and when you think you have reached its current you are suddenly possessed by another.'
>
> (Tucker 1995: 4)

Even apparently closed narratives may 'manage to undermine their meanings somehow, either by presenting alternative endings or by questioning the meaning or formal potency of any ending' (Leitch 1986: 123). *Operation Shylock* well illustrates this. Although there is a Preface and Epilogue (ostensibly from Roth, the writer), the reader is left in doubt as to the text's status as fact or fiction and, consequently, where the narrative as presented actually ends. The Epilogue which follows the 'conclusion' of the novel might be read as an attempt at closure: but 'Roth' is finally depicted as unsure whether or not to keep the money which Smilesburger has brought him. And the last words go to Smilesburger:

> 'Philip, pick up the attache case, take it home, and put the money in your mattress. Nobody will ever know.'

'And in return?'
'Let your Jewish conscience be your guide.'

In *The Book of Daniel*, the ambiguity surrounding the Isaacson/Rosenberg trial and execution, including Daniel's suspicion that the actual spies got away, establishes the impossibility of closure in the introductory section of the book. The question of his parents' guilt or innocence continues to trouble Daniel and is never resolved. The narrative conveys the impression that Daniel has moved a good way towards finding himself, but when the book ends, on the page, Daniel's story is clearly not finished.

Daniel's strivings – as with the ambiguity of 'Roth's' involvement in Operation Shylock, Aaron's authorial attempt to fix Sachs, or Oedipa's to find meaning – correspond to Siegle's typification of 'the archetypal narrator's belief that *some* technical stratagem, some confluence of conventions, and some squiggle on the conceptual schematic exists that will offer hope of pulling phenomena within the narratable – if also problematic – margins of cultural comprehension'. However, these characters *also* come to realize something like the thought that 'preconceived plots provided by rational conceptions and whole systems of thought . . . provide only the illusion of access to some stable and universal "true" order to which individuals and events may be meaningfully assimilated' (Siegle 1986: 97).

Closure and the matter of endings represent a problem for narrative identity. Often 'it is *our* closure that we force upon the narrative and by our closure we mean our temporality, our need for order and completion' (Schweizer 1990: 17);[5] but any desire for completion is likely to go unmet. Commenting on *The Book of Daniel*'s ending on the page while clearly not finished, Linda Hutcheon suggests that 'perhaps we need a rethinking of the social and political (as well as the literary and historical) representations by which we understand our world. Maybe we need to stop trying to find totalising narratives which dissolve difference and contradiction' (Hutcheon 1988: 70). This may prove a problem for theorizing that hopes to move to conclusion. Political theorists employing narrative mode (as against chronicling, describing, analysing, or other distinctively social scientific modes of expression) or who use narrative fiction in their work may be likely to assume meaning, expressed in closure, as an attribute of narrative. This is, of course, only in line with the theorist's own tendency to work towards definitive meaning. However,

> once the ending is enshrined as an all-embracing cause in which the elements of a narrative find their ultimate justification, it is difficult for analysis to assert anything short of total coherence. One is barred even from suspecting possible discontinuities between closure and the narrative movement preceding it, not to mention possible contradictions and ambiguities within closure itself.
>
> (Miller, D.A. 1981: xiii)

It can in any case be argued that closure is an irrelevant concept for the situated human life.[6] Even if 'we make the hypothesis of a continuous personal identity and of an eventually determinate narrative embodying it', we are often 'too much in the middle of things to make out clearly an ending which would stabilize the story and confirm its superiority to alternative versions' (Cave 1995: 112). The coherence of a life then consists in what pattern or order we can give it as we reflect on and/or narrate it as it proceeds. In practice, an identity story is one that 'never implies an ending as strongly as it implies a world in the middest, a world whose logic resists endings' (Kermode 1967). Taken literally, the narrative self cannot be completely told, or narrative identity be fixed, until death – if then: and concomitantly, identity is always provisional, change is always possible.

For the individual life, it may be said that the only conclusive ending is death. But any separate life is also, socially and politically speaking, an embedded narrative; even death is not an ending as far as the larger story is concerned. To treat narrative identity in terms of movement towards end in the sense of closure is therefore neither helpful nor accurate. Meaning is conveyed not by any conclusive ending but by the attempt to tell coherent stories, establishing identity by way of understanding of and by self and others.

Users of the terminology of 'narrative identity' may be taken to imply thereby pattern, sequence, a movement towards closure, whereas, if the term is unpacked, narrative may well indicate lack of pattern, non-sequentiality and absence of closure. Lack of closure can then be added to the other challenges to conventional or simplistic views of narrative and narrative identity which I discuss.

Narrative unity

The readings in this study show how identity is problematized by narrative to the extent that narrative identity may be characterized as uncertain, fragmented, disunified. As these novels variously demonstrate, the ordering process of narrative does not equate with, or produce, an unproblematically unified life. That is most obviously so, for instance, in *Leviathan*. Although Sachs feels himself to achieve a certain wholeness, this is a story of a non-unified life, narrated in a disunified way, of a protagonist whose 'entire life fell apart in mid-air' and who comes to a shattered and inexplicit end. Yet narrative identity is associated with narrative unity. In what, then, does that unity consist – or, properly, what goes to make up a coherent (narrative) identity?

Narrative is commonly associated with unity: conceptions and usages of the narrative self and narrative identity implicitly assume or are explicitly built on this idea. For McCormick, 'the unity of a life is what constitutes the identity of a person' (McCormick 1988: 232; cf. Harrison 1991: 199). Benhabib asserts that identity 'is constituted by a narrative unity, which integrates what "I" can do, have done, and will accomplish with what you expect of "me", interpret my acts and intentions to mean, wish for me in the future etc.' (Benhabib 1992: 5). The connection is especially prominent in Alasdair MacIntyre's formulations – and in those many theorists who cite MacIntyre in this regard, including Taylor and Benhabib (cf. Taylor 1989: 17, 47–9; Ricoeur 1991: 195; Beiner 1983: 125–6; Hauerwas and Jones 1989: 2–11; Connolly 1987: 6).

MacIntyre's conception of narrative unity

Attempting to establish the parameters of narrative identity in the context of political theory, in the Anglo-American tradition at least, would seem, prima facie, to demand attention to MacIntyre's conceptualization of the narrative unity of a life. MacIntyre claims that, '[N]arrative history of a certain kind turns out to be the basic and essential genre for the characterisation of human actions'; persons are essentially storytelling animals, telling stories that 'aspire to truth'; 'the concept of a person is that of a character abstracted from a history'; and thus to 'the narrative concept of selfhood'. Then 'personal identity is just that identity presupposed by the unity of the character which the unity of a narrative requires' (MacIntyre 1985: 217, 218).

'In what does the unity of a human life consist? The answer is that its unity is the unity of a narrative embodied in a single life' (MacIntyre 1985: 216–18). Unity, in MacIntyre's account is not to be confused with unity of consciousness or perception, a state of being, but is rather a matter of the integrated, ordered life consequent on articulating that life in narrative terms. (So while order is, narratively speaking, only necessary methodologically in order to convey the story, for MacIntyre it appears to be of value as such.) Identity consists in being able to give an account of oneself. MacIntyre himself holds that 'all attempts to elucidate the notion of personal identity independently of and in isolation from the notions of narrative, intelligibility and accountability are bound to fail' (MacIntyre 1985: 218).

In MacIntyre's account 'intelligibility' is the central connecting concept between action and narrative. Actions are expected to be intelligible, and intelligible actions take a narrative form; human agents are accountable through conversation as enacted narrative. The relationship between the concepts of narrative, intelligibility and accountability, each presupposing 'the applicability of the concept of personal identity', and vice versa, 'is one of mutual presupposition' (MacIntyre 1985: 217–18).

'Narrative' – synonymous with 'story' – is taken as simply and unproblematically descriptive of a way of telling a sequence of events – hence 'a concept of a self whose unity resides in the unity of a narrative which links birth to life to death as narrative beginning to middle to end' (MacIntyre 1985: 204, 205). Each action takes place in a setting that has a history, so that in explaining actions, persons are involved in composing a narrative history.

That narrative history is embedded in a social context, and 'the unity of a human life is the unity of a narrative quest' (MacIntyre 1985: 211). 'Identity' is a matter of the person's place in a narrative history, a story, in which each person is a character.

Such a usage of narrative as indicative of a certain type of self or identity, associated with the idea of unity, may be valid as MacIntyre uses it, to express the interconnectedness of events and experiences as against isolated moments and moral relativism, where each incident is judged separately, with no regard to setting or context. However, that is MacIntyre's argument, and his understanding of the narrative self is distinctive to that argument. MacIntyre's account of narrative is subservient to his wider purpose in *After Virtue* (1985), an argument for the restoration of the Aristotelian virtues. The account of narrative identity that can be derived from that argument is limited by the constraints inherent in the argument within which it is contained. To use the term more generally, the implications of the term have to be explored both more widely and more deeply. It is naïve and misleading merely to extract the term from MacIntyre's argument for use in other rather different contexts and arguments.

For instance, human experience is not necessarily so dominated by linear sequentiality, let alone so unified as MacIntyre suggests (and a residually Whiggish view of history as progressive might rather easily attach itself to MacIntyre's conceptualization). For instance, taking a life 'lengthwise', as MacIntyre does (following Aristotle) may not be the only or the best way to consider 'a whole human life':

> [I]t is quite common to think of the unity or wholeness of a life vertically, so to speak: as the complex of interrelationships between a person's functioning, behaviour, actions and activity, considered either over a large stretch of time, or at some particular moment (or moments) in some particular set of circumstances, or, most commonly, both.
>
> (Goldberg 1993: 279)

Goldberg points out the extent to which 'constructing a lengthwise "narrative" is largely a matter of discovering the interrelationships over time between many vertical analyses and evaluations of life'; and his gloss on this is especially pertinent in my context – that a narrative life 'does not have any special veridical advantage over, say, the imaginatively explorative analysis of the life; indeed, many narratives imply or point out how many and how different are the "narratives" that could claim to tell the same life' (Goldberg 1993: 279).

It might also be argued that unity resides no more in the narrative as such – the drawing together of episodes, which is MacIntyre's concern – than in the experience of, and involvement in, those episodes by the same person, the self who tells the story and/or about whom the story is being told. Although identity is dependent on others – '"Who I am" is an external feature, it is created by the other, by the story told' – still, 'the "who" is unique and one . . . since she is always the protagonist of her story' (Guaraldo 1998: 265). This would correspond to a standard philosophical position on identity – 'the idea that a person is not a single determinate entity of any sort whatsoever but a more or less unified, although indeterminate collection of continuous and/or connected experiences' (McCormick 1988: 226).

Post-realist and experimental fictions as exemplars of narrative and of narrative in practice do much to challenge MacIntyre's idea of narrative unity. The fictions I refer to contribute to that challenge: the examples of doubling and of multiple identities, of internal divisions of consciousness – depictions of persons divided in themselves – call the unified self into question (independently of judgements on the moral status of the self – its goodness, or adherence to the virtues). For example, 'Roth' provides an instance of the *non*-unified nature of the narrative self. 'Roth' worries about the failure to achieve a 'whole, harmonious character', existing in 'a plot of sequential integrity'. Just such 'failure' may, though, be consonant with the idea of narrative identity, though incompatible with understandings of the subject as unified self. It may, indeed, come to seem that a stable, non-divided identity is only possible as an abstraction, 'achieved' by a process of extraction from the lives and actions of persons in actual situations.

The modern self, as depicted in modern novels, is no longer to be regarded as akin to the autonomous author/narrator of nineteenth-century classic realism, a figure comparable to that of the self as presented in liberal theory, nor to the unified character (Taylor 1989: 449, 461, 462, 464, 465), a figure also related to the liberal chooser moving and progressing 'from birth to death'. Various parts of my discussion of modern narratives amount to a critique of MacIntyre; aspects of narrative characteristic of modern novels run counter to MacIntyre. For example, narrative sequentiality contradicts his insistence on a linear progression of beginning-middle-end.

Alford accounts MacIntyre's view of the narrative unity of a life a 'noble lie', the danger of which lies in the 'splitting off and denying all those aspects of the self that contradict the ideal of unity'. For Alford, '[T]he truth is that the constructed self is real, albeit so lacking in unity that it is generally in a state of desire for itself – for the unity it lacks' (Alford 1991: 188), as Oedipa's story well demonstrates. However, Alford suggests that '[T]o construct the unity of the self by an act of imagination (or by countless acts of imagination stretching over many years) that connects in a realistic way who one is with who one wants to be' is a viable enterprise – approximating to Oedipa's frequent cry, 'Shall I project myself?' This account may be 'constructed in full awareness that it is partial, provisional, serving to give the illusion of unity to what is actually a fragmented subject'. Alford acknowledges then that 'unity' may be held to be illusory; but it is 'constructed with will and consciousness'. Rather than an illusion, this unity constitutes a 'noble lie' – and noble lies are sometimes permissible – and may be all that is possible. The 'lie about the narrative unity of the self' is permissible because it restores the self, the subject, against those 'lies' that sublimate self to the social order (Alford 1991: 187, 188–90). This may be so, but narrative identity offers a way of avoiding even the 'noble' lie.

An answer to the meaning of unity in narrative terms is offered by Alford's contention, in discussion of MacIntyre, that the unity lies in the telling rather than in the life as such. 'The narrative unity of the self is more about the unity of narratives than the unity of the self' (Alford 1991: 16). The person cannot tell their story as a whole – narrative identity is in that sense provisional, and consists in the telling and not in the tale that is told. This understanding compares with the supposition among literary critics and theorists that it is form as such that conveys unity, or, as Lamarque and Olsen remark, the creation of form 'imposes on the subject a coherence it has not possessed beforehand' (Lamarque and Olsen 1994: 265). Narrative identity may be associated most productively not with unity but with coherence – but coherence understood in narrative terms, not as a technical requirement for texts or descriptions but as a quality, and conceptually descriptive of what narrative is able to produce.

Coherence

In his development of MacIntyre's ideas, Charles Taylor comments on the development of the modern novel, including a new time-consciousness, an 'objectification of time', which allows the reader to cope with '(provisionally) unconnected events' that occur simultaneously. This, in turn, has its effect on identity: it becomes more difficult to take over a ready-made story from 'canonical modes and archetypes'.[7] Instead, it has to be drawn from 'the particular events and circumstances of this life'. There are two interrelated aspects to this: that 'the life at any moment is the causal consequence of what has transpired earlier', and that 'since the life to be lived has also to be *told*, its meaning is seen as something that unfolds through the events'. Taylor comments that these are not easy to combine: the first 'seems to make the shape of a life simply the *result* of the happenings as they accumulate'; the second 'seems to see this shape as something already latent, which emerges through what comes to pass'. However, both are 'inescapable': 'We are made what we are by events; and as self-narrators, we live these through a meaning which the events come to manifest or illustrate' (Taylor 1989 288–9).

Taylor's view of narrating is criticized for involving 'reasoning in transitions', a matter of 'justifying the path one's life is taking by showing that the choice of certain personal commitments brings about a transition that makes sense from the perspective established after one has passed through it' (Anderson 1996: 29). The use of the present tense, the understanding that life is experienced *in media res* (as Taylor does recognize), is important. But thence a problem then arises, though, how to reconcile the need for an ongoing coherence with post hoc justification, or imposition of coherence.

Taylor himself says that 'we want the future to "redeem" the past, to make it part of a life story which has sense or purpose, to take it up in a meaningful unity' (Taylor 1989: 50). The desire for unity could just as well be expressed as an aspiration to – and for narrative identity the necessity of – coherence.

Inasmuch as modernist fiction disrupts the sense of self, and post-realist experimental fiction disrupts the sense of self in the world, so there is, apparently, a loss of coherence, and, hence, disorder; but modernism has also been characterized as a search for wholeness. The relevance to politics of a conception of narrative identity based on such an understanding would seem very dubious. The characters met with here are indeed 'searching for wholeness' – but they can hardly be said to achieve unity; nor, importantly, does their capacity for agency depend on such an achievement. Benhabib says that 'the individual with a coherent sense of self-identity is the one who succeeds in integrating these tales and perspectives into a meaningful life history' (Benhabib 1992: 198): she and other theorists want to claim that the benefit of narrative is to bestow unity and thence enable agency. The presumption must then be no unity, no capacity for an active political life. However, the narrative process, as I have suggested, has of itself the potential to cope with – not eliminate but encompass – disorder and fragmentation. If that is so, narrative identity may be associated with coherence – as expressed, for example, in Benhabib's own formulation – but not unity (cf. Shapiro, I. 1990: 24, 27, 54), despite strong theoretical associations of telling a coherent story with a unified, stable or integrated, identity (Nash 1994a; and cf. Nash 1994b, especially 211–12).

The crucial question is what is meant by coherence. Coherence is, like most of the terms employed in discussion of narrative, a debatable term. Technically, coherence 'derives from the relations that the parts of a text bear to one another and to the whole text, as well as from the relation that the text bears to other texts of its type'. A text is 'coherent' if its parts – words, phrases, sentences or larger units – are in 'proper' relation to one another and to the text as a whole, and/or if the text as a whole is 'a recognizable and well-formed text *of its type*' (Linde 1993: 12). Most generally, narrative as such is considered 'by-and-large as a technique for getting coherence', where 'getting' could be either 'the discovery or the production of coherence' – this is an open question (Nash 1994a: xiii). Coherence does not necessarily equate to unbroken narrative flow. Narrative *per se* does not provide sequence, imposing linear development, from 'beginning' to 'middle' to 'end'. Much that I have shown of narrative so far works against that – for example Daniel's book ends by going back to the beginning, as does Aaron's (cf. Polonoff 1982: 49, 49, n. 3). In literary terms, coherence may be a state achieved over time, or through form, narrative structure, style and techniques, or it may consist in the ordering process whereby even an apparently disordered narrative is intelligible (Kermode 1967), as against rigid literary-philosophical requirements such as logical succession, causality or sequentiality.[8]

Such an understanding is a long way from the philosophical position – and, by derivation therefrom, notions of coherence in the social sciences – whereby a coherence theory of truth emphasizes the requirement of the coherence of propositions with one another, coherence understood as a relation among propositions, not just consistent in the sense of non-contradictory but mutually supporting (Hospers 1967: 117). Furthermore, coherence theory often slides into correspondence theory, so that propositions are not only to be mutually supporting but are also required to be verifiable by reference to (external) 'facts' (Edwards 1977: 130–3; Hospers 1967: 116–17). But coherence need not be defined on rigorous philosophical or epistemological principles and the literary version of narrative has something to offer to more general or theoretical ideas of coherence – for instance, a way of accounting for change, for incorporating contingency into coherent accounts of lives and actions.

As literary studies recognize, coherence as a term applying to the lives of persons need not be tied to truth verification criteria (Lamarque and Olsen 1994: 197–202). (Narrative(s) shows that there may be versions of the truth – as in Sach's story.) While there must be some connection with the world of the listener/reader, strict correspondence is not necessarily required. For instance, *The Book of Daniel* offers three possible endings to the action – though none to the narrative overall; *Operation Shylock* and *The Crying of Lot 49* 'end' inconclusively. But literary coherence is about internal agreement rather than scientific forms of proof which end in QED, so that overall coherence is maintained as long as all possible endings are feasible, in respect of what has gone before, for the story that has been told, as long as they are imaginable and intelligible. That is, where narrative is understood as not necessarily working towards an end, it is not incoherent to have more than one ending (whereas a theoretical text may want or need to work towards a conclusion).

The criterion for coherence may be a 'commonsense' one, a 'correspondence' with ordinary experience. Joseph Femia – commenting on Quentin Skinner's work on coherence as between different texts by the same author, but pertinent in the context of narrative identity as well – expresses what happens:

> In everyday conversation we leap from expression to expression, filling gaps, removing apparent inconsistencies, drawing inferences, and so develop an intellectually elaborated result which is our understanding of what the other person has said. Moreover, when we try to understand an individual *as such* – his character, his thoughts, and so on – it never occurs to us to confine ourselves to his own self-image; on the contrary, we strive to uncover the *hidden premises* (psychological or social) as well as the *consequences* (logical or practical) of his behaviour and statements.
> (Femia 1988: 172)

This usefully summarizes both how the text is read and how identity is understood. What matters for the person is that their life is capable of coherent explanation, and thence understanding, and that there is a degree of coherence between the story they can tell about themselves and the stories of which they perceive themselves to be a part – which in turn need to be coherent.

That is ostensibly similar to the idea of coherence as probability – whether a story hangs together. '*Homo narrans*' will have an 'inherent awareness of narrative probability' which depends on argumentative or structural coherence, material coherence and characterological coherence – a matter of the reliability of characters as narrators and actors:

> not only is narrative prone to unreliable narration, but the general requirement is too stringent – Coherence in life and in literature requires that characters behave characteristically. Without this kind of predictability, there is no trust, no community, no rational human order.
>
> (Fisher 1989: 47)

As narratives have demonstrated, narrative and narrative identity can cope with unpredictability and still retain coherence. One of Bruner's 'narrative universals' is 'historical extensibility', the capacity of narrative to cope with change. Stories expand, to apply to different circumstances. 'We construct a "life" by creating an identity-conserving Self who wakes up the next day still mostly the same. . . . We impose coherence on the past, turn it into history.' Bruner explains that '[O]ne thing that makes this . . . possible is the conception we seem to have about "turning points", pivotal events in time when the "new" replaces the "old"' (Bruner 1996: 143–4). He refers to historical narratives, but the same might be said of literary narratives, and thence of narrative identity – that coherence is created by the incorporation of change into an ongoing narrative. For all the characters met here – Daniel, Roth, Hillela, Clarissa, Sachs and Aaron, Oedipa – 'turning points' occur and are incorporated into their narrative.

> The accrual of history is an extraordinarily narrative enterprise . . . it seems to be dedicated to finding some intermediate ground where large-scale, almost incomprehensible forces can be made to act through the medium of human beings playing out a continued story over time.
>
> (Bruner 1996: 146)

Inasmuch as identity represents a history, all or part of the story of the person as they wish to present it, or as it is understood by others, the act of narrating necessarily incorporates, makes room for and sense of, changes of direction and new facets of experience.

Uncertainty, disunity, instability, fragmentation, doublings and multiple identities are component parts of, and problems for, the concept of narrative identity. But even though modern identity is characterized by such features, for author/narrator or listener/observer there must be some degree – at least a local level – of coherence if the story is to be told and/or understood at all. So Pynchon's characters are said to 'make connections in the anticipation that eventually everything will have a place in a fully coherent scheme, and they discover local and contingent relationships in the process of straining toward this final explanation' (Hite 1983: 24, 25). There are two aspects to this: 'the degree to which a person's identity is well-defined overall depends on the degree of cohesiveness of his narrative as a whole' and 'the more a particular action, experience, or characteristic coheres with the rest of a person's narrative . . . the greater the degree to which it contributes to the overall intelligibility of that narrative' (Schechtman 1996: 98). In *The Book of Daniel*, Doctorow shows that Daniel is misled about himself – about his own identity – but he also shows his passage to a more coherent life: 'We see the turmoil within Daniel finally cohere and organize itself into a pattern for integrating internal psychological development and external political events' (Girgus 1988: 86). In *Leviathan* Sachs needs to find, and Aaron needs to relate, a coherent story.

'Coherence' might indicate a degree of consistency between self and identity – between the story one tells oneself, the story one tells others and the stories they can tell about one. The self-narrated story is a basis for interpretation and, if necessary, negotiation, or as a requirement for recognition, by others. Consistency, however, is in this context as debatable a concept as coherence itself. Situations so diverse as Ziad's haranguing of Roth as to his duty as a Jew, Sachs's reaction to the threat to the stranger who had given him a lift which results in his killing a man and thence changing his life, or Hillela's choice of lifestyle in order to fulfil a commitment to her dead husband, Whaila, all suggest that neither establishing consistency between internal beliefs, nor between those beliefs and the external world guarantees coherent identity.[9] Or as the examples show, inconsistency can permit, even allow for (the achievement of) an overall coherence.

Both Ziad and Roth act irrationally, both by each other's criteria and by reference to commonly held presumptions of rational behaviour – for instance, what an American-educated academic 'ought' to do, or what a parent ought to do for his wife and son, or what a famous writer ought to do for 'his' people. Ben Sachs might be held to have a political duty to express ideas in his writing (or even by conventional political activity) rather than by the blowing-up of replicas of the Statue of Liberty. Hillela walks away from an influential position in a relief agency to become one of a deposed African leader's women. Anderson offers a theoretical example:

> although I might recognize the general, objective, importance of protecting wilderness areas – indeed, at one point, that ideal might even have held out the prospect of becoming the organizing project of my

life – owing to the contingent turns that my life has taken or perhaps to an urban upbringing, it happens not to have much importance *for me*.
(Anderson 1996: 28)

Then 'explaining why other personal commitments are, in fact, central to my identity will involve telling a story that highlights other equally contingent elements in my particular life-history' (Anderson 1996: 28). That latter comment is a helpful gloss on the idea that identity may be revised or reinterpreted, and not thereby lose its coherence. It also emphasizes the idea that for the person, coherence may be bound up with the attempt to establish meaning, of trying to work out some degree of coherence between their perception of themselves and their world (which process will also include others' perceptions of them), of striving to construct a viable identity within a given context.

The story the person tells about themself needs to be minimally coherent, both for their own satisfaction and to satisfy others – to make it intelligible to others; and that requirement also applies to the stories others tell about the self – they must be intelligible *and* minimally consistent with the known history of the person. Coherence may therefore be defined as some degree of consistency between self and identity, for which intelligibility and reciprocity are necessary. While the narrative construction of the self entails a minimal degree of internal consistency, in order to persuade ourselves, narrative construction of identity requires a more stringent level of coherence or intelligibility. We need to persuade others of our stories and be persuaded by theirs to the extent that we are willing to incorporate them into our own, to adjust our own to fit with theirs.[10] Coherence is the outcome of co-operative effort. Theorists as diverse as Lacan and Arendt are said to 'decenter the "I" or the private identity in favor of a second self' which is 'constituted through a plurality of judgments and narratives of others' grounded in 'the plural and variable character of human interaction'; and this self 'possesses a degree of substance and reality precisely because, determined by language, not biology, it can acquire a distinctive, coherent, and stable identity' (Dolan, F.M. 1995: 342).

Coherence as a function of narrative has to be reconciled with what have been identified as the disruptive elements of narrative. If narrative is able to produce coherent accounts of identity, how is that compatible with narrative identity characterized by uncertainty, fragmentation and the like? Even in post-realist novels, pattern is observable beneath overtly disorganized plot and characterization. It becomes apparent that coherence is going to be an outcome of narrative organization, 'the imposition of form' (Lamarque and Olsen 1994: 265), plotting. The emphasis here is again on the narrative whole: for narrative identity, coherence is achieved by way of the patterning and structuring produced by plotting, whereby what characters do, how the plot progresses, is coherent – explicable – given all that is being shown. ('Shown' rather than 'told' because this is more than a matter of narrative voice, but rather the total narrative effect – so, for instance, recurrent imagery may contribute to coherence.)

Emplotment

> What [Graham] Swift seems to like about the structure of a story is its jigsaw nature: not just that it should fit, or that it should be divisible into parts, but that a piece you shuffled past in the box ten minutes ago happens to slip neatly into the top left hand corner.
>
> (Wood 1996: 20–1)

Plotting is 'the activity of shaping', the 'dynamic aspect of narrative.' It is, in Brooks's standard definition, 'that which makes a plot "move forward", and makes us read forward, seeking in the unfolding of the narrative a line of intention and a portent of design that hold the promise of progress towards meaning' (Brooks 1984: xi, xiii). It is, though, by no means guaranteed that meaning will be found. What is significant is the process of arranging events into a coherent or patterned narrative, rather than the understanding of plot as overall design with a predetermining effect on the story being narrated, and as leading inexorably to meaning and closure.

'It is emplotment that gives significance to independent instances, not their chronological or categorical order. And it is emplotment that translates events into episodes' (Somers 1994: 616). In relation to self and identity, this can be glossed by the comment that some people have 'no tendency to see their life as constituting a story or development. Some merely go from one thing to another, living life in a picaresque or episodic fashion', whereas Strawson takes the alternative to be people who 'live in narrative mode', those who 'experience their lives in terms of something that has shape and story, a narrative trajectory' (Strawson 1996: 21–2). Narrative identity is then the product of a process of narrating, telling – in the course of which events, episodes, are woven into the narrative. Hence the readings here of novels that show identity in the process of construction but not necessarily completed – and not in any case identity that could not be other.

Emplotment does not entail any grand design, let alone foreordained end known by an omniscient author/narrator. There is only patterning and process, not a desired and/or achieved end. In Pynchon's novel, Oedipa's constant finding of patterns and connections as she follows up the clues deriving from the originating event of Inverarity's death and her position as his executor is of itself a structure, regardless of whether or not she can find meaning, or any kind of closure. She constantly seeks meaning, but failing to find any she tries to assimilate the many clues or strange signs that she encounters into her search. The corresponding theoretical position would be something like the observation that '[A] community's political identity then is neither unalterable and fixed, nor a voluntarist project to be executed as it please, but a matter of slow self-recreation within the limits set by its past' (Parekh 1995b: 264).

Many of the features of narrative identity that I have identified contribute to the uncertainty of identity – instability, splitting, fragmentation – presenting a problem for the construction of identity and suggesting the difficulty, if not impossibility, of a unified self (cf. Connolly 1991: 172–3). However, narrative has the capacity for 're-contextualizing the fragments', and in that sense can 'contain' disunity: '[T]he recontextualisation of fragments replaces chronological narrative of the subject's itinerary through life as the dominant formal strategy of fiction' (Smyth 1991: 142, 144). The subject of narrative identity may remain fragmented, splitting still occurs, but the fragments are contained, held in place, within a framework; and splitting is not necessarily destructive of identity. Alford comments – on MacIntyre's assumption that the unity of the self is a direct relation of the unity of its tradition – that the activity of splitting 'is not just a *response* to a fragmented tradition but a way of coping with the intensity of our hopes and fears'; and 'when traditions do split us, they do not just split us into pieces' but the 'patterns to these splits, resulting from the internal dynamics of the self in interaction with its environment' produce 'particular types of selves which in turn create particular types of worlds' (Alford 1991: 17).

MacIntyre's adoption of the term 'narrative' as part of an argument against moral relativism tends, among other things, and not least in its limited choice of narrative genres as examples, to obscure the fact that for modern lives as depicted in modern literature there is indeed fragmentation but that same literature does not deny the fragmentation but pulls together the fragments by way of the narrative process itself.

Narratives tend to violate the systematic nature of theory: they remind theory of the sheer *messiness* of much lived existence but they also, co-incidentally, connect the fragments, through emplotment, the process of narrative construction. Cave has suggested that identity is to be understood as an 'amalgam' of component parts ('awkward to analyse even though we seem to be able to get along with it reasonably well in everyday life') (Cave 1995: 116, 117). Modern fictions correspond to this understanding in that however diverse or disjointed their elements, they are coherent narratives. As Cave says, fictions are 'a model of the processes whereby we seek to comprehend that which borders on the incomprehensible. Fictional narratives represent the awkward couplings of experience non-analytically, holistically, and . . . in all their cultural and historical particularity' (Cave 1995: 118).

Post-realist narratives disturb assumptions about sequentiality and causation; they allow for contingency and coincidence; they demonstrate the disordered or inaccurate recall of events that is a feature of lived life, if not of theory. There is problematic narration: who is telling the story – in whose voice, from whose point of view; what certainty does the narrative allow? Fragmentation and gaps prevent a single, unassailable characterization to be arrived at; identity may be multiple, split, disunified. Narratives allow for – indeed, plot may hinge on – chance, coincidence and (the effects of) contingency. Experimental, post-realist novels show that the unified character set out by an omniscient author/narrator is unrealistic, outmoded, and not *true* in any sense to which fictional narratives can usefully contribute.

My examination of narrative identity by way of such narratives is meant to suggest not only that the conceptualization of narrative identity is less straightforward than might be presumed but also that 'problems' encountered in these readings need not be so regarded: that is, apparently problematical aspects of narrative identity are not necessarily so. These novels are readable; and in that sense at least, they are coherent: their presentation of narrative identity is comprehensible – and persuasive. Their characters are recognizable; and despite the uncertain or unstable aspects of their lives and identities, these bearers of narrative identity are able to act.

The idea of narrative identity carries with it both the presentation of the modern self as uncertain, non-unified, fragmented, and the possibility of coherence achieved by the narrative process. Disorder is containable via narrative telling. In arguing that this is the case, various difficult and contentious questions have emerged which quite clearly impinge on the interests and concerns of political theory; the final chapter of this study addresses some of those issues. Many of the questions are left open at this stage; and this study does not move towards conclusion (indeed, to do so would be disappointing, if not downright contradictory, given my emphasis on open, 'process', texts) – there is no closure.

7 Narrative, identity and politics

In this final chapter, I want to suggest what consequences for politics might follow from unpacking the idea of narrative identity. Some aspects of narrative identity as I have described it are already recognized in or supported by political theory. However, as the citations in the substantive chapters of this study suggest, these connections or correlations are widely scattered across the range of what can be labelled political theory; they are not generally followed through or brought together in such a way as to interrelate with a full and coherent account of narrative identity. I suggest that some political theorizing could profitably begin from narrative identity, seeing what then follows. In doing this, I unavoidably raise yet more questions.

Current political theory is, not surprisingly, interested in identity; is somewhat aware of narrative; and has taken rather less notice of narrative identity. Peter Euben asks

> how it is we become who we are. What forces, internal and external, shape our actions and wants, our speech and our gestures? In what sense and under what circumstances are we initiators, complicitors, or simply victims of our character and our destiny? Can we tell our own story or must we leave it, necessarily, to others to say and portray 'who we are'? To what degree can we understand how identities are formed, our own and others, as persons and cultures?
>
> (Euben 1990: 100)

Euben goes on to suggest answers, the alternatives corresponding, more or less, to the understandings of identity current in political theory: 'as self-conscious largely autonomous beings possessing a unified will and stable self we can, to a large degree, define ourselves and control the consequences of our action and the meaning of our lives'; or, 'we are socially constructed individuals or historically constructed subjects who lack any fixed identity apart from the institutional matrices and forms of discourse that shape regimes of power-knowledge' (Euben 1990: 100).

On another dimension, analytically speaking, attention to identity in political theory has taken two distinct forms: an interest in personal identity –

the self – and in political identity. The former has been associated with the current debate, said to be dominant in contemporary political theory, between liberals and communitarians (Strong 1990: 2). Meanwhile, the attention paid to political identity in the study of politics has taken certain characteristics – notably race, gender and ethnicity – whereby persons can be grouped for political purposes, as the relevant features for political analysis (disregarding individual characteristics of separate persons) (Rajchman 1995). Identity is thus regarded, crudely speaking, as either a matter of self-awareness and/or the relationship of the person to the political order or a characteristic attributed to (members of) groups regarded as significant in the political process.

Charles Taylor's *Sources of the Self* and *The Ethics of Authenticity* combine these two meanings inasmuch as they seek to establish the modern self as a being with specific features of identity which demand recognition as affirming that identity, with 'authenticity' as a function of self-affirmation of that identity.[1] These understandings provide a basis for treating the recognition of that self-identity in terms of group identity – identity politics. As the study and definition of politics have widened beyond (or behind) the formal institutions and processes of regimes, so 'the politics of identity', as inherent in the social aspects of identity and/or recognized in the civil status of persons as members of political regimes, covers a range of socio-political behaviour and action (cf. Calhoun 1994; Laffan 1996: 81–102; *Journal* 1995).[2]

In addition (and as I have indicated at various points in my discussion), political theorists have extended the usage of political identity from single persons to extra-personal entities, particularly the nation. On that specific form of political identity, Parekh has suggested that 'the central organizing principles, the constitutive characteristics' which make a polity the kind of polity it is constitute 'the most coherent and comprehensive' sense of political identity. The other meanings of political identity that he identifies – as characterized by (a) difference, whereby identity is established by reference to 'what makes it distinct and distinguishable from others'; (b) self-conception or self-understanding; or (c) 'deeply cherished values, goals and commitments' – 'emphasize specific aspects of identity and mistakenly equate these with the whole' (Parekh 1995b: 256). That political identity can be so characterized does not sit easily with the attention to narrative identity already present in political theorizing.

There is a degree of understanding of narrative in political theory. I have referred to the work of major political theorists and philosophers as proponents of the turn to narrative. Although some aspects of their attention to narrative are pertinent to my discussion, it moves away from or beyond them. For instance, Arendt makes plain two major qualifications which largely rule out her advocacy of storytelling in my context. She speaks of life-stories, as against 'a fictional story, where indeed an author pulls the strings and directs the play'. For her, '[T]he distinction between a real and a fictional story is precisely that the latter was "made up" and the former not made at all' (Arendt 1958: 186).[3] There are no authors but only subjects. And she speaks of 'the various forms of reification in art works', 'acting', where acting and speaking become associated with imitation and repetition. Arendt does not so much object to this as to isolate drama among the (narrative) art forms: '[t]he theater is the political art par excellence; only there is the political sphere of human life transposed into art' (Arendt 1958: 184–8). While this is hardly surprising, given her context, the essentially public nature of politics, my attention to the novel as a prime instance of narrative directly contradicts her opinions.

In general where narrative is recognized by political theorists, the emphasis tends to be on patterning, sequence – and hence, again, unity. Often the term narrative is used methodologically, as for instance in discussion of various aspects of national identity. The assumptions are, again, sequentiality, the patterning of events, and storytelling as an unproblematic activity. To reiterate and emphasize: political usages do not usually stipulate a definition, apparently taking the meaning as self-evident, though often implying that it is synonymous with story or storytelling.

What then of narrative identity in current political theory? MacIntyre's and Taylor's attention to narrative and identity is well known in Anglophone political theory. Taylor goes further than MacIntyre in specifying types of narrative and the different ways in which they might order human lives, tracing the historical development of connections between the four terms which he thinks make up the modern identity – ideas of the good, understandings of self, conceptions of society and narrative forms. There are also aspects of the political theorizing of identity for which the terminology of narrative is directly relevant, where the term is utilized in specific political arguments, beyond use as mere metaphor or passing phrase.[4] An example is Bridges' treatment of civic identity, whereby '[A] capacity for civic freedom consists of a capacity to incorporate into every narratively constructed identity or self a recognition and affirmation of its own narratively constructed status' (Bridges 1994: 175). Group identity is considered in narrative terms: in the building of identity by nationalist groups, for example, identity narratives are weapons in the struggle for power, and can also (therefore) be instruments 'for constructing an "imagined community"' (Martin, D.-C. 1995: 10, 13).

For the most part, the relatively few direct references to narrative identity current in political theorizing resemble Alford's observations on the self in social theory: that is, they are to be found in, can be extracted from, or derive from, theory that is primarily focused on some other object, activity or political issue.

> The key problem with so many accounts of the self is that they render the self the dependent variable – the last thing to be explained, formulated

to fit the theorist's favorite concepts but in effect having no reality independent of these concepts.

(Alford 1991: 20)

And hence, accordingly, these usages are relatively underdeveloped. Alford's claim for beginning from the self which I take as a model for beginning from identity includes the observation that for classical political theorists, and those who have derived theory from or against these 'greats', '[C]onceptualizing the self as an abstract metaphysical entity leads to a way of thinking that in the end values not the self but the abstract principles from which it is derived' (Alford 1991: 2). Similarly, identity is frequently taken as subservient to some wider or larger concern, for instance, nationhood, gender politics, or a discussion of otherness and difference. As I have said, MacIntyre's much-cited attention to narrative is dependent on his turn to that concept in support of his broader argument against modern relativism and for the restoration of the virtues. Similarly, Arendt's conception of identity, associated with storytelling as a method, is said to arise from 'her attempt to articulate the nature of action' (Dolan, F.M. 1995: 326, 342).

By analogy with Alford's argument, to begin with a conception of narrative political identity might have some interesting results for political thinking. Rather than deriving ideas of identity from political instances or problems, or attaching narrative identity to a specific political argument, much might be gained for political understanding by beginning from the idea of narrative identity.

Narrative identity in/for political theory

There are benefits to be had across a wide range of approaches in political theory from focusing directly on narrative identity in the political context, and from drawing out the meanings and implications of narrative political identity. For instance, apart from the particular ways in which narrative identity relates to the political, there are general methodological advantages. One of these is a synthesizing function. I have already indicated where relevant elements of narrative are compatible with lines of argument in current political thought, so that various points of my discussion will not necessarily come as any great surprise to many political theorists. However, although much in political theory supports this discussion of narrative identity, that support is not necessarily recognized as such: the theorists cited are not usually themselves talking about narrative identity. Furthermore, those various aspects of theory I have cited are just that – separate strands of theorizing, attached to a wide range of political subjects, and often not connected in any way within the work of political theory. Narrative identity offers certain interconnections of themes and issues of interest to political theorists; the elements of narrative identity offer a way of synthesizing or integrating disparate parts of the study of politics, or of showing up contradictions and tensions. This is so in the case of certain clusters of concepts which narrative identity brings together: for example, narrative identity draws considerations of recognition, coherence, embedment or inter-textuality, into understandings of both agency and order.

Not only does beginning from, or focusing on, narrative identity have the benefit of pulling certain strands of theory together, showing the connections between them, but that process may of itself have a mediative capacity, offer-ing a way of holding the balance between otherwise opposing points of view or disparate strands or approaches in political theorizing, as for example, between libertarians and communitarians. That stories of identity are in part (self)narrated but are also embedded, that the self is situated but also exercises choice as to what to affirm or deny in what is given – 'The situ-ated and gendered subject is heteronomously determined but still strives towards autonomy' (Benhabib 1992: 214) – are in effect arguments against strong versions of both liberal and communitarian thought. An understand-ing of narrative construction could help to hold the ring between con-ventional and radical/postmodern theories on this controversy. Or again, a narrative conception of identity has the capacity to mediate the distinction between *self*-identity, as perceived and narrated by the self, and identity in the sense of perception by others of that which makes the self recognizable to those others, often theorized politically as a matter of group characterization.

Apart from such general considerations, when narrative identity is looked at in detail, various narrative elements and characteristics have something to offer political theory. For instance, just as some political theory supports the theorizing of narrative identity, so, conversely, conceptualizations of narrative identity relate to understandings already present in political theorizing, especially where theorists critique liberal and mainstream politi-cal theory. Some elements of narrative are especially relevant to a political understanding of identity, as has been indicated in discussion of those features. The characterization of narrative identity as embodied, embedded, interrelational, presenting a 'thick' character distinguished by certain parti-cularities, relates to debates on the nature of the political subject. Narrative identity understood as identity in process, fluid, and changing in the telling, lack of closure, and the significance of emplotment disturb assumptions about conclusive explanations.

Narrative identity works to refine or extend features of identity already in use in political theory as, for example, in the case of ascription, identification and recognition, which are central to identity politics. The narrative treat-ment of multiple identity adds to the discussion of multiplicity already in process – narrative form indicates how multiplicity is expressed, for instance by multivocal narratives. It also extends the discussion, for example by showing that ascriptions or recognitions may vary, so stories may vary, and thence another dimension of multiplicity. Narrative identity is able to incorporate, 'contain', multiplicity and splitting, and is able to cope with and, indeed, respond positively to, change and contingency. The narrative process frames and contextualizes disruption, allowing the interaction of identity with agency and action despite instability or uncertainty. For instance, where political identity refers to nations or states, narrative political identity would allow for the telling or re-telling of stories that contain – in a double sense – coups, acts of secession and other threats to the stability of the political order. The narrative 'solution' is the narrative process itself.

The idea of narrative identity does not merely interact, in some form of matching exercise, with political theory (as though confirmation of the political implications of the idea were necessary from the theoretical standpoint). Narrative political identity offers new ideas to political theory. Overall, identity is presented as composite, and hence attention is to be paid to the nature and form of the compositing. Theory has not paid much attention to the figure of the narrator as such, but certain facets of that role are interesting in a political context: for example, that narrating may be self-revealing that there is a choice of what to tell or not to tell – narrative gaps are a common feature of narrative telling. Emplotment draws episodes together but there is no predetermined plot, no grand design (no 'master narrative'): unity or, as I argue, coherence, is not given merely by reference to a narrative but has to be (re)constructed by the narrative process, or, by reflection – and subsequent telling – as the life proceeds. Distinguishing emplotment from plot removes even the hint of a teleological cast to storytelling as a political device, and emphasizes process. Narratives end but there is not necessarily closure; conversely, to impose closure may be artificial – unrealistic. Narrative content suggests that there may be no need to fix an identity and related aspects of narrative, such as lack of closure, establish uncertainty as a feature of identity. That, together with the understanding of narrative identity as embedded, works against totality or totalizing accounts.

Narrative telling and politics

Narratives are also suggestive, not only in terms of content but also by way of the features basic to narrative. Beyond general issues or applications, particular elements and characteristics of narrative identity are also new to and potentially suggestive for political theory. This is especially the case with the idea of narrative telling essential to narrative identity, where a number of questions arise for politics. Some of these are the familiar questions of political theory recast, but some are newly posed by this unfamiliar language. To employ narrative in political theory raises certain issues relating to characteristic features of narrative telling, for instance as to narration, narrative voice and point of view. In particular it raises the question of who tells the political story, or what is entailed in the requirement that identity stories need to be coherent, at least by way of mutual intelligibility.

The primary requirement of narration is a narrator and hence attention to narrative voice and point of view. However, this straightforward require- ment can prove problematic in the political context. For instance, the problems around multiplicity already alluded to also point to difficulties of narration – how to characterize political identity by way of who tells the story, single or collective voices, conflicting accounts and so on. Attention to narrative identity encourages identification of the author, and evaluation of their authoring, narrative telling. For example, does the author seek agree- ment – consent? (Carr 1986: 157). This is a difficult but fascinating, and potentially very fruitful, line of enquiry for political theory. 'Who tells the political story?' Each bearer of political identity might be expected to tell their story – in conjunction with others; but can a political system remain stable if everyone tells their own story (Carr 1986: 156–7), or maintains the right to edit or amend the collective story? If not a story told by each and every person, then who: should communities tell their own stories; or should dominant groups; or leaders of dominant groups; or government; or the poli- tical theorist (Bürger 1992: 107)? In the political world, identity, especially that of groups, may be multi-authored (as, for instance, when politicians, journalists and political theorists all tell stories about a group).

In democratic or associative politics, 'ordinary citizens' 'who acquire the capacities of political judgment and initiative in the process of self- organisation' (Benhabib 1992: 124–5) could be expected, correspondingly, to tell their own stories. But what of minority or excluded groups whose story is not heard? The ascription of identity to groups within the political process results in a problem highlighted by questions of authorship – loss of voice. The exclusion of certain groups is attributable to a dominant narrative voice. In a critique of identity politics, Benhabib notes the tendency to turn claimants into victims – where 'any definition of a group's identity not in terms of its own constitutive experiences but in terms of its victimization by others reduces that group's subjectivity to the terms of the dominant discourse' (Benhabib 1992: 69; cf. Brown 1995; Norton 1988: 4, 53).

To recast political discussion in narrative terms immediately draws attention to the necessary presence of 'listeners'. To whom the story is told, and for what purpose, are obviously pertinent issues to political identity (and there are implicit connections to recent developments in political theory such as dialogical, communicative and discourse theories). Narrative identity challenges or complicates some of the commonplaces of politics. For instance, is authority automatically attributed to the teller of the story; or does the political story depend – equally perhaps – on audience response; and if the latter, does this strengthen communitarian ideas? Such consider- ations open up the question as to what kind of political order can accom- modate narrative identity. That is, it might be argued that (the working out of) narrative political identity requires a democratic system – if not a 'face-to-face society' – if the terms of the formulation are to have practical application beyond theoretical (or metaphorical) use. If narrative is dialogic or relational, how much political applicability does it have if, for instance, tellers at any level other than one-to-one relationships may not know who their listeners are?[5] Or, again, to what extent can the political story as told by ruling groups be modified by other stories? If modification is not possible, such a story becomes a master narrative, ruling out the relevance of any other story(ies)? If 'the explanation of human action must always include – and perhaps even take the form of – an attempt to recover and interpret the meanings of social actions from the point of view of the agents performing them' (Skinner 1985: 6), then stories below the level of the dominant discourse should be listened to – or does it have to be conceded that political identity beyond that of the single person is not narrative identity, even though storytelling is involved?

These questions also imply (positive) answers, at least in that they may suggest thinking through narrative identity presents a way of analysing the political. 'Narrative' analysis could, for example, explain disorder in terms of dissonant stories told by actors within a specific political situation. That is demonstrated in part by work in narrative policy-making which has shown the political implications of conflicting stories told by different groups within the policy-making process (cf. Roe 1994; Kaplan 1986).

The applicability of narrative and narrative identity may also, and similarly, be shown by focusing on the concerns of political theory as such. Although much theoretical work on identity is concerned with the identity of the person, political theory is just as interested in the identity 'of the extra-personal, the entities that make up the political realm. If narrative is the appropriate form for the construction of identity, does the construction of the identity of the state or, indeed, political order at any level also depend on the capacity to tell a story, to construct an intelligible narrative that will convince the 'readers' (cf. Martin, D.-C. 1995: 5–19, 11)? Classic concerns of political theory, the activity of the state and the relationship between the individual and the state can be understood in terms of story, interlocking stories, episodes in containing narratives. 'Rational authority' may then be understood as a matter of coherent narrative, and political order may be said to depend on the regime's ability to tell an appropriate story (narratively speaking, appropriate to the expectations of the readers, or to the genre, for instance). The political body needs to tell a compelling story, to gain the assent of its listeners, in order to establish its identity. The language of narrative can be brought into political use; conversely, political language could be rethought in narrative terms. For example, familiar political terms in the cluster state, authority and legitimacy, can be associated with narrative where that is concerned with recognition or intelligibility.

Claims to legitimacy may be construed as a matter of storytelling; the achievement – or construction and maintenance – of legitimacy may be interpreted as the capacity for giving an account. Just as authority has been understood theoretically as entailing the requirement that reasons can be given, so legitimacy in a narrative mode rests on the ability 'to tell a true tale'. The listener must understand the story, and it should be credible. What then of a credible but fantastic story, a story with internal coherence, but with little or no correspondence to external verifications? Listeners need not relate a story to real life, as every reader of modern narratives knows; but then, again, the question is not only do we understand the story, do we *like* it, but do we trust the storyteller?

Does the listener understand the story being told: is it coherent, rational, intelligible, true? By what criteria does the listener judge the validity of the story – and does it matter whether the story is 'true', or only that it is plausible? Are the storyteller(s) reliable – how to avoid being gulled by a persuasive but generally unreliable storyteller? To present the state's claims to legitimacy as a matter of telling a story suggests that the breakdown of legitimacy, crises of legitimacy, occur and are made manifest when the story is patently untrue or when it is incoherent.

Beginning to theorize from narrative identity not only offers new concepts or fresh slants on familiar themes but also effectively critiques existing theory. The most obvious instance is the effects of interaction between narrative identity and political identity, the narrativization of political identity; following from that, narrative identity also has an impact on political understandings of the relationship between the self and the political system, and identity and agency.

Narrativizing political identity

Narrative identity problematizes certain conceptions of political identity: what would be the effect of applying narrative to standard formulations of political identity – for example, the individual rational chooser or group membership?

The autonomous self is associated with 'a unified life', assuming that 'lives well-lived are orderly, consistent, holistically patterned, rationally and deliberately constructed by a self . . . A self divided or disordered is untenable territory for autonomy' (Di Stefano 1993: 4). What I have said of narrative identity as 'divided or disordered' makes the autonomous self 'untenable territory' for narrative identity. Furthermore, the characterization of narrative identity as relational, situated, embodied and embedded, works against surviving versions of the predominantly autonomous self (Crittenden 1992).

Political theorists may want to separate out a specific political identity which disregards all else about the person except their status and behaviour in the political realm. For instance, citizenship is treated not as a facet of identity, or a mediating concept between personal and political identity, but as a separate 'civic' identity, conferred on, not stemming from the person. 'Who and what we are as citizens can be seen as a production or imposition' (Shapiro, M. 1988: 5); not then a particular manifestation of identity in a political context, but an artificial construction abstracted from the actual person as bearer of an identity which includes reference to their membership of a cultural community. Bridges acknowledges that the 'first and primary identity of any citizen' is their identity as 'members of particular class, ethnic and religious communities' but asserts that this 'must be transformed in the process of developing a civic identity' (Bridges 1994: 86, 35–9, 54–7 and *passim*; cf. Mouffe 1995a: 37, 38). (Ironically, Bridges suggests narrative means for achieving this: the transformation can be produced by 'the development and cultivation of linguistic and moral capacities that are not conceived of by modernist philosophies as capacities for reasoning at all . . . produced only through the exercise of certain forms of narrative imagination and self-understanding' (Bridges 1994: 86, 112).)

Nancy Rosenblum says that 'the problem with orthodox liberal thought is that some men and women cannot recognize themselves in it' (Rosenblum 1987: 3; cf. Digeser 1995; Johnston 1994). Whereas modern liberal theory has focused on the individual, the autonomous self, in contrast, post-liberal – or post-Rawlsian – theorists have substituted a conception of the situated self. Then citizen identity cannot constitute a 'universal' political identity because persons are 'unique, self-creating, and creative individuals, and because they originate in, and live in, differing cultures within the political whole' (with a nice echo of the narrative understanding of the containment of fragments) (Gutmann 1994b: 6; Taylor 1994: 43–4). Discourse theory has postulated identity as product, in part at least, of the community – a 'negotiated' identity, politically dependent on the existence of a political realm where 'conversation' as 'free and equal agents' is possible (Taylor 1991: 47–50). The embedded self of narrative identity equates to the theoretical understanding of the situated self.

As against conceptualizations of political identity which take persons for political purposes to be 'free of all attachments', or 'individuals who are conceived to be entirely equal units, living in a cultural and historical vacuum' (Scott 1995: 9), narrative identity is constructed with reference to the past, drawing on memory, and related to present context. Warren talks of 'how we assign meaning to duration' doing this 'partly by situating ourselves within a narrative of the self', and 'partly by borrowing stories that are already part of our culture' (Warren 1990: 622). Oedipa's experience with the tapestry makes the point in a different way: it is not sufficient to fabricate a story or a self; the person needs grounding – to be situated, indeed. Embedment may be compared to intertextuality, the understanding that there is a narrative tradition in which any one narrative is situated and to which it responds. The abstracted, free-standing self is ruled out by the idea that any story draws from and responds to other stories. Narrative identity offers an alternative specification to the characterization of the modern individual as alienated, cut off from social and political ties. Narrative identity is inter-relational and in that respect tied in to community (though not thereby communitarian), as against the individual pitted against otherness regarded only as different and threatening.

Single lives can be regarded as episodes in a containing and continuing narrative, or narratives, one of which is the political story; and the stories of person, group and regime interlock. As with groups within pluralist, multi-cultural states, '[T]he larger identity is grounded and energized by the particular, and the particular fulfils itself and finds a safe nest in the larger unit' (Parekh 1995a: 150). The very idea of narrative identity directs attention to that which is publicly shown, in interaction with others.

The identity of political entities beyond the single person is liable to all the same constraints inherent in narrative identity as have been identified for the theoretical figure of the free-standing individual. However, when group identity is in question, two further, interlinked considerations apply. Theorists are liable to deal in abstractions, including treating persons as units for analysis rather than particular(istic) selves. And the process of ascription often associated with group identity both accentuates that tendency as well as raising problems of itself (cf. Appiah 1997). (Both problems are already identified and critiqued in recent political theory but, again, narrative identity is particularly helpful in advancing that critique – and especially so where narratives are taken as instances of the process of the construction of narrative identity.)

On the first, political identity understood in terms of groups tends to depersonalize. Narrative political identity would require that the person is recognized as such, not just aggregated by some characteristic or other into group identification. Even where political identity is a group identity, the persons making up that group retain their own, singular, identity – otherwise, 'If what matters about me is my individual and authentic self, why is so much contemporary talk of identity about large categories – race, gender, ethnicity, nationality, sexuality – that seem so far from the individual' (Waldron 1998: 13, quoting Appiah and Gutmann 1998). Political analysis may tend to focus on groups as existing for common causes but neglect the fact that those groups include disparate persons who have their own stories to tell. They also have, in this sense, multiple identities (which may, therefore, affect the behaviour of the group in the course of attempting to, or failing to, reconcile those identities) (cf. Smith 1995: 130). This is problematic where identity politics attributes political identity by way of one distinct characteristic (cf. Appiah 1995: 110). I have emphasized the relational and social aspects of narrative identity; for group identity, it is equally necessary to emphasize that the basis of identity remains the person's own story.

Literary criticism suggests that 'the rise of the novel is synonymous with the rise of the modern fictional character, whose identity is highly individualized and who is often a first person narrator embarked on a restless search for an adequate sense of self.' This 'historical commonplace opens up a crucial issue in the broader understanding of identity'. It is not that 'the inward turn has replaced other ways of constructing identity', but that there is 'a delicate and difficult balance' between 'internal and external co-ordinates or criteria, between personal identity as individual differentiation and personal identity as constituted by belonging to one or more groups' (Cave 1995: 105). It is that delicate balance which narrative identity mediates – the identity of the self as a single person and as a political agent.

Where there is a potential or actual disparity between the singularity/ one-dimensionality or abstraction of political analysis and the particularity and multiplicity of experience of the person(s) affected, literary fictions prove especially helpful, focusing as they do on *characters*. It is now some time since it was stated that '[I]n the place of what ought to be problems, political philosophers still put metaphysical placeholders' (Warren 1988: 155). Inasmuch as theorists do continue to work from assumptions about given and stable identities, they can only do so on the basis of abstraction from the real person, located in space and time – thus producing a more fictional character than those in works of fiction. Narrative identity should at least remind political theory that groups are composed of persons, bearers of distinct identity, characterized by particulars.

Narrative identity works to enlarge the scope of the political: one of its functions in this respect is the insistence on bringing the complete person into politics rather than a partial incorporation, merely treating the person as bearer of politically-relevant characteristics – the choosing agent of liberal political theory, for instance, or the gendered or racially-identified unit of identity politics. Contrarily, narrative political identity takes the self out of the narrowness of the philosophical or literary world in that it associates identity with choice and agency, linked to embedment in the political world.)

The second problem attached to group identity is that the theoretical ten-dency to abstract and the assimilation of the separate self into group identity are closely linked to the practice of ascription, which also raises problems for political identity. While the relational aspect of narrative identity entails that the person cannot completely control the construction of identity, it is also the case that the person cannot be identified only by ascription. Despite the possibility of multiplicity or splitting in the person, there is a sense in which narrative identity entails consideration of the complete person. That is, in the political context, reference to one characteristic, as in ascriptions of group identity (or to one aspect of behaviour as in assumptions of citizenship) is not sufficient. To identify certain characteristics and then to suppose that a story – a coherent, mutually intelligible story – can be told about that group based solely or primarily on extrapolation from those selected charac-teristics will quite possibly be to miss the 'true' – or, more accurately, the fuller – story.

In the political context, as elsewhere, there may well be a discrepancy between self-narrated and ascribed identity or identification. Ascribed identity may have the effect of making the person or other political entity invisible – or, replaced by a stereotype, a case of misperception, non-recognition. The classic case for the person is that recorded by Ralph Ellison in *Invisible Man* (cf. Stone 1999). A nice political example is the observation that the 'story' of Trieste is bound up with certain perceptions of situation (place), culture and use of language concerning

> a place to the east imagined as Balkan, 'Slav' terrain. . . . 'Slav' was a convenient term for ignoring cultural specificity and emphasizing instead Bolshevism, barbarism and backwardness. Conversely, 'Balkan' contained the idea of fragmentation. When juxtaposed with 'Slav', it indicated an essential inability to unite or represent a coherent identity.
>
> (Sluga 1996: 25)

There are many groups for whom identity is or has been precarious, and has to be renegotiated. For instance, it is said of French Jews in the 1940s that most were 'happy to be defined by General de Gaulle as French citizens, nothing more, nothing less, who had suffered under the Nazis, like all French patriots' (as against identifications in terms of Jewish essentialism) (Buruma 1998: 4). In the 1990s the Hong Kong Chinese had to decide whether or not they were 'Chinese' (Buruma 1997). Some identifications 'become politically salient for a time in certain contexts'; but identity 'is an ongoing process of differentiation, relentless in its repetition . . . but also subject to redefinition, resistance and change' (Scott 1995: 3–12, 11). Scott's comment confirms the understanding that stories of identity are not fixed. References such as Scott's, together with the many references to non-fixed identity cited throughout this study, and consonant with my understanding of narrative identity, are in clear contrast to the fixed point at which the subject of political interest is frozen for the purposes of theorizing, captured at a static moment of time, and in a particular focus. Politics can slip into an assumption of identity as stable or predictable on the basis of the given-ness or continuity of the specific characteristic(s) taken as the basis for grouping. But for narrative political identity, all the elements of narrative which indicate instability and uncertainty remain operative, whatever the process of ascription/affirmation. Narrative identity is identity in process. Process is effectively the key term here: narrative as process allows for theorizing about identity in interaction with, and as a facet of, the dynamics of the political process, as against a static or snapshot view of identity (subservient to some particular political argument).

The relationship between the self and the political system

Narrative identity suggests that this relationship can be considered in terms of the embedment of the self in the political system; the person's response to the system, and vice versa, involving mutual recognition and intelligibility; and the possibility of discrepancy between stories told at different levels of the political, potentially productive of disorder.

It is inherent in a narrative conception of identity that identity is not free-standing. It therefore draws attention to the context of identity: and so for narrative *political* identity, attention to the political context with which the bearer of identity interrelates and within which they operate. For any given person, their identity is somewhat a political matter: they operate – or not – in a political world, their identity is affirmed, recognized, in part by their political status or activity, their (potential) behaviour as political actor. That much is evident from the novels. Much of what I have said about the narrativization of political identity relates to embedment as characteristic of narrative identity; and indeed, the fact of embedment constitutes the most basic level of interaction between the person and the political. Personal stories of identity are embedded within a larger narrative about the past and the present of the culture, the socio-political world in which the person lives. The frequency with which the identity of the person is tied up with the identity of the (American) nation in the novels makes the point.

Recognition and intelligibility are necessary elements in the political relationship – and mutually so where that relationship is, actually or ideally, a democratic or egalitarian one. Conventionally speaking, interaction between the person and the political realm is negotiated by way of the processes and behaviour encapsulated in concepts such as legitimacy, authority, obligation and consent (as suggested above). These traditional political expressions of the relationship carry connotations of initiative from the political, eliciting response from the individual. However, narrative terminology makes clear that each side is both teller and listener, and that each will benefit or lose according to the intelligibility of the stories each is telling. Even if the conventional view of the relationship is maintained, and the person as subject or citizen listens to the story which the political authority tells, narrative opens up a variety of possible responses. The art of storytelling again becomes politically germane: the reception of the story may link to the conventions of a particular genre; problematic reactions are possible – wandering attention, boredom with a familiar, often-told story.

Both persons and political bodies construct narratives to order and explain themselves; and order for both person and political group, state, regime or other political entity may depend on mutually understandable narratives, on giving an account, telling a coherent story. However, a central understanding to be gained from narrative identity is that there may well be discrepancies between stories told by or about the person, or the political order; and recognitions may differ similarly. The stories told by the political order and the person may be incompatible in the sense that one cannot hear the other, or because the integrity of the one is compromised if they allow credibility to the other.

Identity and agency

Narrative identity opens up aspects of agency as understood politically – the standard figure of the unified agent is put in doubt; the particularistic approach of narrative enlarges the scope of agency; contingency is not necessarily a hindrance; the understanding of coherence available from narrative links to an understanding of the capacity for action. 'On a societal level, the establishment of personal identity is never an end in itself, but a pressing historical prerequisite for making forms of activity clear' (Hoffmann-Axthelm 1992: 206) – politically speaking, the relevant consideration is political agency. 'Politics is about many things, but it is partly about the abilities of people to choose and make a difference, about people as *political agents*' (Warren 1988: 6). If the establishment of identity – the ability to tell a coherent story about the self – is a necessary prerequisite for political agency, then such storytelling and its implications, the necessary conditions of acting, are the conditions for *political* identity. Conversely, that identity is achieved through telling stories in the political realm. The search for meaning typified, to an extreme, by Oedipa Maas is a search for order both on a personal level and on the level of the political system within which action may be possible.

Agency may be associated with the figure of a unified agent, but the examples in the novels read here of doubling and of multiple identities, of internal divisions of consciousness, depictions of persons divided in themselves, immediately call the unified self into question. By their depiction of a fragmented self as a typical modern figure, modern narratives contest any continuing assumption that only the unified self is capable of political agency; however, literary narrative also presents an antidote to fragmentation by offering the possibility that narrative itself can unite the fragments. Both processes challenge theoretical aspirations to the conception of a unified self as political agent. Together with the effects of contingency, narrative identity may exhibit characteristics of splitting, instability, multiplicity and fragmentation – in a word, it may be disordered. And yet the fragments be contextualized, presented coherently, by way of the storytelling entailed in the use of narrative.

Drawing on the understanding of narrative political identity outlined here, the elements of narrative – for example, who tells the story and for what purpose – and the narrativization of political identity combine to show that narrative conveys no impetus towards unity; and yet – as characters in the literary readings have demonstrated – the non-unified character can still act; and, conjointly, identity is achieved through action (cf. Kareb 1984: 8; Honig 1988).

Narrative identity points towards a different conception of agency than that implied by Barron's report on the conventional view of citizenship: that it 'describes the identity assumed by the subject as a participant within the political realm, and is conceived of in terms of a capacity for autonomous action which is shared by all' (Barron 1993: 80). At the least, the assumption of equality would be modified by the insistence of narrative on the recognition of particulars. The attention to particularity inherent in narrative identity can work towards a move 'from universal notions of agency to more particularistic identities – a shift that endows the previously marginalized with a powerful new sense of subjectivity' (Somers 1994: 634). In so far as the theoretical focus remains on the individual as rational chooser, conceptualizations of 'agency', with strong theoretical links to rationality and responsibility, are liable to ignore or consign to a group categorization such persons as have from time to time been deemed to lack the qualities for agency, such as women, the poor or foreigners (cf. Rajchman 1995).[6] The concept of agency is also liable to exclude facets of identity that are apparently beyond consideration in respect of agency such as ethnicity, gender or religion. Narrative identity, though, in drawing from the complete person, does not so exclude, and can allow for agency by those defined as 'marginal', 'deviant' or 'anomalous'.

Narrative identity suggests a strong link between situated identity and agency. Furthermore it resolves the problem of the deficiencies of a theoretical, abstracted, 'thin' self as political subject or agent, as I have indicated for political identity in general, by directing attention to the socially-constructed and socially-focused, culturally embedded person. Despite the disunified and disorderly aspects of identity which modern novels present, the bearers of that kind of identity, as depicted in the novels, are capable of action, of taking their place in the political world, in a way that the liberal self typical of the realist novel has been shown not to be. Paradoxically, sequentiality of form and movement towards closure are apt to inhibit the individual from taking action. Self-consciousness as to the necessity of proceeding progressively towards a goal traps such individuals in anxiety about making the 'correct' choices in pursuit of that goal, and questions of motive or intention and outcome become so closely related with cause and effect that these individuals dare not act (Whitebrook 1995; cf. Arblaster 1984: Chapter 17).

Arendt's theory of action (already referred to in Chapter 5) is again relevant here, because of its linkages between agency, action, narrative and identity. Narratives tell of action, and action, in the Arendtian formula, is productive of identity: thus the query 'whether the identity of any human self can be defined with reference to its capacity for agency alone', and the answer, that '[I]dentity does not refer to my potential for choice alone, but to the actuality of my choices' (Benhabib 1992: 161). Benhabib takes 'the narrative structure of actions and personal identity' as a central premise in *Situating the Self*. 'All action . . . is narratively constituted. The what of our actions and the who of the doer are always identified via a narrative, via the telling of what one does and who one is'. That latter – who one is – 'emerges in the process of doing the deed and telling the story'; and action is a process of invention (Benhabib 1996: 125, 129–30; cf. Canovan 1977: 59; Beiner 1983: 13, 125–8): 'who we are is revealed in the narratives we tell of ourselves

and of our world shared with others. Narrativity is constitutive of identity'
(Benhabib 1992: 92). The 'immersion of action in a web of human relationships' – 'narrativity' – is 'the mode through which the self is individuated
and acts are identified'; and the 'wholeness' of the self is 'constituted by the
story of a life – a coherent narrative of which we are always the protagonist,
but not always the author or the producer' (Benhabib 1992: 127; cf. Disch
1994). The connections Benhabib summarizes are very strong:

> Human actions are always identified in terms of 'such and such has done
> so and so'. Actions, unlike things and natural objects, live only in the
> narrative of those who understand, interpret, and recall them. The
> narrative structure of action also determines the identity of the self.
>
> (Benhabib 1992: 127, 92)[7]

Coherence is a necessary prerequisite for agency: narrative identity
suggests new approaches to the type and level of coherence necessary in the
achievement of identity to allow the political subject to operate in the political realm. The degree of coherence necessary for political life is linked to
issues of mutual intelligibility and recognition, interaction between the self
and others – in this case, between the self and the political context. Narrative
identity may be inconclusive as to ends or endings, but it is required to be
coherent in the telling, mutually intelligible as between tellers and listeners
and between the various contributors to the story/stories of an identity. In
political terms this is a stringent requirement: intelligibility is required
between different levels of the political arena – persons and political entities
from the inter-personal to the global level.

Without some coherent sense of the self and recognition by others, the
person is unable to act. If, in the social and political world, the person has
no clear conception of who they are, cannot present a coherent account of
themselves, then they cannot act – or cannot act effectively; and if others –
their fellows or their leaders and rulers – do not know who they are, if they
are not recognizable or recognized, they will not be able – be allowed or
given opportunities – to act. The same could be said of political entities
beyond the self: so, for instance, on national identity, Jacqueline Rose's
remark on the Israeli–Palestinian problem – also, she says, applicable to central Europe, querying

> how the grounds of national entitlement can ever be definitively secured.
> For if national assertion is precisely *self*-affirmation, it rhetorically
> and ritually blinds itself to the other on whose recognition its claim finally
> depends. . . . The viability of a nation does not rest with its own self-
> imagining, but on whether the other can (chooses, wants) to recognize *me*.
>
> (Rose 1996: 85)

Northern Ireland is another clear instance of her remarks.

Further developments

Applying understandings of narrative identity to pre-existing topics of interest does not exhaust what politics can make of narrative political identity. Other lines of enquiry might be developed out of this study: memory and remembrance; truth and fiction, and the fictional and the real; the way in which persons model themselves on literary, fictional models; imagination; the responsibility of both tellers and listeners; interpretation. Again, there are interconnections that need exploring. For example, the place of imagination in the construction of a narrative identity may have a particularly political significance: together with the retrospective character-istic of narrating, attention to remembrance and memory, narrative political identity might also need, for effective political agency, to imagine the future, on the basis of an understanding of present and past (thus reinforcing the understanding of narrative identity as not fixed). Or, both interpretation and responsibility relate to the question of the dependence of narrative iden-tity on recognition: and that in turn relates to the degree of co-operation, mutuality and reciprocity involved in narrative identity. The disordering of (conventional ideas of) time and sequence is a distinctive feature – 'fictional order sustained against consecutive story' (Bradbury and McFarlane 1976: 50; and cf. Taylor 1989: 463).

The connections between the modern self, modernity and modernism deserve working out in political as well as literary terms. Modernist novels could be examined as a genre in relation to the question of 'the modern self as a subject', that self whose identity is 'crucial to modern practices of free-dom, knowledge, responsibility and democracy' (Connolly 1987: 111).

From the content of narratives, themes not usually accounted as politically relevant such as home, love and death are both relevant to narrative identity and (thence) suggestive for political understanding. For example, the understanding of ending and closure in narrative identity can be connected to attitudes to death represented in fictions – as for instance in the way in which Whaila's death proved a beginning for Hillela.

Narrative and political order

The most pressing case for development is the treatment of the political concept of order in relationship to narrative and narrative identity. What would be the effects for a basic issue in politics, order – its basis, construction and maintenance, and its status as a political good – if it were to be examined from the perspective of narrative identity? The number of issues raised in this study that relate to order suggests that a full examination could be made of the connections and implications. For instance, political under-standing of 'disorder' could be radically extended by attention to the way in which narrative brings disunity, disorder, into the frame. This is obviously important in respect of narrative identity inasmuch as that is understood to be disunified, uncertain and potentially unstable.

It is also the case that the conceptualization of narrative identity as such has a bearing on this issue. Identity consists in being able to give an account of oneself, and that narrative history is embedded in a social context – other stories. The story any person tells is always a sub-plot in the larger socio-political story; there is thus always some connection between the story the person tells and stories being told by or about the political order in which they are situated. However, the requirement of contextuality for narrative political identity is a precarious one: if context and identity are inseparable, the threat is that if one is destroyed, then so is the other (Laclau 1995). The intermeshing of political identities is particularly problematic. If personal identity is public identity then there is always a basis for conflict, because identity is constructed within a pre-existing narrative framework – that told by the political regime – which may be especially restrictive. There is no equivalent on the personal level of the justification and (attempted) legitimation of the political order by way of supposedly self-evident propositions about 'the need for order' and/or organization. But that in itself means that the person and the political authority give different types of account of their respective behaviour, and in that sense at least tell different – and quite possibly incompatible – stories. Similarly, the story associated with group identity may include aspects which the person as member of the group cannot easily accommodate in their own story of identity.

Narratives provide models for explanation; and narrative structure allows for a variety of modes of explanation which despite their variety all have a basis in coherent ordering. Different understandings of order (narrative order) are appropriate to, or can be derived from, different types of novel. Realist novels generally display tight control, associated with the concept of the omniscient author: characters 'know their place' in a plot narrated sequentially and *apparently* fully. (Though post-realist features precede post-realist novels as categorized in the twentieth century: narrative gaps, flashbacks, non-sequentiality are all to be found in so-called classic realist novels.) Experimental and modernist novels, on the other hand, are more loosely ordered. Attention to modern narrative fictions reminds political theory that 'order' is a more complex concept than might be suggested by simplistic assertions of the 'need' for order, and assumptions of its synonymity with stability, or law, or good government. If narratives present what appears to be a lack of order in characters, plot, setting, or the mode of narration, and if narrative as a method or process does not require absolute order or shun disorder, then what then of *political* order? And what connection(s) are possible between narrative order and political order, between narrative and political theory?

Narrative political identity calls closure – and a conventional conception of coherence – into question, disturbs assumptions about sequentiality and causation and allows for the disordered or inaccurate recall of events that is a feature of lived life, if not of theory. As I have already said (in Chapter 6), narrative coherence does not rule out unpredictability – but narrative can cope with change. Narrative identity is identity in process; it is open to revision; but such openness may run counter to political expectations of order. Narrative political identity may be associated with disorder rather than order. Narrative works towards an overall coherence: an overall order subsumes internal dissonances, disorder. Narrativity is characterized as a way of making sense of reality; but at the same time it has a 'scandalous, incoherent, chaotic dimension' which allows it to be 'a way of unleashing a healthy disorder' (Mitchell 1981: viii–ix). There is 'a rejection of both individual and collective order in the interests of "open form" which precludes narrative closure and its attendant certainties about meaning' (Martin, W. 1986: 83). Politics does not match narrative in this understanding that varieties of disorder may be more than merely tolerable/containable – that they may actually add to the overall order.

Attention to narrative suggests the need for a re-interpretation of order, relating that concept to the ways in which narrative patterns, emplots and contextualizes the fragments. (There is a potential for imposing total order: it is possible that aligning political order with emplotment as used in the argument here could be suspected of smuggling the idea of master narratives back into theorizing that has attempted to move away from the need for such containing inclinations. Political theorists would be right to be suspicious if advocating some usage of narrative worked out as recourse to an overarching story that unifies. That has not been my intention – again I stress that the capacity of narrative to encompass disunity is about a process not a given or completed whole (Hutcheon 1988: 70).)

That reinterpretation might include the understanding that if identity is conceived of as narrative identity, then it represents a patterned – ordered – story for public presentation; however, it also represents a story in the making, subject to change and revision, *not* moving towards a pre-determined end – as, for example, in the political process where a group moves from opposition to power. And in that respect, it has much to say to politics about disorder. On the structural level, the possibility of disorder could be examined by way of an understanding of the plurality of order. That is, there may well be a disparity between an overall order and the order – or disorder – of the constitutive elements of that order. And such an understanding would allow for revision of suppositions about the need for consistency between personal and regime order – more scope for dissonance within the political order writ large might be imagined than previously thought possible.

Some indication of the possibility of beginning to theorize political order and disorder from the basis of narrative identity is given in Tracy Strong's introduction to his collection *The Self and the Political Order*. His simple proposition is that the self and the political order interact, based on the idea that politics shapes both. He is then interested in 'the complexity of the manner in which they are co-determined'. However, although he refers (in respect of his own writing on Nietzsche) to the possibility of 'finding the order in disorder', what is missing is any explication of 'order' as such (Strong 1992: 4, 7, 17). Like the majority of other theorists, Strong leaves the term unspecified (other than that he generally refers to 'a' or 'the' political order, apparently meaning by that a system of order – 'law and order', government?). The relative neglect of such a basic concept in political theory encourages the thought that an exploration of its meaning for politics could be a major development from narrative identity.

Much of the argument in this chapter has been directed at the theorizing of the identity of the self: and that is not an inappropriate place to begin. To move on to this issue of the implications of narrative identity for political order necessarily and helpfully widens the focus to other aspects of the political beyond the self as political subject or agent. For example, if narrative identity is less 'unified' than has been presumed (or hoped), then narrative political identity may pose certain problems for the political realm – of unpredictability, for instance. Correspondingly, the narrative identity of social movements, or nations, may appear relatively unstable or fragmented – and again, unpredictable and possibly threatening to political order. However, such an extension of the argument would need to pay more attention to two aspects of the interconnections I am suggesting, both of which have already been noted in passing. There will be areas of political theory where the application of the themes and issues associated with narrative identity is just not appropriate; and there will be instances where the general direction is reversed, and aspects of political theory can critique or modify the understanding of narrative identity.

On inapplicability, political theorists may perceive disadvantages in such focusing on narrative identity as I encourage; perhaps there are aspects of theorizing the political where narrative political identity is not altogether helpful. I am certainly not claiming that 'narrative identity' should amount to something like a master narrative which envelops all possible theorizing. Not all identity is *narrative* identity. For example, at the most basic level, narrative political identity cannot encompass that understanding of political identity whereby identity is based in the group, where 'a passive sense of "group identity" is a "primary good" that equals or even precedes the importance of universal human rights' (Fierlbeck 1996: 4). Or

> [W]hile collective identities are composed of individual members, they are not reducible to an aggregate of individuals sharing a particular cultural trait. Similarly, from a description of the elements composing a collective cultural identity one cannot read off the probable actions or dispositions of individual members, only the kinds of contexts and constraints within which they operate.
>
> (Smith 1995: 130)

If this is the case, then narrative identity is not for use in this area of theory.

On the possibility that political theory might modify 'narrative', an obvious case is the understanding – to be derived from some of the more radical recent political theory – that 'narrative' is not necessarily an innocent or neutral term, and may be associated with power, is a topic central to politics. Warren speaks of identity as 'the articulate self, whose identity is formed by the roles that a prevailing discourse with its associated power relations has to offer (citizen, soldier, patriot . . .)' (Warren 1992: 15); and '[I]dentities, whether racial or other, are not permanently fixed. Rather, they are socially constructed and inscribed with particular meanings within the context of existing power relations' (Kellner 1995).

Other connections are possible. As I pointed out in introduction to this study, the range of themes and issues is very wide, and other theorists will see other connections, arising from but going beyond what I have laid out in the substantive chapters of this book. I only suggest what might be done to draw out the implications of my argument for political theory. I have indicated the relevant questions and some ways in which they could be followed through – though still not necessarily conclusively answered. To take narrative identity seriously within the study of politics will involve applying what I have made of narrative identity in specialist work in the sub-disciplines of the study of politics. Where I make general points, specialists can specify and exemplify.

To an extent what is advocated is not so much new work as new approaches to political theorizing. For instance, there could be analytical interest in identity construction – *that* identities are constructed and examined in terms of *how* they are: for example examining a narrative account of a political topic for narrative voice or point of view, and forming judgements as to the reliability of the narration, or question who is narrating, from what point of view, and whether or not they are reliable – what can be gained from the narrative that the narrator does not intend or know. Or the work could be descriptive, studying instances of narrative identity in the political context: for example by observing and describing split identity, as demonstrated, for instance, in political leaders, or in the behaviour of political regimes; or recognizing the effects for persons of ascription of identity. Such approaches would operate within a general framework of awareness of the ubiquity – and implications – of the narrative process in the construction of political identity.

However, beyond this kind of application of narrative to political theorizing, what I have shown also allows for a more fundamental or radical revisioning of theory in the light of narrative political identity. This discussion of narrative identity in effect offers a response to the query inherent in a comment on Connolly who, in contrast to politicized identity which 'reiterates the structure of liberalism in its configuration of a sovereign, unified, accountable individual' suggests 'although it is not clear what would motivate identity's transformed orientation, a different configuration of identity – one which understood itself as contingent, relational, contestatory and social' (Brown 1993: 225, n. 17). Narrative identity offers one possibility for the 'what would motivate' – and as such offers more than just another contribution to the post-liberal attack on the liberal self, extending to a critique of other aspects of political theory (including post-liberal theory itself), and speaking directly to the experience – including the narrative construction of identity – of selves and groups in the real world of politics.

8   Postscript

I have suggested that other connections could be made from this discussion of narrative identity to themes and issues of political concern, across a range of what is labelled as political theory. One obvious move would be to extend the arguments and methods here to postmodern narrative(s) and political theory. In introduction to this study I briefly alluded to the reasons internal to it for my exclusion of the avowedly postmodern and/or the Continental philosophers. In declining postmodernist approaches for this study, and in respect of those philosophers commonly labelled postmodern, I do not so much contest the value of their work as note that they are moving in rather different directions (and with different intentions), so that to attend to these philosophers would be beyond – not coterminous with – this study.

I only attempt here to begin the process of moving theory and theorists on from the suggestive but relatively undeveloped uses of narrative and narrative identity in political theory, to open up those terms for potential use in political studies. In that respect, this study might be the necessary precursor to work that develops the contribution of narrative theory to, say, the question of identity, where subjectivity itself is in question, or of agency *vis à vis* the loss of subjectivity in postmodernism, or the relationship of self to other.

Narrative political identity draws attention to the other who is an essential partner in the formation of identity; and this alone can be taken to suggest that my argument has strong links with much postmodern theory. (Though, as I have pointed out, interest in the other is also a feature of modernism.)[1] Distinctively 'postmodernist' concerns such as relationships between the self and the other are already known to political theory. William Connolly's work, particularly *Identity\Difference*, and other radical and feminist theory have addressed these relationships, including their import as constitutive of identity. Connolly's attention to identity, difference and otherness requires a measure of self-understanding: to know the self in order to know the other, to recognize difference within in order to cope with difference between. Self-examination and interrogation can enable the recognition of difference in self and others while avoiding converting that difference to otherness or evil. And so to the development of an 'ethic of identity' – 'an ethic in which

adversaries are respected and maintained in a mode of agnostic mutuality'
(Connolly 1991: 166). Or, in another version,

> In postmodern investigations of human subjectivities the self can be split
> into selves to probe the particularities of self. One autobiographical
> detail of the author's life can become a detail in a character's life that
> the narrator records in the story that he tells. Instead of a unified self we
> have then a self that can radiate towards infinite possible relations. As it
> radiates, it questions those relations.
>
> (Barone 1995: 15)

Postmodern attention to the relationship self–other, and the creation of
otherness in the construction of identity, could be further developed for
political theory. For instance, Anne Norton's treatment of otherness and
difference emphasizes ambiguity rather than 'contradiction' or conflict.
'Individual and collective identities are created not simply in the difference
between self and other but in those moments of ambiguity where one is
other to oneself, and in the recognition of other as like'; and 'Here, as elsewhere in politics, it is in difference that one assumes a form common to
others. It is through the confrontation with the other that one comes to
know oneself.' This is an understanding well in keeping with narrative
identity. 'There is no choice in this ambivalent constitution, between self
and other, identity and difference, partiality and impartiality, for each is
entailed in the other' (Norton 1988: 7, 189–90, 194).

When Dienstag refers to the 'sea of claims about narrative' in which
political theory is presently awash, he notes that he thinks it likely that

> this episode of cultural anthropology itself results from a dissatisfaction
> with rationalism and an attempt to flee into its opposite or 'other'. This
> discovery of narrative in other cultures or subaltern groups, then, would
> itself rest on the Western philosopher's dichotomy between reason and
> narrative and would represent, largely, an attempt simply to resolve the
> poles of this dichotomy.
>
> (Dienstag 1997: 248, n. 13)

This is an interesting proposition. Among the possible digressions from the
main lines of argument of this study is the large topic of the relationship(s)
of narrative with imagination, truth, reason and rationality. In so far as postmodernism has been associated with a divorce from 'Western philosophy's'
reliance on rationality and reason, more could be done in this respect.
Narratives – stories as such – may be helpful: 'Some literature may be a
revolt against the limitations of reason that opens up dimensions of human
existence which are inaccessible to philosophers' (Weinstein 1982: 68; see
also 67–70, 84–5 and *passim*).

I take Calvin Schrag's *The Self after Postmodernity* to be most apposite for my decision – risking accountability as a 'failure' – not to engage with post-modernism directly or unequivocally. Schrag mounts what I take to be a convincing case for moving beyond postmodernism. One of his basic propositions is that 'it is the telling of a story in which the self is announced as at once actor and receiver of action' (Schrag 1997: 1). He notes, though, that 'the mosaic of messages dealing with the death of man, the demise of the author, and the deconstruction or dissimulation of the subject' makes that kind of proposition difficult, whereas Schrag supposes that there is no need for 'a jettisoning of every sense of self' (Schrag 1997: 9). Within that framework, he addresses the position whereby postmodernism eschews modernity's project, to reunite the domains of science, morality and art divided by Kant, in the face of heterogeneity and difference. Then, his project 'takes the direction of an inquiry toward the portrait of the self as subject *after* post-modernity' (Schrag 1997: 28). One form of that self, remarkably similar to the bearer of narrative identity as I have discussed that figure, is 'a narrating self, a *homo narrans*, a storyteller who both finds herself in stories already told and strives for a self-constitution by emplotting herself in stories in the making'. And narrative 'encompasses the domain of human action', so that the narrative self is also 'the self in action' (Schrag 1997: 26, 43, 75).

Schrag goes beyond postmodernism: my discussion might be read as 'staying behind' – and thus in a sense remaining within the boundaries of modernism and modernity. To the extent that that is so – though it could also be said to join Schrag in a kind of post-postmodernism – it has been in order to show that political theory which is 'pre-postmodern' – the work of theorists who do not regard themselves as 'postmodernist' or continue to address themselves to the modernist project – can still benefit from some of the understandings that are commonly claimed or thought to be distinctively postmodern. That this is so, is shown, for instance, by the extent to which this discussion of narrative political identity addresses those same objections to 'the project of modernity' which Schrag identifies as claimed for post-modernism. I have suggested how this discussion can be extended: it remains for political theorists working in a variety of areas, across the range of political studies, and from a variety of approaches – from 'mainstream liberal' to 'radical postmodernist' as it were – to take up the argument for a conception of narrative political identity which I present here.

Notes

1 Introduction

1 To avoid an excessive number of notes to this study, I use the Harvard reference system: but note that such references may be to quotations or direct references, as normal, but may also be to additional, or comparative, material.

2 I do not enter here into the debate on what constitutes 'politics' or 'the political', though I do maintain that an essential characteristic is that it refers to speech, behaviour, actions in public, and to collective action (Whitebrook 1996: 40). Throughout this study, the meaning is to be taken from the context, either as referring to institutions and activity connected to the political process as conventionally understood – state, government and the like – or, more broadly, as concerning action in the public sphere. 'Political' may also refer to the activity or to political theory's analysis and interpretation of it.

3 Throughout this study, 'political theory' and 'political theorists' refer both to 'first-order' theorizing, that issuing in major texts generally recognized as classic and seminal ('from Plato to Rawls') and to the ongoing process of commentary on and interpretation of these works. Miller claims that it is no longer possible to make general arguments about political theory because the range of work is so diverse (Miller, D. 1990; cf. Held 1991: 19 and *passim*; see also Horton and Baumeister 1996: 5–6; Plant 1991). While I refer in the main to what Miller categorizes as conceptual and/or normative theory, I also try to indicate something of the wider range where it is relevant to narrative identity – my approach crosses several of the boundaries Miller and Held identify and is analogous to Miller's stipulation of the benefit of the conceptual history approach, that 'we will have avoided the naivety of thinking that our conceptual framework stands in no need of defense; we will have become more self-conscious about the ideas we use and the assumptions they embody' (Miller, D. 1990: 426).

4 For a representative range of views on identity, see Harris 1995; Barry 1986; Rorty, A. 1976.

5 The relevant distinction here is not the familiar private/public but interior(self)/ public: cf. Flathman's remark that 'a strongly voluntarist liberalism might shift from "public versus private" to language such as "public versus personal", or better, to a distinction between that which is general, shared, or common and that which is individual' (Flathman 1992: 208); see also Chapter 4, 82, and 156n10). The difference is crucial to my understanding of the distinction to be made between self and identity. The former is concerned with what the self tells the self together with what that self (is prepared to) confirm(s) of what others tell about it. Identity, on the other hand, requires recognition, from outside of

the self, of the person. Most often, of course, there is, as Norton points out, a simultaneity of self and public recognition (Norton 1988).

6 'The concept of autonomy captures, in an especially compelling and efficient way, the modern discovery and valuation of freedom, reason, and agency housed within a new conception of the self as an independent and reflexive rational chooser' (Di Stefano 1993: 3). This self is always prior to its situation, has a sense of self-command, and chooses rather than discovers its ends. 'Liberal individuals seek to run their lives themselves, to make their own choices, to form their own beliefs and judgments, to take nothing for granted or as given' (Parekh 1992: 161–2; cf. Bellamy 1992: 244–8; Gray, J. 1993: 307–9; Christman 1989; Raz 1986). The theoretical construct of the autonomous individual is already under attack in political theory: this study offers, among other things, an alternative line of critique.

7 In practice the usage of 'narrative' or 'story' is, as Randall suggests, largely a matter of preference: story is emotionally attractive because it is 'the term to which most of us most readily turn in referring to our experience of life as a whole', whereas 'narrative', as a technical term 'is attractive to those who wish to develop a respectable science from the study of stories' (Randall 1995: 85–6). Randall also points out that in an academic context, story 'can signify a pattern or trend, a theory or a theme' (Randall 1995: 84).

8 Charles Jencks suggests that 'Post-modernism' tends to get used for '*everything* that was different from High Modernism' (Jencks 1987: 10) – for literature, 'post-modern' might then be better reserved for a specific genre such as Hutcheon's 'historiographic metafiction' (Hutcheon 1989).

9 For a general overview see Critchley and Schroeder 1998 and West 1995. Excluding these philosophers may appear to emphasize a certain Anglophone slant to my work (cf. Miller, D. 1990: 422); this is not especially significant given that I similarly 'neglect' Anglo-American philosophers and theorists of narrative, and of identity, where they are not directly relevant to this discussion of narrative political identity.

10 That the work is complete in itself should not be confused with the claim that novels are closed worlds and therefore cannot be extrapolated from for theoretical (or any other) purposes. This is the argument that there is 'nothing beyond' the world created by the novelist, that the novel constitutes a self-contained universe, in which all that happens is logical, has a point, for that world (but only for that world) (Johnson, P. 1988: 178; Barth 1984: 19, 22; Horton 1996). It is asserted that 'narratives present the moral and political world "pre-packaged"', and that 'the authority of the text' allows 'only those disagreements for which there is textual warrant' (Mendus 1996: 59, 60) and that 'once we have read a novel we know how things turn out (in so far as they turn out at all) but it is a rather significant feature of our deciding and acting in the world that it is always accompanied by a host of uncertainties' (Horton 1996: 84). However, such claims are difficult to sustain for anything but the classic realist novel; objections to the use of literature for theorizing are primarily about content rather than narrative construction as such; and they often they refer to didactic, realist novels, rather than the more open narratives I work with in this study.

2 The narrative construction of identity

1 E.L. Doctorow, *The Book of Daniel*, Picador 1982 [1971]: all further references in the text are to this edition.

2 The term 'control' in the context of authoring is a matter for debate – and caution. There are well-founded objections to the equation of authorship with control;

however, there is also a justifiable sense of control inherent in narrative structuring in that, it is argued, without narrating 'we are unable to exercise even the slightest degree of control, or power, in relation to the world. It is our internal narrative faculty that makes it possible for each of us perpetually to construct and reconstruct our sense of our selves as individuals located socially and in time and space' (Hanne 1994: 8; see also Siegle 1986: 170—5, 198).

3 Literary texts are commonly 'dialogic', 'incorporating many different styles or voices, which "talk" to each other, and to other voices outside the text, the discourses of culture and society at large', whereas expository prose on the other hand is usually 'monologic', 'striving to impose a single vision, or interpretation of the world by means of single unitary style' (Lodge 1992: 128). One significance of the narrative concept of voice for theory lies in the thought that there is more opportunity in narrative for multiple voices, whereas theoretical expression, especially that dominated by strict coherence criteria, is more likely to be univocal; compare Wendy Brown's remark on her own writing that different voices 'appear not as a literary device but because they are all inescapably present in a political, feminist, student of political theory and the world' (Brown 1988: xi–xii).

3 Uncertain identity

1 Philip Roth, *Operation Shylock: A Confession*, London: Vintage 1994 [1993]. All further references in the text are to this edition.

2 The double – 'The apparition of a living person, a double, a wraith' (*Shorter Oxford English Dictionary*) – is a problematic concept both generally and specifically in this novel. Roth himself does not help: 'I have never found out what was hidden in this stranger's trickery or what his secret was', though he says that he considered him 'deformed, deranged, craven, possessed, an alien wreck in a state of foaming madness – someone, in short, who isn't really human at all' (Roth 1993; and cf. Kauvar 1995: 435–7, 441, 435, n. 15).

3 Compare the case of a political scientist who describes how at different times it has been more or less acceptable within the political science community to assert her identity as Jewish, lesbian, or female – whichever of these characteristics she has felt able to articulate. This well illustrates the relationship of the presentation of identity to different times and contexts – in which story does one find oneself a character and, because character-ship is a self-conscious position, which characteristics does one decide to affirm or deny at any particular point. The problem is how to reconcile the different identities or aspects in a life in practice (Acklesberg 1993).

4 On national identity generally, see Smith 1995. Smith deals with 'the various ways in which national identities are formed and analyses how this process is shaped by the interplay of cultural inheritance, political expediency, and myth'.

4 Gaps and fragments

1 Nadine Gordimer, *A Sport of Nature*, London: Jonathan Cape, 1987. All further references in the text are to this edition.

2 Ascription of political identity, particularly within identity politics, is frequently based on what are held to be given characteristics of the person. Counter-arguments – from feminist theory, for instance (cf. Ashenden 1996; Shanley and Pateman 1991; Hekman 1999; Dean 1996) – would assert that even givens can be negotiated. Even more fundamentally, it can be argued that supposedly fixed attributes may be regarded as social constructs. This is so for gender (cf. Butler 1990; Lorraine 1990) and for race and ethnicity, where the construction of concrete

regional or historico-linguistic identity may be connected to distinct cultural practices and beliefs (cf. Griffith *et al*. 1995; Appiah 1995).

3 There are some problems with Connolly's account of contingent identity: Chabot
comments that '[B]y "contingency" Connolly means that identity is not, as is
commonly believed, something one chooses on the basis of careful reflective
thought; it is, rather, the reflection (or interiorization) of society's mechanisms
for discipline and control' (Chabot 1993: 21) – it should be noted that his conceptualization of identity overall, including his treatment of contingency, derives
from advancing that argument (cf. Chabot 1993, also this volume, Chapter 5,
p. 99).

4 A creature who does not run true to type: '*Lusus naturae* – Sport of Nature. A plant,
animal, etc., which exhibits abnormal variation or a departure from the parent
stock or type . . . a spontaneous mutation; a new variety produced in this way'
(*Oxford English Dictionary*, used by Gordimer as epigraph to the novel).

5 For instance, ascription of group identity is frequently practised by theorists who
do not recognize themselves as belonging to a group 'ascribers' – a group of
those who do not need to recognize their identity as academic, articulate, Western
and mainly male. Similarly, policy-makers and politicians use 'ethnic' as referring
to groups other than themselves. Both cases are instances of 'the majoritarian pri-
vilege of never noticing oneself' (Williams, P. 1997; cf. Benhabib 1992: 69).

6 By referring to *Mrs Dalloway* in particular, and to modernism and late-modernism
in general, I do not mean to get embroiled in debate or discussion of modernism
as a literary movement – that is well done in a vast amount of critical work, attention to which is, though interesting *per se*, not directly relevant to this study. Nor
do I mean to suggest that modernism is the predominant twentieth-century
genre or, still less, that it is of special importance for this study. See also p. 85.

7 Virginia Woolf, *Mrs Dalloway*, with an Introduction and Notes by Elaine
Showalter, text edited by Stella McNichol, London: Penguin Books 1992 [1925].
All further references in the text are to this edition.

8 References to 'the Armenians' recur in this novel, typically when Clarissa
Dalloway is challenged as to the worth of her social and party-giving life; they
are 'hypothetical' only in the sense that they are so used by Clarissa. The facts
are that in 1915–16 the entire Armenian population of Anatolia was targeted for
deportation and death, in order to rid the Ottoman Empire of a potentially
treacherous minority. The precise figures are unclear, but it is thought that
between 800,000 and 1.3 million Armenians were killed. Nothing was done
'to help the Armenians'. In 1939, Hitler remarked, 'who now remembers the
Armenians?'; but even in the early 1920s, in the Dalloways' world, there were
few who recalled the Armenians as against the belief, or hope at least, that the
Great War had been fought to create a world 'safe for democracy'. Clarissa's
point is that although there was much talk and much agonizing about how to
help, little or nothing was actually done.

9 Compare the observation that for Arendt, the political means 'an expanding web
of relationships between various *fields* of public life, which includes much beyond
our usual restrictive concept of politics, poetry, literature, perhaps religion' in
which people get the opportunity 'to play a role, participate, and to be responsible'. Furthermore, 'Arendt assumes that what characterizes political life is the
constant *passage from field to field* – from action in common to art enjoyment, from
art enjoyment to thought, from thought to poetry, from poetry to action etc.'
(Herzog 1999).

10 See Chapter 1, n. 5: but note that the private/public distinction is viewed
positively in liberalism –

A complete human being has two faces, one a communicative, consensus-seeking, politically active, reasonable face, in the sense of 'reasonable' that is opposed to fanatical, the other a private and autonomous, perhaps detached and secretive, uncompromising face of a person pursuing his own distinctive good, perhaps guided in this by a comprehensive morality.

(Hampshire 1993: 45)

5 Contingency, identity and agency

1 Paul Auster, *Leviathan*, New York: Viking Penguin, 1992. All further references in the text are to this edition.
2 The nature of his political activity and/or the possible objection that it is irresponsible or futile need not detract from this identification of political action;

> His phantom life is more effectively political and public than his previous life as a writer . . . his secret life embodies the directive implied in the novel's epigraph: if 'Every actual State is corrupt,' then 'good men must not obey the laws too well'.
>
> (Osteen 1994: 90, cf. 87)

3 There is a sense in which Sachs's identity could be said to be primarily achieved at second-hand – narrated by Aaron, eventually realized by taking on Dimaggio's identity, and thoroughly grounded throughout in American history and tradition, culminating in this taking on the identity of various historical characters in order to carry out his subversive activity as the Phantom Bomber.
4 Despite this kind of (mis)understanding of contingency across a range of theorists, the concept has received more positive attention from theorists such as Merleau-Ponty and Deleuze; and see Connolly (1988: 159, and Chapter 5 *passim*), on Nietzsche's affirmation of contingency. A particular understanding of contingency, in the context of his argument on liberal irony, is expounded and defended in Rorty, R. 1989 (though note Connolly's comment: 'It is notable to me that the issue of the resentment of contingency gets little play in his recent work' (Connolly 1991: 226, n. 11, cf. 176–9)).
5 Theoretical distinctions are made between narrative and causal explanations, but these are often needlessly rigid – for example, the difference might be that narrative makes 'connections of causality . . . between widely separated events' (Lodge 1992: 75; cf. Booth, W. 1991 [1983]: 19). Narrative causation is not a matter of mere sequentiality, and attention has to be paid to the logic *of* the narrative rather than necessarily expecting logic *in* the narrative – a 'logical' plot, for instance. There may be a 'logic of implication' or, even if a narrative does not follow a linear progression, a causal sequence of events can be recovered from it (Leitch 1986: 121–2; cf. Dunn 1980: 24–6). Charlotte Linde suggests (in discussion of narrative causality with respect to life stories) that narrators have to establish 'a chain of causality that is neither too thick nor too thin' – 'Too thin an account suggests that one's life has proceeded at random, without direction. Too thick an account suggests that the speaker implicitly accepts a deterministic or fatalistic theory of causation'. Narrative may employ complex strategies for 'establishing rich multiple causality' (Linde 1993: 127, 128, 138, 139).
6 Narratives present decision-making as embedded, as against the extreme case of theoretical abstraction whereby characteristically modern (post-Enlightenment) rationalist approaches, 'characterizations of human agency as a knowing subject and rational actor' by pluralists, neoclassical economists, rational actor theorists, 'those working within the Kantian tradition of liberal political thought', including

Rawls and Dworkin, all 'turn the problem of rational agency into a metaphysical assumption' whereby '[T]he agent becomes an abstraction (in this case a necessary presupposition) divorced from the social and cultural contexts that make agents what they are' (Warren 1988: 152–3, 155); rationality is held to be a central tenet of modernity (McCormick 1988: 305; Avinieri and de-Shalit 1992: 2–4).

7 This character is based on the conceptual/performance artist Sophie Calle. Much of Calle's work represents this kind of controlled chance, as for example in her Venetian project where she shadowed and photographed a stranger who told her in a casual conversation at a party that he was going to Venice. Calle has customarily used such chance encounters or events to structure her own life.

8 Rather, that is, than being an example or illustration of the view that literary works are 'closed worlds' (see Chapter 1, n. 10), where 'contingency' is hardly a relevant term in that everything in the work contributes to the end in view, or, to the author's intention – then 'chance' 'intrudes only to be tamed', and anything apparently not 'emerg[ing] from the causal chain', 'yet accomplishes what the design requires' (Morson 1998).

9 Cf. the debate in historical studies on the distinction, or not, between historical and fictional narratives (see, for example, White 1981; Scholes 1981; Mink 1981; Carr 1986; Kramer 1989).

6 Coherent identity

1 Cover summary, Thomas Pynchon, *The Crying of Lot 49*, London: Pan Books, 1979 [1966], quoting from Norman Shrapnel in *The Guardian*.

2 Cover summary, Thomas Pynchon, *The Crying of Lot 49*, New York: Harper & Row, 1986 [1966].

3 Thomas Pynchon, *The Crying of Lot 49*, London: Pan Picador, 1979 [1966]. All further references in the text are to this edition.

4 Modern, open (literary) narratives – fictions – are thus to be distinguished from genres with a greater claim to completeness such as historical chronicles or quests, types in which there is a level of predetermination or preknowledge of the outcome of the tale that is being told, and not necessarily much surprise – that is, the pattern is familiar, and there is little suspense in the form of the telling ('Well, how *did* he find the Grail then?'). They differ too from nineteenth-century novels moving towards a disposition of characters within expectations based on marriage and property as desirable outcomes; or from the continuing genre of the conventional detective story which must 'disclose meaning' by the end of the story. Conversely, lack of closure, along with retrospective narration, disassociates narrative identity from life-plans which are not strictly speaking narrated but described or predicted, and commonly have a definite goal in view.

5 Cf. Nash's remarks on the identity of Demjanjuk – see Chapter 3, p. 6.

6 I concentrate here on the lack of closure. It might also be noted that post-realist novels are said to be characterized by lack of beginning: 'A modernist novel has no real "beginning" since it plunges us into a flowing stream of experience with which we gradually familiarize ourselves by a process of inference and association' (Lodge 1977: 45). More generally, it can be held that beginnings are arbitrary, the choice of the writer to begin at some point in a story – an idea relating to embedment and intertextuality.

7 Cf. 'Our individual identity is embedded in communal stories', including the literary canon (MacIntyre 1985: 11): this relates to what can only be a side-issue for this study, the commonplace that the shaping of identity is frequently based on fictional models – both in the most general sense of MacIntyre's supposition

that lives are lived as quests, and in specific reference to admired types or characters. McCormick notes how this allows a person to imagine different possibilities in the future for themselves (McCormick 1988: 29). Siegle notes the way in which 'narrative constitutes identity within its characters and, by extension, its reader, who necessarily assimilates narrative's implicit models for conceiving of selfhood and subsequently or correlatively conceive themselves' (Siegle 1986: 122).

8 It appears to be difficult for theorists of narrative to avoid the presumption of linear sequence – not only is this central to MacIntyre's treatment of narrative, but Kerby, also much cited, speaks of 'developmental followability' – achieved by giving a beginning, middle and end structure to the narrative. He maintains that 'this particular narrative way of sequentialising is basic to the process of human understanding' and that '[T]o understand a life is to trace its development upon a narrative thread, a thread that unites otherwise disparate or unheeded happenings into the significance of a development, a directionality, a destiny' (Kerby 1991: 39, 40; cf. Fish 1995: 10–11).

9 In previous work I claimed that some consonance of values was necessary for individual and political order (Whitebrook 1995: 133, and Chapter 6 *passim*). I was wrong to make a strong claim of that kind (and I failed to acknowledge the conservative implications of such a claim). My discussion here of coherence is not intended to suggest, explicitly or implicitly, any notion of 'integration' – as I go on to say in Chapter 7, the stories told by persons and their political authorities may, as I have suggested for all identity stories, vary or, indeed, prove incompatible.

10 The dependence of narrative identity on some measure of co-operation with others is problematical both empirically – the extent to which such reciprocity is possible – and theoretically – the extent to which such a requirement is compatible with conceptualizations of other(s), as for instance in Connolly's seminal *Identity\Difference*. That is a topic for development from this study, but in the context of this discussion it can be assumed that some co-operation is both possible and necessary – the latter resting on the basis of the truism that at least a minimal degree of mutuality – simply, conversation – is a prerequisite for the existence of any social order at all.

7 Narrative, identity and politics

1 See also *Constellations* 1996, and comments by Wolf, Rockefeller, Walzer in Gutmann 1994a for a critique of Taylor's views; also see Cooke 1997.

2 'Identity politics', where identity is the ground of the political approach – and hence an underlying presumption of given characteristics – can be contrasted with 'the politics of identity' which interrogates the formation of identity by the processes of exclusion, understanding identification as an active process – and hence allowing that there is some choice about the characteristics of identity. The contrast may be expressed in terms of the former as (more) modernist and the latter (more) postmodernist.

3 The relationship of narrative and narratives to 'the real' cannot be examined fully here – but see Lamarque and Olsen 1994.

4 Michael Bell claims that MacIntyre's use of 'narrative' must be only metaphorical, because 'narrative has to be a different kind of thing from lived temporality or there is no point in drawing any analogy between them'. Even if this is conceded, Bell's argument depends on his contention that in narratives, everything is put there by the author and therefore 'the elements of narrative are intrinsically meaningful', whereas elements and events in life 'do not have this intrinsic

meaningfulness' (Bell 1994: 174–5). Not only do I read modern literature against the 'closed world' view of the novel (see Chapter 1, n. 10) but the very basis of turning to narrative in this respect is the contention that it is narrating which 'gives point'. Stephenson's view is more pertinent: 'Narration is not life but life has no meaning without narration' (Stephenson 1998: 11).

5 A nice twist to this question is given by the argument – ironically enough, employing a fictional model, Crusoe – that politics may not need anyone other than the single person if politics is construed as policy-making. Then the lone person on the desert island would have a political function as, for instance, in deciding an environmental policy (Burns 2000). That idea, if pursued, would raise some further interesting questions on splits – and power-struggles? – within the person.

6 Compare Kariel's review of Strong's *The Idea of Political Theory* (Strong 1990): Strong examines the ways in which modernity has 'perverted' political life, with the danger of a Rousseauian theatrical 'politics of unreality', whereas it is 'only in some form of nontheatrical politics' that individuals can 'achieve a wholeness that does not sacrifice diversity'. Kariel remarks on the form of Strong's 'reflections' and concludes by pointing out that Strong 'makes no scene, creates no disturbance, shapes no transgressive language for including homeless others seething on the other side of respectability' (Kariel 1992). On this account – 'Kariel together with Strong' – narrative identity seems to offer something both more specific and more inclusive than does Strong's attempt to rescue political agency within modernity.

7 As the references to Benhabib, and particularly to her *Situating the Self* in this study suggest, her treatment of narrative is generally helpful for my argument excepting only – and this is a crucial proviso, given my argument overall – that she wants to follow MacIntyre in associating narrative identity (positively) with unity.

8 Postscript

1 Siegle suggests that postmodernism might be confused, or confusing, in respect of its interest in otherness when he 'teasingly' points out that designating 'the other' is a case of drawing boundaries; 'if we can draw that margin', then '"the other" would be present and knowable', or 'we cannot draw such a margin, in which case notions of boundaries or categories', including that of 'the other', are 'part of a fundamental cultural mythology' (Siegle 1986: 98). Interestingly, Siegle suggests that since the first option is 'clearly nonsensical', 'the other' represents 'those elements of its own experience it chooses to deny' – a case of splitting as I have understood it in relation to narrative identity.

References

Acklesberg, M.A. (1993) 'Identity politics, political identities: reclaiming politics', unpublished paper presented at the Annual Meeting of the American Political Science Association, Washington DC.

Alford, C.F. (1991) *The Self in Social Theory: a Psychoanalytic Account of Its Construction in Plato, Hobbes, Locke, Rawls and Rousseau*, New Haven, CT, and London: Yale University Press.

Allen, W. (1964) *Tradition and Dream: the English and American Novel from the Twenties to Our Time*, London: Phoenix House.

Altieri, C. (1994) *Subjective Agency: a Theory of First-person Expressivity and Its Social Implications*, Oxford: Blackwell.

Amis, M. (1995) *The Information*, London: Flamingo.

Anderson, J. (1996) 'The personal lives of strong evaluators: identity, pluralism, and ontology in Charles Taylor's value theory', *Constellations* 3(1): 17–37.

Appiah, K.A. (1995), 'African identities' in L. Nicholson and S. Seidman (eds) *Social Postmodernism: Beyond Identity Politics*, Cambridge: Cambridge University Press.

—— (1997) 'The multiculturalist misunderstanding', *New York Review of Books*, 9 October: 30–36.

Appiah, K.A. and Gates Jnr, H.L. (eds) (1996) *Identities*, Chicago, IL and London: University of Chicago Press.

Appiah, K.A. and Gutmann, A. (1998) *Colour Conscious: the Political Morality of Race*, Princeton, NJ: Princeton University Press.

Arblaster, A. (1984) *The Rise and Decline of Western Liberalism*, Oxford: Basil Blackwell.

Arendt, H. (1958) *The Human Condition*, Chicago, IL: The University of Chicago Press.

Aronowitz, S. (1995) 'Reflections on identity' in J. Rajchman (ed.) *The Identity in Question*, New York: Routledge.

Ashenden, S. (1996) 'At the boundaries of the political: feminism beyond identity politics?' in J. Lovenduski and J. Stanyer (eds) *Contemporary Political Studies*, vol. 3, Belfast: Political Studies Association, 1853–62.

Auster, P. (1992) *Leviathan*, New York: Viking Penguin.

Avinieri, S. and de-Shalit, A. (1992) 'Introduction' in S. Avinieri and A. de-Shalit (eds) *Communitarianism and Individualism*, Oxford: Oxford University Press.

Avnon, D. and de-Shalit, A. (eds) (1998) *Liberalism and Its Practice*, London: Routledge.

Bainbridge, Beryl (1998) *Master Georgie*, London: Abacus.

Baldick, C. (1990) *The Concise Oxford Dictionary of Literary Terms*, Oxford: Oxford University Press.

Ball, T. (1995) *Reappraising Political Theory: Revisionist Studies in the History of Political Thought*, Oxford: Clarendon Press.

Banville, J. (1997) 'A life elsewhere' [review of J.M. Coetzee, *Boyhood: Scenes from Provincial Life*], *New York Review of Books*, November 20: 24–6.

Barber, B. (1984) *Strong Democracy: Participatory Politics for a New Age*, Berkeley, CA: University of California Press.

—— (1988) *The Conquest of Politics: Liberal Theory in Democratic Times*, Princeton, NJ: Princeton University Press.

Barone, D. (1995) 'Introduction: Paul Auster and the postmodern American novel' in D. Barone (ed.) *Beyond the Red Notebook: Essays on Paul Auster*, Philadelphia, PA: University of Pennsylvania Press.

Barron, A. (1993) 'The illusions of the "I": citizenship and the politics of identity' in Alan Norrie (ed.) *Closure and Critique: New Directions in Legal Theory*, Edinburgh: Edinburgh University Press.

Barth, J. (1984) *The Friday Book: Essays and Other Nonfiction*, New York: G.H. Putman.

Barry, B. (ed.) (1986) 'Symposium on Derek Parfit's *Reasons and Persons*', *Ethics* 96: 4.

Baumann, Z. (1993) *Postmodern Ethics*, Oxford and Cambridge, MA: Blackwell.

Beiner, R. (1983) *Political Judgment*, London: Methuen.

Bell, M. (1994) 'How primordial is narrative?' in C. Nash (ed.) *Narrative in Culture: the Uses of Storytelling in the Sciences, Philosophy and Literature*, London: Routledge.

Bellamy, R. (1992) *Liberalism and Modern Society*, Oxford: Polity Press.

Benhabib, S. (1992) *Situating the Self: Gender, Community and Postmodernism in Contemporary Ethics*, Cambridge: Polity Press.

—— (1996) *The Reluctant Modernism of Hannah Arendt*, Thousand Oaks, CA/London/New Delhi: Sage.

Bennett, W.L. (1998) 'The uncivic culture: communication, identity, and the rise of lifestyle politics', *PS: Political Science and Politics* 31(4): 741–61.

Berman, M. (1992) 'Why modernism still matters' in S. Lash and J. Friedman (eds) *Modernity and Identity*, Oxford, UK and Cambridge, MA: Blackwell.

Bernstein, J.M. (1994) 'Self-knowledge as praxis: narrative and narration in psychoanalysis' in C. Nash (ed.) *Narrative in Culture: the Uses of Storytelling in the Sciences, Philosophy and Literature*, London: Routledge.

Bloom, H. (1994) 'Operation Roth', *New York Review of Books*, 22 April: 45–48.

Booth, J. and Rosamond, B. (1996) 'Who on earth are "we"? globalisation, localisation and identity' in B. Axford and G. Browning (eds) *Modernism/Postmodernity: from the Personal to the Global*, Oxford: Thamesman.

Booth, W. (1991) [1983] *The Rhetoric of Fiction*, 2nd edition, London: Penguin.

Bordo, Susan (1993) *Unbearable Weight: Feminism, Western Culture and the Body*, Berkeley, CA: University of California Press.

Bradbrook, F. (1964) 'Virginia Woolf: the theory and practice of fiction' in B. Ford (ed.) *The Modern Age*, vol. 7 of the Pelican Guide to English Literature, Harmondsworth: Penguin.

Bradbury, M. (1982) *Saul Bellow*, London and New York: Methuen.

Bradbury, M. and McFarlane, J. (1976) 'The name and nature of modernism' in M. Bradbury and J. McFarlane (eds) *Modernism 1890–1930*, Harmondsworth: Penguin.

Brettschneider, M. (1996) *Cornerstones of Peace: Jewish Identity Politics and Democratic Theory*, New Brunswick, NJ: Rutgers University Press.

Bridges, T. (1994) *The Culture of Citizenship: Inventing Postmodern Civic Culture*, Albany, NY: State University of New York Press.

Brodsky, C.J. (1987) *The Imposition of Form: Studies in Narrative Representation and Knowledge*, Princeton, NJ: Princeton University Press.

Brooks, P. (1984) *Reading For the Plot: Design and Intention in Narrative*, New York: Harvard University Press.

Brown, W. (1988) *Manhood and Politics: A Feminist Reading in Political Theory*, Totowa, NJ: Rowman & Littlefield.

—— (1993) 'Wounded attachments', *Political Theory* 21(3): 390–410.

—— (1995) *States of Injury, Power and Freedom in Late Modernity*, Princeton, NJ: Princeton University Press.

Bruckner, P. (1995) 'Paul Auster, or the heir intestate' in D. Barone (ed.) *Beyond the Red Notebook: Essays on Paul Auster*, Philadelphia, PA: University of Pennsylvania Press.

Bruner, J. (1987) 'Life as narrative', *Social Research*, 54(1): 11–32.

—— (1991) 'The narrative construction of reality', *Critical Inquiry*, 18: 13–21.

—— (1996) *The Culture of Education*, Cambridge, MA, and London: Harvard University Press.

Buckler, S. (1996) 'Hamlet and Hannah Arendt's theory of action', in J. Lovenduski and J. Stanyer (eds) *Contemporary Political Studies* vol. 3, Belfast: Political Studies Association, 1566–76.

—— (1998) 'Literature and politics as vocations: the case of the Spanish Civil War', unpublished paper presented at the Political Studies Association Annual Conference, University of Keele.

Buj, L. (1996) 'Croatia constructed', *The European Legacy*, 1(2): 415–20.

Bürger, P. (1992) 'The disappearance of meaning: essay at a postmodern reading of Michel Tournier, Botho Strauss and Peter Handke' in S. Lash and J. Friedman (eds) *Modernity and Identity*, Oxford, UK, and Cambridge, MA: Blackwell.

Burns, T. (2000), 'What is politics? *Robinson Crusoe*, deep ecology and Immanuel Kant', *Politics* 20(2): 93–8.

Buruma, I. (1997) 'Selling out Hong Kong', *New York Review of Books*, August 14: 26–7.

—— (1998) 'The Afterlife of Anne Frank', *New York Review of Books*, 19 February: 4–8.

Butler, J. (1990) *Gender Trouble: Feminism and the Subversion of Identity*, New York: Routledge.

—— (1995) in J. Rajchman (ed.) *The Identity in Question*, London and New York: Routledge.

Cadava, E., Connor, P. and Nancy, J.-L. (eds) (1991) *Who Comes after the Subject?*, New York: Routledge.

Calhoun, C. (ed.) (1994) *Social Theory and the Politics of Identity*, Oxford: Blackwell.

Calvino, I. (1996) *Six Memos for the Next Millennium*, London: Vintage.

Canovan, M. (1977) *The Political Thought of Hannah Arendt*, London: Methuen.

Carr, D. (1986) *Time, Narrative and History*, Bloomington, IN: Indiana University Press.

Cave, T. (1995) 'Fictional identities' in H. Harris (ed.) *Identity: Essays Based on Herbert Spencer Lectures Given in the University of Oxford*, Oxford: Clarendon Press.

Chabot, D. (1993) 'In defense of "moderate" relativism and "skeptical" citizenship', unpublished paper presented at the American Political Science Association Meeting, Washington DC.

Chatman, S. (1978) *Story and Discourse: Narrative Structure in Fiction and Film*, Ithaca, NY, and London: Cornell University Press.

Chénetier, M. (1995) 'Paul Auster's pseudonymous world' in D. Barone (ed.) *Beyond the Red Notebook: Essays on Paul Auster*, Philadelphia, PA: University of Pennsylvania Press.

Christman, J. (ed.) (1989) *The Inner Citadel: Essays on Individual Autonomy*, New York: Oxford University Press.

Cohan, S. and Shires, L.M. (1988) *Telling Stories: A Theoretical Analysis of Narrative Fiction*, New York: Routledge.

Connolly, W. (1987) *Politics and Ambiguity*, Madison, WI: University of Wisconsin Press.

—— (1988) *Political Theory and Modernity*, Oxford: Basil Blackwell.

—— (1991) *Identity\Difference: Democratic Negotiations of Political Paradox*, Ithaca, NY, and London: Cornell University Press.

Constellations (1966), 3(1),'Identity and the Politics of Recognition' section.

Cook, T.E. (1997) 'The making of identities: self, dyad, subnational group, nation and transnation', unpublished paper presented at the American Political Science Association Annual Meeting, Washington DC.

Cooke, M. (1997) 'Authenticity and autonomy: Taylor, Habermas, and the politics of recognition', *Political Theory* 25(2): 258–88.

Cooper, B. (1990) 'New criteria for an "abnormal mutation"? an evaluation of Gordimer's *A Sport of Nature*' in M. Trump (ed.) *Rendering Things Visible: Essays on South African Literary Culture*, Athens, OH: Ohio University Press.

Creeley, R. (1994) 'Austerities', *Review of Contemporary Fiction*, Special Issue Paul Auster: Danilo Kis, 16(1): 35–9.

Critchley, S. and Schroeder, W.R. (eds) (1998) *A Companion to Continental Philosophy*, Oxford: Blackwell.

Crites, S. (1986) 'Storytime: recollecting the past and projecting the future' in T.R. Sarbin (ed.) *Narrative Psychology: the Storied Nature of Human Conduct*, New York: Praeger.

Crittenden, J. (1992) *Beyond Individualism: Reconstituting the Liberal Self*, Oxford: Oxford University Press.

Dean, J. (1996) *Solidarity of Strangers: Feminism after Identity Politics*, Berkeley, CA: University of California Press.

Di Stefano, C. (1990) 'Dilemmas of difference' in L. Nicholson (ed.) *Feminism/ Postmodernism*, New York: Routledge.

—— (1993) 'Autonomy and abjection, or, the haunting at Koenigsberg', unpublished paper presented at the American Political Science Association Annual Meeting, Washington DC.

Didion, J. (1991) 'New York: sentimental journeys', *The New York Review of Books*, 17 January: 45–56.

Dienstag, J.F. (1997) *Dancing in Chains: Narrative and Memory in Political Theory*, Stanford, CA: Stanford University Press.

Digeser, P. (1995) *Our Politics, Our Selves? Liberalism, Identity and Harm*, Princeton, NJ: Princeton University Press.

Disch, L. (1993) 'More truth than fact: storytelling as critical understanding in the writings of Hannah Arendt', *Political Theory* 21(4): 665–94.

—— (1994) *Hannah Arendt and the Limits of Philosophy*, Ithaca, NY and London: Cornell University Press.

Doctorow, E.L. (1982) [1971] *The Book of Daniel*, London: Picador.

Dolan, F. (1994) *Allegories of America: Narratives – Metaphysics – Politics*, Ithaca, NY: Cornell University Press.

Dolan, F.M. (1995) 'Political action and the unconscious: Arendt and Lacan on decentring the subject', *Political Theory* 23(20): 330–52.

Dunn, John (1980) *Political Obligation in its Historical Context: Essays in Political Theory*, Cambridge: Cambridge University Press.

—— (1985) *Rethinking Modern Political Theory: Essays 1979–83*, Cambridge: Cambridge University Press.

—— (1990) *Interpreting Political Responsibility: Essays 1981–1989*, Cambridge: Polity Press.

Dupriez, B. (1991) *A Dictionary of Literary Devices*, translated and adapted by Albert W. Halsall, New York: Harvester Wheatsheaf.

Echevarria, R.G. (1985) *The Voice of the Masters: Writing and Authority in Modern Latin American Literature*, Austin, TX: University of Texas Press.

Edwards, L. (1977) 'War and roses: the politics of *Mrs Dalloway*' in A. Diamond and L.R. Edwards (eds) *The Authority of Experience: Essays in Feminist Criticism*, Amherst, MA: University of Massachusetts Press.

Elshtain, J.B. (1987) *Women and War*, New York: Basic Books.

Ettin, A.V. (1992) *Betrayals of the Body Politic: the Literary Commitments of Nadine Gordimer*, Charlottesville, VA and London: University Press of Virginia.

Euben, J.P. (1990) *The Tragedy of Political Theory: The Road Not Taken*, Princeton, NJ: Princeton University Press.

Ezrahi, Y. (1995) 'The theatrics and mechanics of action: the theater and the machine as political metaphors', *Social Research* 62(2): 299–322.

Feibleman, J.K. (1968) 'Disorder' in P.G. Kunz (ed.) *The Concept of Order*, Seattle, WA: University of Washington Press.

Femia, J. (1988) 'An historicist critique of "revisionist" methods for studying the history of ideas' in J. Tully (ed.) *Meaning and Context: Quentin Skinner and His Critics*, Cambridge: Polity Press.

Fierlbeck, K. (1996) 'The ambivalent potential of cultural identity', *Canadian Journal Of Political Science* 29(1): 3–22.

Fish, S. (1995) *Professional Correctness: Literary Studies and Political Change*, Oxford: Clarendon Press.

Fisher, W.R. (1989) *Human Communication as Narration: Toward a Philosophy of Reason, Value and Action*, Columbia, SC: University of South Carolina Press.

Fishman, E.M. (1989) *Likely Stories: Essays on Political Philosophy and Contemporary American Literature*, Gainesville: University of Florida Press.

Flathman, R.E. (1992) *Willful Liberalism: Voluntarism and Individuality in Political Theory and Pràctice*, Ithaca, NY and London: Cornell University Press.

Flax, J. (1994) 'Is Enlightenment emancipatory?' in J. Flax *Disputed Subjects: Essays on Psychoanalysis, Politics and Philosophy*, London: Routledge.

Fowler, D. (1992) *Understanding E.L. Doctorow*, Columbia, SC: University of South Carolina Press.

Fowler, R. (ed.) (1973) *A Dictionary of Modern Critical Terms*, London: Routledge & Kegan Paul.

Friedl, H. (1988) 'Power and degradation: patterns of historical process in the novels of E.L. Doctorow' in Herwig Friedl and D. Schulz (eds) *E.L. Doctorow, a Democracy of Perception: a Symposium with and on E.L. Doctorow*, Essen: Verlag die Blaue Eule.

Furman, A. (1995) 'A new "other" emerges in American Jewish literature', *Contemporary Literature* 36(4): 633–53.

Gallie, W.B. (1964) *Philosophy and the Historical Understanding*, London: Chatto & Windus.

Gath, D. (1989) 'What a lark! What a plunge! Fiction as self-evasion in *Mrs Dalloway*', *Modern Language Review* 84(1): 18–25.

Giddens, A. (1991) *Modernity and Self-Identity: Self and Society in the Late Modern Age*, Cambridge: Polity Press.

Gill, E. (1986) 'Goods, virtues and the constitution of the self' in A.J. Damico (ed.) *Liberals and Liberalism*, Lanham, MD: Rowman & Littlefield.

—— (1992) 'Autonomy and the encumbered self', unpublished paper presented at the American Political Science Association Annual Meeting, Chicago.

Girgus, S. (1988) 'In his own voice: E.L. Doctorow's *The Book of Daniel*' in Herwig Friedl and D. Schulz (eds) *E.L. Doctorow, a Democracy of Perception: a Symposium with and on E.L. Doctorow*, Essen: Verlag die Blaue Eule.

Goldberg, S.L. (1993) *Agents and Lives: Moral Thinking in Literature*, Cambridge: Cambridge University Press.

Gordimer, N. (1987) *A Sport of Nature*, London: Jonathan Cape.

—— (1988) *The Essential Gesture: Writing, Politics and Places*, edited and with an introduction by Stephen Clingman, New York: Alfred A. Knopf.

Gray, J. (1989) *Liberalisms: Essays in Political Philosophy*, London: Routledge.

—— (1993) *Postliberalism: Studies in Political Thought*, New York and London: Routledge.

Gray, M. (1992) *A Dictionary of Literary Terms*, Beirut: Longman, York Press.

Griffith, E.E.H., Blue, H.C. and Harris, H.W. (eds) (1995) *Racial and Ethnic Identity: Psychological Development and Creative Expression*, New York: Routledge.

Guaraldo, O. (1998) 'Identity and storytelling' [review of Adriana Cavarero, *Tu Che Mi Guardi, Tu Che Mi Racconti*], *Finnish Year Book of Political Thought*, 2: 261–7.

Gubar, S.(1997) *Racechanges: White Skin, Black Face in American Culture*, New York: Oxford University Press.

Gutmann, A. (ed.) (1994a) *Multiculturalism: Examining the Politics of Recognition/Charles Taylor et al.*, Princeton, NJ: Princeton University Press.

—— (1994b) 'Introduction' in A. Gutmann (ed.) *Multiculturalism: Examining the Politics of Recognition/Charles Taylor et al.*, Princeton, NJ: Princeton University Press.

Habermas, J. (1994) 'Struggles for recognition in the democratic constitutional state' in A. Gutmann (ed.) (1994) *Multiculturalism: Examining the Politics of Recognition/ Charles Taylor et al*, Princeton, NJ: Princeton University Press.

Hagen, W.M. (1995) '*Operation Shylock*: a confession', *World Literature Today* 69(1): 142–63.

Haight, G. (ed.) (1956) *The George Eliot Letters*, London: Oxford University Press.

Hampshire, S. (1992) [1989] *Innocence and Experience*, Harmondsworth: Penguin.

—— (1993) 'Liberalism: the new twist' [review of John Rawls's *Political Liberalism*] *New York Review of Books*, August 12: 43–8.

Hanne, M. (1994) *The Power of the Story*, Oxford: Berghahn Books.

Hardwick, E. (1997) 'Paradise Lost' [review of P. Roth's *American Pastoral*], *New York Review of Books*, June 12: 12–14.

Hardy, B. (1987) *The Collected Essays of Barbara Hardy Volume 1, Narrators and Novelists*, Brighton: Harvester Press.

Harpham, G.G. (1995) 'Who's who' [review of C. Altieri's *Subjective Agency*], *London Review of Books*, 20 April: 12–14.

Harré, R. (1998) *The Singular Self: An Introduction to the Psychology of Personhood*, London/Thousand Oaks, CA/New Delhi: Sage.

Harris, H. (ed.) (1995) *Identity: Essays Based on Herbert Spencer Lectures Given in the University of Oxford*, Oxford: Clarendon Press.

Harrison, B. (1991) *Inconvenient Fictions: Literature and the Limits of Theory*, New Haven, CT, and London: Yale University Press.

Harrison, R. (ed.) (1979) *Rational Action: Studies in Philosophy and Social Science*, Cambridge: Cambridge University Press.

Hauerwas, S. and Burrell, D. (1989) 'From system to story: an alternative pattern for rationality in ethics' in S. Hauerwas and L.G. Jones (eds) *Why Narrative? Readings in Narrative Theology*, Grand Rapids, MI: William B. Eerdmans Publishing Co.

Hauerwas, S. and Jones, L.G. (eds) (1989) *Why Narrative? Readings in Narrative Theology*, Grand Rapids, MI: William B. Eerdmans Publishing Co.

Hawthorn, J. (1992) *A Concise Glossary of Contemporary Literary Theory*, London: Edward Arnold.

Hekman, S. (ed.) (1999) *Feminism, Identity and Difference*, London: Frank Cass.

Held, D. (ed.) (1991) *Political Theory Today*, Cambridge: Polity Press.

Herzog, A. (1999) 'The poetic nature of political disclosure: Hannah Arendt's story-telling' unpublished paper presented at the ECPR Workshop 'The Political Uses of Narrative', Mannheim, Germany.

Hilfer, T. (1992) *American Fiction since 1940*, London and New York: Longman.

Hite, M. (1983) *Ideas of Order in the Novels of Thomas Pynchon*, Columbus: Ohio State University Press.

Hoffmann-Axthelm, D. (1992) 'Identity and reality: the end of the philosophical immigration officer' in S. Lash and J. Friedman (eds) *Modernity and Identity*, Oxford UK and Cambridge, MA: Blackwell.

Holloway, J. (1963) 'The literary scene' in B. Ford (ed.) *The Modern Age*, vol. 7 of the Pelican Guide to English Literature, 2nd edition, Harmondsworth: Penguin.

Honig, B. (1988) 'Arendt, identity and difference', *Political Theory* 16(1): 86–90.

Horne, P. (1992) 'It's just a book', *London Review of Books*, 17 December: 20–1.

Horton, J. (1996) 'Life, literature and ethical theory: Martha Nussbaum on the role of the literary imagination in ethical thought' in J. Horton, and A. Baumeister (eds) *Literature and the Political Imagination*, London and New York: Routledge.

Horton, J. and Baumeister, A. (1996) 'Literature, philosophy and political theory' in J. Horton, and A. Baumeister (eds) *Literature and the Political Imagination*, London and New York: Routledge.

Hospers, J. (1967) *An Introduction to Philosophical Analysis*, 2nd edition, London: Routledge & Kegan Paul.

Hutcheon, L. (1988) *A Poetics of Postmodernism: History, Theory, Fiction*, London and New York: Routledge.

—— (1989) *The Politics of Postmodernism*, London and New York: Routledge.

Hyvärinen, M. (1992) 'Narrative analysis and political autobiography', *Journal of Political Science* 20: 51–70.

Ingle, S. (1979) *Socialist Thought in Imaginative Literature*, London: Macmillan.

Jackson, B.E. (1994) 'Legal theories and legal discourse' in C. Nash (ed.) *Narrative in Culture: the Uses of Storytelling in the Sciences, Philosophy and Literature*, London: Routledge.

Jackson, S.J. (1996) 'A disjunctural ethnoscape: Ben Johnson and the Canadian crisis of racial and national identity', unpublished paper presented at the International Crossroads in Cultural Studies Conference, Tampere, Finland.

Jencks, C. (1987) *Post-modernism: the New Classicism in Art and Architecture*, New York: Rizzoli International Publications.

Johnson, B. (1994) *The Wake of Destruction*, London: Blackwell.

Johnson, P. (1988) *Politics, Innocence, and the Limits of Goodness*, London: Routledge.

—— (1996) 'Three theories of narrative gaps' in J. Lovenduski and J. Stanyer (eds) *Contemporary Political Studies*, vol. 3, Belfast: Political Studies Association, 1352–7.

Johnston, D. (1994) *The Idea of a Liberal Theory*, Princeton, NJ: Princeton University Press.

Jones, E.C. (1992) 'Figuring Woolf', *Modern Fiction Studies* 38(1): 1–14.

Journal of Arts Management, Law and Society, The (1995) 'Art and the politics of identity', Special Issue, 25(1).

Kaplan, T.J. (1986) 'The narrative structure of policy analysis', *Journal of Policy Analysis and Management* 5: 4.

Kariel, H. (1992) [review of Strong, *The Idea of Political Theory*] *Political Theory* 20(2): 345–8.

Kateb, G. (1982) *Hannah Arendt: Politics, Conscience, Evil*, Towota, NJ: Rowman & Allanheld.

Kauvar, E.M. (1993) 'An interview with Cynthia Ozick', *Contemporary Literature* 34(3): 359–94.

—— (1995) 'The doubly reflected communication: Philip Roth's "Autobiographies"', *Contemporary Literature* 36(3): 412–46.

Kearney, R. (1995) 'Narrative imagination: between ethics and poetics', *Philosophy and Social Criticism* 21(5/6): 173–90.

—— (1998) *Poetics of Imagination*, Edinburgh: Edinburgh University Press.

Kellner, D. (1995) *Media Culture: Cultural Studies, Identity and Politics Between the Modern and the Postmodern*, London: Routledge.

Kerby, A. (1991) *Narrative and the Self*, Bloomington, IN: Indiana University Press.

Kermode, F. (1967) *The Sense of an Ending: Studies in the Theory of Fiction*, New York: Oxford University Press.

King, R. (1988) 'Between simultaneity and sequence' in Herwig Friedl and Dieter Schulz (eds) *E.L. Doctorow, A Democracy of Perception: a Symposium with and on E.L. Doctorow*, Essen: Verlag die Blaue Eule.

Kinzer, S. (1992) 'Self-portrait of a revolutionary' [review of Tomas Borge, *The Patient Impatience: From Boyhood to Guerrilla: a Personal Narrative of Nicaragua's Struggle for Independence*], *New York Review of Books*, 3 December: 17–18.

Kirkegaard, P. (1993) 'Cities, signs and meanings in Walter Benjamin and Paul Auster: or, never sure of any of it', *Orbis Litterarum, International Review of Literary Studies, Copenhagen* 48(2–3): 161–79.

Kramer, L. (1989) 'Literature, criticism, and historical imagination: the literary challenge of Hayden White and Dominic LaCapra' in L. Hunt (ed.) *The New Cultural History: Essays*, Berkeley, CA: University of California Press.

Kundera, M. (1988) *The Art of the Novel*, trans. Linda Asher, New York: Harper & Row.

Kuntz, P.G. (ed.) *The Concept of Order*, Seattle, WA: University of Washington Press [for Grinnell College].

Kymlicka, W. (1990) *Contemporary Political Philosophy: an Introduction*, Oxford: Oxford University Press.

Laclau, E. (1995) 'Universalism, particularism and the question of identity' in J. Rajchman (ed.) *The Identity in Question*, New York: Routledge.

Laffan, B. (1996) 'The politics of identity and political order in Europe', *Journal of Common Market Studies* 34(1): 81–102.

Lamarque, P. and Olsen, S.H. (1994) *Truth, Fiction and Literature: a Philosophical Perspective*, Oxford: Clarendon Press.

Lane, A. (1997) 'Hannah Arendt: theorist of distinction(s)', *Political Theory* 25(1): 137–59.

Leavis, F.R. (1972) *Nor Shall My Sword: Discourses on Pluralism, Compassion and Social Hope*, London: Chatto & Windus.

Leftwich, A. (ed.) (1990) *New Developments in Political Science: an International Review of Achievements and Prospects*, Aldershot: Edward Elgar.

Leitch, T.M. (1986) *What Stories Are: Narrative Theory and Interpretation*, University Park, PA: Pennsylvania State University Press.

Levine, P. (1985) *E.L. Doctorow*, London and New York: Methuen.

—— (1988) 'E.L. Doctorow: the Writer as Survivor' in Herwig Friedl and D. Schulz (eds) *E.L. Doctorow, A Democracy of Perception: a Symposium with and on E.L. Doctorow*, Essen: Verlag die Blaue Eule.

Lieblich, A. and Josselon, R. (eds) (1994) *Exploring Identity and Gender. The Narrative Study of Lives*, vol. 2, London: Sage.

Linde, C. (1993) *Life Stories: the Creation of Coherence*, New York: Oxford University Press.

Livingston, P. (1991) *Literature and Rationality: Ideas of Agency in Theory and Fiction*, Cambridge: Cambridge University Press.

Lloyd, G. (1993) *Being in Time: Selves and Narrations in Philosophy and Literature*, London: Routledge.

Lodge, D. (1977) *The Modes of Modern Writing: Metaphor, Metonymy and the Typology of Modern Literature*, London: Edward Arnold.

—— (1992) *The Art of Fiction Illustrated from Classic and Modern Texts*, London: Penguin.

Lorraine, T. (1990) *Gender, Identity, and the Production of Meaning*, Boulder, CO: Westview.

Love, N. (1993) 'Am I that performance?' unpublished paper presented at the American Political Science Association Annual Meeting, Washington DC.

McCormick, P.J. (1988) *Fictions, Philosophies and the Problems of Poetics*, Ithaca, NY: Cornell University Press.

Macdonald, S. (1994) 'Identity complexes in Western Europe: social anthropological perspectives', in S. Macdonald (ed.) *Inside European Identities*, Providence, RI: Berg.

McHale, B. (1987) *Postmodern Fiction*, London: Routledge.

McFarlane, J. (1976) 'The mind of modernism' in M. Bradbury and J. McFarlane (eds) *Modernism 1890–1930*, Harmondsworth: Penguin.

MacIntyre, A. (1985) *After Virtue: a Study in Moral Theory* 2nd edition, London: Duckworth.

—— (1988) *Whose Justice? Which Rationality?*, Notre Dame, IN: University of Notre Dame Press.

Madsen, D.L. (1991) *The Postmodernist Allegories of Thomas Pynchon*, Leicester and London: Leicester University Press.

Mantel, H. (1996) 'Murder and memory', *New York Review of Books*, 19 December: 4–9.

Martin, D.-C. (1995) 'The choices of identity', *Social Identities* i(1): 5–20.

Martin, W. (1986) *Recent Theories of Narrative*, Ithaca, NY: Cornell University Press.

Mendus, S. (1995) 'Human rights in political theory', *Political Studies*, XLIII: 10–24.

—— (1996) 'What of soul was left, I wonder? The narrative self in political philosophy' in J. Horton, and A. Baumeister, (eds) *Literature and the Political Imagination*, London and New York: Routledge.

Miller, D. (1990) 'The resurgence of political theory', *Political Studies* 38: 421–37.

—— (1995) 'Reflections on British national identity', *New Community* 21(2): 153–6.

Miller, D.A. (1981) *Narrative and Its Discontents: Problems of Closure in the Traditional Novel*, Princeton, NJ: Princeton University Press.

Mink, L. (1981) 'Everyman his own annalist' in T.W.J. Mitchell (ed.) *On Narrative*, Chicago, IL: The University of Chicago Press.

Mitchell, T.W.J. (1981) 'Foreword' in T.W.J. Mitchell (ed.) *On Narrative*, Chicago, IL: The University of Chicago Press.

Morrison, Toni (1982) *Sula*, London: Triad.

Morson, G.S. (1998) 'Contingency and poetics', *Philosophy and Literature* 22: 286–308.

Mouffe, C. (1995a) 'Democratic politics and the question of identity' in J. Rajchman (ed.) *The Identity in Question*, New York: Routledge.

—— (1995b) 'Feminism, citizenship and radical democratic politics' in L. Nicholson and S. Seidman (eds) *Social Postmodernism: Beyond Identity Politics*, Cambridge: Cambridge University Press.

Mulhall, S. and Swift, A. (1996) *Liberals and Communitarians; an Introduction*, 2nd edition, Oxford: Blackwell.

Nash, C. (1994a) 'Introduction' in C. Nash (ed.) *Narrative in Culture: the Uses of Storytelling in the Sciences, Philosophy and Literature*, London: Routledge.

—— (1994b) 'Slaughtering the subject: literature's assault on narrative' in C. Nash (ed.) *Narrative in Culture: the Uses of Storytelling in the Sciences, Philosophy and Literature*, London: Routledge.

Newton, A.Z. (1995) *Narrative Ethics*, Cambridge, MA: Harvard University Press.

New Yorker (1992) Review of *Leviathan*, 9 November.

Nicholson, L. (1995) 'Interpreting gender' in L. Nicholson and S. Seidman (eds) *Social Postmodernism: Beyond Identity Politics*, Cambridge: Cambridge University Press.

Norton, A. (1988) *Reflections on Political Identity*, Baltimore, MD, and London: The Johns Hopkins University Press.

Nussbaum, M.C. (1990) *Love's Knowledge: Essays on Philosophy and Literature*, New York: Oxford University Press.

O'Donnell, P. (1992) *Echo Chambers: Figuring Voice in Modern Narrative*, Iowa City, IA: University of Iowa Press.

O'Sullivan, N. (1997) 'Difference and the concept of the political in contemporary political philosophy', *Political Studies* 45: 739–54.

Oates, J.C. (1993) 'Introduction' in J.C. Oates (ed.) *The Oxford Book of American Short Stories*, Oxford: Oxford University Press.

Osteen, M. (1994) 'Phantoms of liberty: the secret lives of *Leviathan*', *Review of Contemporary Fiction* 14(1): 87–91.

Parekh, B. (1992) 'The cultural particularity of liberal democracy', *Political Studies*, XL: 160–75.

—— (1995a) 'Introduction', *New Community* 21(2): 147–51.

—— (1995b) 'The concept of national identity', *New Community* 21(2): 255–68.

Parker, D. (1994) *Ethics, Theory and the Novel*, Cambridge: Cambridge University Press.

Pecora, V.P. (1989) *Self and Form in Modern Narrative*, Baltimore, MD: The Johns Hopkins University Press.

Pitkin, H. (1981) 'Justice: on relating private and public', *Political Theory* 19(3): 327–52.

Plant, R. (1991) *Modern Political Thought*, Cambridge, MA: Blackwell.

Pocock, J.B. (1975) *The Machiavellian Moment: Florentine Political Thought and the Atlantic Republican Tradition*, Princeton, NJ: Princeton University Press.

Polonoff, D. (1982) 'Self-deception', *Social Research* 54: 46–53.

Poole, R. (1996) 'On being a person', *Australasian Journal of Philosophy* 74(1): 38–56.

Pynchon, T. (1996) [1979] *The Crying of Lot 49*, London: Picador.

Rajchman, J. (1995) 'Introduction' in J. Rajchman (ed.) *The Identity in Question*, New York: Routledge.

Rainwater, M. (1995) 'Refiguring Ricoeur: narrative force and communicative ethics', *Philosophy and Social Criticism* 21(5/6): 99–110.

Rancière, J. (1995) 'Politics, identification and subjectivisation' in J. Rajchman (ed.) *The Identity in Question*, New York: Routledge.

Randall, W.L. (1995) *The Stories We Are: an Essay on Self-Creation*, Toronto: University of Toronto Press.

Rawls, J. (1972) *A Theory of Justice*, Oxford: Oxford University Press.

Raz, J. (1986) *The Morality of Freedom*, Oxford: Clarendon Press.

Rex, J. (1995) 'Ethnic identity and the nation state: the political sociology of multi-cultural societies', *Social Identities* 1(1): 21–7.

Ricoeur, P. (1991) 'Narrative identity' in D. Wood (ed.) *On Paul Ricoeur: Narrative and Interpretation*, London: Routledge.

Roe, E. (1994) *Narrative Policy Analysis: Theory and Practice*, Durham, NC. and London: Duke University Press.

Rorty, A.O. (ed.) (1976) *The Identity of Persons*, Berkeley, CA: University of California Press.

Rorty, R. (1989) *Contingency, Irony and Solidarity*, Cambridge: Cambridge University Press.

Rosamond, B. and Booth, J. (1995) 'The globalisation of the state' in J. Lovenduski and J. Stanyer (eds) *Contemporary Political Studies*, vol. 2, Belfast: Political Studies Association, 924–31.

Rose, J. (1996) *States of Fantasy*, Oxford: Clarendon Press.

Rosenau, P.V. and Bredemeir, H.C. (1993) 'Modern and postmodern conceptions of social order', *Social Research* 60(2): 341–9.

Rosenblum, N. (1987) *Another Liberalism: Romanticism and the Reconstruction of Liberal Thought*, Cambridge, MA: Harvard University Press.

Ross, A. (1973) 'Narrative', in R. Fowler (ed.) *Dictionary of Modern Critical Terms*, London: Routledge & Kegan Paul.

Roth, P. (1989) *The Facts: a Novelist's Autobiography*, London: Jonathan Cape.

—— (1993) 'A bit of Jewish mischief', *New York Times Book Review* 7 March: 1, 20.

—— (1994) [1993] *Operation Shylock: A Confession*, London: Vintage.

Rycroft, C. (1968) *A Critical Dictionary of Psychoanalysis*, Harmondsworth: Penguin.

Said, E. (1984) 'Permission to narrate', *London Review of Books*, 29 February: 247–94.

Sakwa, R. (1996) 'Russian studies: the fractured mirror', *Politics* 16(3): 175–86.

Saltzman, A. (1995) '*Leviathan*: post hoc harmonies' in D. Barone (ed.) *Beyond the Red Notebook: Essays on Paul Auster*, Philadelphia, PA: University of Pennsylvania Press.

Sandel, M.J. (1982) *Liberalism and the Limits of Justice*, Cambridge: Cambridge University Press.

Schaar, J. (1981) *Legitimacy in the Modern State*, New Brunswick, NJ: Transaction Books.

Schechtman, M. (1996) *The Constitution of Selves*, Ithaca, NY and London: Cornell University Press.

Scholes, R. (1981) 'Language, narrative, and anti-narrative' in T.W.J. Mitchell (ed.) *On Narrative*, Chicago, IL: The University of Chicago Press.

Schrag, C.O. (1997) *The Self after Postmodernity*, New Haven, CT, and London: Yale University Press.

Schulz, D. (1988) 'E.L. Doctorow's America; an introduction to his fiction' in Herwig Friedl and Dieter Schulz (eds) *E.L. Doctorow, a Democracy of Perception: a Symposium with and on E.L. Doctorow*, Essen: Verlag die Blaue Eule.

Schwab, G. (1994) *Subjects without Selves: Transitional Texts in Modern Fiction*, Cambridge, MA and London: Harvard University Press.

Schweizer, H. (1990) 'Introduction' in F. Kermode (ed.) *Poetry, Narrative, History*, Oxford: Basil Blackwell.

Scott, J. (1995) 'Multiculturalism and the politics of identity' in J. Rajchman (ed.) *The Identity in Question*, New York: Routledge.

Shanley, M.L. and Pateman, C. (eds) (1991) *Feminist Interpretations and Political Theory*, University Park, PA: Pennsylvania State University Press.

Shapiro, I. (1990) *Political Criticism*, Berkeley, CA: University of California Press.

Shapiro, M.J. (1988) *The Politics of Representation: Writing Practices in Biography, Photography and Policy Analysis*, Madison, WI: University of Wisconsin Press.

Shklar, J. (1991) [review of Taylor's *Sources of the Self*] *Political Theory* 19(1): 105–9.

Siegle, R. (1986) *The Politics of Reflexivity: Narrative and the Constitutive Poetics of Culture*, Baltimore, MD: The Johns Hopkins University Press.

Skinner, Quentin (1985) 'Introduction' in Q. Skinner (ed.) *The Return of Grand Theory in the Human Sciences*, Cambridge: Cambridge University Press.

—— (1991) 'Who are "we"? Ambiguities of the modern self', *Inquiry* 34(2): 133–53.

Sluga, G. (1996) 'Inventing Trieste: history, anti-history and nation', *The European Legacy* 1(1): 25–30.

Smith, A.D. (1995) 'The formation of national identity' in H. Harris (ed.) *Identity: Essays Based on Herbert Spencer Lectures Given in the University of Oxford*, Oxford: Clarendon Press.

Smyth, E.J. (ed.) (1991) *Postmodernism and Contemporary Fiction*, London: Batsford.

Somer, D. (1991) *Foundational Fictions: the National Romances of Latin America*, Berkeley, CA: University of California Press.

Somers, M. (1994) 'The narrative construction of identity: a relational and network approach', *Theory and Society* 23(5): 605–49.

Stephenson, S. (1996) 'Narrative, self and political theory', unpublished PhD thesis, University of Southampton.

—— (1998) 'Graham Swift and the politics of integrity', unpublished paper presented at the Political Studies Association Annual Conference, Keele.

Stevenson, R. (1986) *The British Novel since the 1930s: an Introduction*, London: Batsford.

—— (1992) *Modernist Fiction: an Introduction*, London: Harvester Wheatsheaf.

Stone, R. (1999) 'Ellison's promised land' [review of Ralph Ellison's *Juneteenth*] *New York Review of Books*, 12 August: 16–18.

Strawson, G. (1996) 'The sense of the self', *London Review of Books*, 18 April: 21–22.

Strong, T. (1990) *The Idea of Political Theory: Reflections on the Self in Political Time and Space*, Notre Dame, IN: Notre Dame University Press.

—— (1992) 'Introduction' in T. Strong (ed.) *The Self and the Political Order*, Cambridge, MA, and Oxford: Blackwell.

Sturgess, P.M. (1992) *Narrativity: Theory and Practice*, Oxford: Clarendon Press.

Tambling, J. (1991) *Narrative and Ideology*, Milton Keynes: Open University Press.

Tanner, T. (1982) *Thomas Pynchon*, London: Methuen.

Taylor, C. (1985) 'What is human agency?' in C. Taylor *Human Agency and Language: Philosophical Papers*, Cambridge: Cambridge University Press.

—— (1989) *Sources of the Self: the Making of the Modern Identity*, Cambridge: Cambridge University Press.

—— (1991) *The Ethics of Authenticity*, Cambridge, MA, and London: Harvard University Press.

—— (1994) 'Multiculturalism and the politics of recognition' in A. Gutmann (ed.) *Multiculturalism: Examining the Politics of Recognition/Charles Taylor et al*, Princeton, NJ: Princeton University Press.

Trenner, R. (ed.) (1983) *E.L. Doctorow: Essays and Conversations*, Princeton, NJ: Ontario Review Press.

Tucker, E. (1995) [letter], *London Review of Books*, 19 October: 2.

Turner, J. (1993) 'Nicely! Nicely!', *London Review of Books*, 13 May: 20–21.

Waldron, J. (1998) 'Whose Nuremberg laws?', *London Review of Books*, 19 March: 12–14.

Walkup, J. (1987) 'Introduction', *Social Research*, Special Issue 'Reflections on the Self', 54(1): 3–9.

Warren, M. (1988) *Nietzsche and Political Thought*, Cambridge, MA, and London: MIT Press.

—— (1990) 'Ideology and the self', *Theory and Society* 19: 599–643.

—— (1992) 'Democratic theory and self-transformation', *American Political Science Review* 86(1): 8–23.

Watt, I. (1996) *Myths of Modern Individualism: Faust, Don Quixote, Don Juan, Robinson Crusoe*, Cambridge: Cambridge University Press.

Weber, M. (1970) [1948] 'Politics as a vocation' in H.H. Gerth and C. Wright Mills (eds) *From Max Weber: Essays in Sociology*, London: Routledge & Kegan Paul.

Weinstein, M. (1982) 'Dostoevsky and Unamuno: the anti-modern personality' in B.R. Barber and M.J.G. McGrath (eds) *The Artist and Political Vision*, New Brunswick, NJ and London: Transaction Books.

Wendt, A. (1994) 'Collective identity formation and the state', *American Political Science Review* 88(2): 384–96.

West, C. (1995) 'The new cultural politics of difference' in J. Rajchman (ed.) *The Identity in Question*, New York: Routledge.

White, H. (1981) 'The value of narrativity in the representation of reality' in T.W.J. Mitchell (ed.) *On Narrative*, Chicago, IL: The University of Chicago Press.

—— (1987) *The Content of the Form: Narrative Discourse and Historical Representation*, Baltimore, MD: The Johns Hopkins University Press.

White, S. (1991) *Political Theory and Postmodernism*, Cambridge: Cambridge University Press.

Whitebrook, M. (1995) *Real Toads in Imaginary Gardens: Narrative Accounts of Liberalism*, Lanham, MD: Rowman & Littlefield.

—— (1996) 'Taking the narrative turn: what the novel has to offer political theory' in J. Horton, and A. Baumeister (eds) *Literature and the Political Imagination*, London and New York: Routledge.

Williams, C. (1998) 'Post-structuralism, subjectivity and political theory', unpublished paper presented at the Political Studies Association Annual Conference, Keele.

Williams, P. (1997) *Seeing a Colour-blind Future: the Paradox of Race*, London: Vintage.

Wirth, E. (1995) 'A look back from the horizon' in D. Barone (ed.) *Beyond the Red Notebook: Essays on Paul Auster*, Philadelphia, PA: University of Pennsylvania Press.

Wood, G. (1996) 'Involuntary memories', *London Review of Books*, 8 February: 20–21.

Woolf, V. (1992) [1925] *Mrs Dalloway* with an Introduction and Notes by Elaine Showalter, text edited by Stella McNichol, London: Penguin Books.

Young, I. (1992) 'Identity\difference', *Political Theory* 20(3): 511–14.

Zalewski, M. and Enloe, C. (1995) 'Questions about identity in international relations' in K. Booth and S. Smith (eds) *International Relations Theory Today*, Oxford: Polity.

Ziegler, H. and Bigsby, C. (1982) *The Radical Imagination and the Liberal Tradition: Interviews with English and American Novelists*, London: Junction.

Index